USING MATHEMATICS
Book 5

ANDRIA P. TROUTMAN
Professor, University of South Florida
Tampa, Florida

JAMES J. BEZDEK
Professor of Education, North Texas State University
Denton, Texas

CATHERINE TOBIN
Educational Consultant
Newtonville, Massachusetts

TEACHER–CONSULTANTS

Philip E. Bertoni
Teacher, John F. Kennedy High School
Anaheim Union High School District
La Palma, California

Lula P. Smith
Teacher, Mahalia Jackson School
Chicago Public Schools
Chicago, Illinois

Caroline L. Chin
Teacher, Nathan Hale School
Boston Public Schools
Roxbury, Massachusetts

Alma E. Wright
Teacher, Trotter School
Boston Public Schools
Boston, Massachusetts

LAIDLAW BROTHERS • PUBLISHERS
A Division of Doubleday & Company, Inc.
RIVER FOREST, ILLINOIS

Irvine, California   Chamblee, Georgia   Dallas, Texas   Toronto, Canada

The USING MATHEMATICS Program

USING MATHEMATICS Kindergarten

USING MATHEMATICS Book 1	USING MATHEMATICS Book 5
USING MATHEMATICS Book 2	USING MATHEMATICS Book 6
USING MATHEMATICS Book 3	USING MATHEMATICS Book 7
USING MATHEMATICS Book 4	USING MATHEMATICS Book 8

ACKNOWLEDGMENTS

EDITORIAL STAFF

Project Director: Albert F. Kempf   *Production Director:* LaVergne G. Niequist   *Art Director:* Gloria J. Muczynski
Assistant to the Art Director: Dennis Horan   *Production Supervisor:* Mary C. Steermann
Production Associates: Joyce M. Symoniak, Jeanette Wojtyla   *Photo Researcher:* William A. Cassin

ILLUSTRATORS

George Hamblin; Paul Hazelrigg; Rick Incrocci; Sergei Itomlenskis/John D. Firestone & Associates, Inc.; Donald C. Meighan; Keith Neely; Joseph Rogers; Sam Sirdofsky

PHOTOGRAPHERS

Cover photograph by John Running/After-Image, Inc.; other photographs credited where each photograph appears.

ISBN 0-8445-1205-2

3456789 10 11 12 13 14 15   1098765

CONTENTS

1 Number Concepts

Number Games   8

Checking Subtraction   10

Checking Division   12

Place Value   14

Large Numbers   16

Comparing Numbers   18

Chapter Review   20

2 Addition and Subtraction

Addition   22

Rounding   28

Estimating Sums   30

Several Addends   32

Subtraction   34

Estimating Differences   36

Solving Problems   37

Skills Review   38

Calculator Words   39

Chapter Review   40

3 Multiplication

Multiplication Facts   42

Multiples of Ten   44

Multiplying 10's and 100's   46

Tens, Hundreds, and Thousands   48

Hidden Fruit   49

Estimating Products   50

Multiplication (2- and 3-digit
   by 1-digit)   52

Multiplication (2- and 3-digit
   by 2-digit)   56

Multiplication (3-digit by 3-digit)   60

Multiplication (4-digit by 1-digit)   62

Skills Review   64

Solving Problems   65

Chapter Review   66

4 Division

Division   68

Finding Quotients   70

Remainders in Division   74

Checking Division   76

Skills Review   77

Divisibility Rules   78

Dividing by Multiples of Ten   80

2-Digit Divisors   82

Zeros in the Quotient   88

Solving Problems   89

Division (4-digit by 2-digit)   90

Finding Averages   92

Using a Calculator to Find Averages   94

What Are They?   95

Chapter Review   96

5 Problem Solving

Reading Problems   98

Planning to Solve Problems   100

Computing Answers to Problems   102

Writing Questions   104

Making Up Problems   106

Don't Get Fooled   107

Extra Information   108

Missing Information   110

Skills Review   112

Problems Without Computation   113

Two-Step Problems   114

Chapter Review   116

6 Geometry

Space Figures   118

Lines, Line Segments, Rays   120

Line Segments   122

Angles   124

Measuring Angles   126

Kinds of Angles   128

Drawing Angles   130

Skills Review   131

Congruent Angles   132

Circles   134

Polygons   136

Parallel Lines   138

Perpendicular Lines   140

Chapter Review   142

7 Fractions (×)

Fractions 144
Equivalent Fractions 146
Renaming Fractions 148
Greatest Common Factor 152
Simplest Form 154
Multiplying Fractions 156
Products in Simplest Form 158
How Are They Related? 160

Fractions for Whole Numbers 161
Fractions to Mixed Numerals 162
Mixed Numerals to Fractions 164
Practice 165
Mixed Numerals in Multiplication 166
Solving Problems 168
  Skills Review 170
  Chapter Review 172

8 Fractions (+, -)

Adding Fractions 174
Least Common Multiple 176
Adding Fractions 178
Mixed Numerals in Addition 182
Practice 184
Fast and Easy Addition 185

Comparing Fractions 186
Subtracting Fractions 188
Mixed Numerals in Subtraction 192
  Skills Review 198
  Chapter Review 200

9 Decimals

Decimals 202
Comparing Decimals 206
Adding Decimals 208
Subtracting Decimals 210
Money 212
  Skills Review 214
Multiplying Decimals 216

Money Sense 220
Multiplying With a Calculator 221
Ratio 222
Percent 224
Using Percent 226
Percent and Money 228
  Chapter Review 230

10 Measurement

Measurement 232
Length 234
Finding Measurements 236
Metric Units 240
Capacity 242
Weight 244

Temperature 246
Using Customary Units 248
  Skills Review 250
Solving Problems 251
  Chapter Review 252

11 Perimeter, Area, Volume

Perimeter   254
Area   256
Area of Rectangle   258
Area of a Right Triangle   260
Solving Problems   262

Area and Perimeter   263
Volume   264
Solving Problems   268
  Skills Review   270
  Chapter Review   272

12 Graphs

Grid Game   274
Ordered Pairs   276
Secret Messages   278
World Grid   279
Making Tables   280
Making Line Graphs   284

Reading Line Graphs   286
  Skills Review   288
Bar Graphs   290
Making Bar Graphs   292
Circle Graphs   294
  Chapter Review   296

13 Probability

Experimenting   298
Chance   300
Probability   302
0 and 1 Probabilities   304
Predicting   306

Probability Experiments   308
Probability and Percent   310
  Skills Review   312
  Chapter Review   313

Review and Practice   314-350

Glossary   351
Table of Measures   356
Index   357

1 Number Concepts

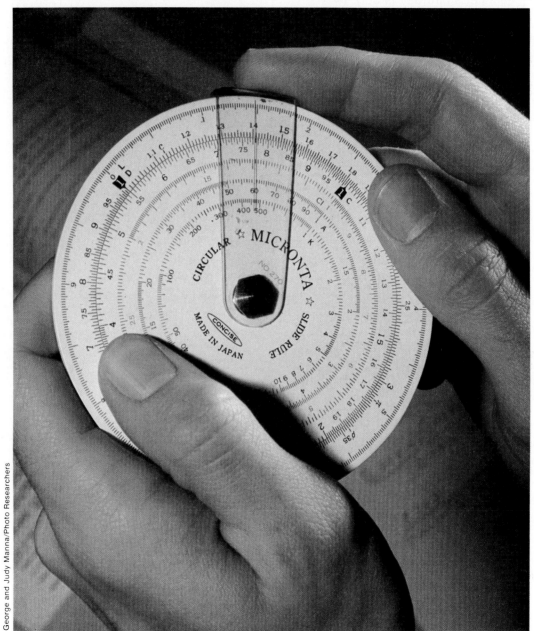

Number Games

Jon's birthday is February 9.

Jennifer's birthday is July 14.

Speech bubble: Write your birthday number. Add 16. Multiply by 5. Subtract 80. Multiply by 2. Then tell me your answer.

	Jon	Jennifer
Birthday number. ➝	9	14
Add 16. ➝	9 +16 25	14 +16 30
Multiply by 5. ➝	25 ×5 125	30 ×5 150
Subtract 80. ➝	125 − 80 45	150 − 80 70
Multiply by 2. ➝	45 ×2 90	70 ×2 140

Jon's answer ⸺⸺⸺⸺
Jennifer's answer ⸺⸺⸺⸺

The magician knew that Jon's birthday number was 9. How did she know?

How can you get Jennifer's birthday number from the answer 140?

What is the birthday number if the answer is 300?

What is the birthday number if the answer is 310?

8

Exercises

Work each number game several times. Try to find the secret for knowing the beginning number.

1. Choose any number.
   Multiply by 6.
   Divide by 3. Subtract
   the original number.
   What is your answer?

2. Choose any number. Add it to the number that comes after it.
   Multiply by 2.
   Subtract 2. Divide by 2.
   What is your answer?

3. Choose a number between 10 and 30. Multiply by 4.
   Add 18. Subtract
   the number you started with.
   Divide by 3. Add 4.
   What is your answer?

4. Choose a number less than 20.
   Subtract that number from 30.
   Multiply by 3.
   Add the number you started with.
   Divide by 2. Subtract 25.
   What is your answer?

Add.

5. 47
   +40

6. 16
   +83

7. 34
   +43

8. 61
   +37

9. 92
   +11

Subtract.

10. 92
    −12

11. 85
    −35

12. 63
    −20

13. 48
    −35

14. 78
    −29

Multiply.

15. 20
    ×4

16. 15
    ×3

17. 36
    ×2

18. 47
    ×3

19. 94
    ×8

Divide.

20. 7)35

21. 3)27

22. 4)64

23. 3)48

24. 7)91

Find each result.

25. 38 + 6

26. 65 × 8

27. 50 − 26

28. 85 ÷ 5

Checking Subtraction

Name ___Don___

Subtract and check.

1.
```
  67◄    33
 −34   +34
  33   └ 67
```

2.
```
  83◄    63
 −26   +26
  63   └ 89
```

3.
```
  63◄     5
 −58   +58
   5   └ 63
```

Name _Lucy_

Subtract and check.

1.
```
   67
 − 34
   33
 + 34
   67
```

2.
```
   83
 − 26
   57
 + 26
   83
```

3.
```
   63
 − 58
   15
 + 58
   73
```

How did Don check each subtraction?

Which problem did Don have wrong?

How did Lucy check each subtraction?

Which problem did Lucy have wrong?

Exercises

Check. If the answer is wrong, correct it.

1.
```
  26
−12
 14
```

2.
```
  78
−63
  5
```

3.
```
  31
−18
 23
```

4.
```
  70
−24
 46
```

5.
```
  93
−52
 49
```

6.
```
  13
−11
 12
```

7.
```
  91
−40
 49
```

8.
```
  57
−32
 25
```

9.
```
  86
−76
 20
```

10.
```
  79
−53
 26
```

Subtract and check.

11.	15 −13	12.	38 −26	13.	82 −60	14.	95 −44	15.	76 −15
16.	62 −36	17.	52 −24	18.	85 −75	19.	74 −69	20.	66 −28
21.	46 −44	22.	18 − 9	23.	97 −59	24.	23 − 8	25.	93 −85
26.	80 −16	27.	68 −49	28.	22 − 3	29.	81 −79	30.	90 − 7

Fran checked some subtraction exercises as shown below. Write the subtraction exercises.

| 31. | 67 +28 ── 95 | 32. | 9 +42 ── 51 | 33. | 47 +27 ── 74 | 34. | 26 +17 ── 43 | 35. | 18 +29 ── 47 |

What Am I?

Find the letter for each number in the name.

| 18 −13 | 39 −18 | 60 −30 | 29 −13 | 52 −30 | 96 −81 | 73 −41 | 89 −76 |
| H | T | L | C | F | A | B | O |

I am a

22–13–13–21–32–15–30–30

16–13–15–16–5.

Checking Division

Divide and check.

1.
```
      16        3
   6)96 ←    16
      6        ×6
     36      └ 96
     36
      0
```

2.
```
      34
   2)78 ←    34
      6        ×2
     18      └ 68
     18
      0
```

3.
```
      19        2
   3)57 ←    19
      3        ×3
     27      └ 57
     27
      0
```

How did Janice check each division?

Which problem did Janice have wrong?

Exercises

Check. If the answer is wrong, correct it.

1.
```
     12
  5)70
     5
    20
    10
     0
```

2.
```
     17
  3)81
     3
    21
    21
     0
```

3.
```
     24
  2)50
     4
    10
    10
     0
```

4.
```
     12
  8)96
     8
    16
    16
     0
```

5.
```
     52
  4)208
    20
    08
     8
     0
```

6.
```
     51
  5)255
    25
    05
     5
     0
```

7.
```
     31
  7)210
    21
    70
    70
     0
```

8.
```
     33
  4)132
    12
    12
    12
     0
```

Divide and check.

9. $7\overline{)35}$ 10. $6\overline{)42}$ 11. $4\overline{)72}$ 12. $5\overline{)95}$

13. $6\overline{)84}$ 14. $5\overline{)100}$ 15. $6\overline{)120}$ 16. $4\overline{)60}$

17. $3\overline{)75}$ 18. $4\overline{)120}$ 19. $8\overline{)160}$ 20. $7\overline{)98}$

21. $7\overline{)147}$ 22. $9\overline{)198}$ 23. $4\overline{)268}$ 24. $8\overline{)192}$

Phyllis checked some division exercises as shown below. Write the division exercises.

25.
$$\begin{array}{r} 23 \\ \times 5 \\ \hline 115 \end{array}$$

26.
$$\begin{array}{r} 34 \\ \times 7 \\ \hline 238 \end{array}$$

27.
$$\begin{array}{r} 19 \\ \times 4 \\ \hline 76 \end{array}$$

28.
$$\begin{array}{r} 62 \\ \times 3 \\ \hline 186 \end{array}$$

29.
$$\begin{array}{r} 50 \\ \times 9 \\ \hline 450 \end{array}$$

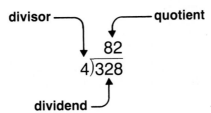

30. To check any division, multiply the ___ by the ___. The result should be the ___.

Can You Do This?

If $76 \div 4 = 19$, then ___ × ___ = $\underline{76}$.

If $98 \div 7 = 14$, then ___ × ___ = ___.

If $a \div b = c$, then ___ × ___ = ___.

Extra Practice—Set B, page 314

13

Place Value

Mr. Frost was going to withdraw $3414 from his savings account. He wanted it in the fewest bills possible. Here is how the teller gave him the money.

$$3 \longrightarrow \$1000 \text{ bills} = \$3000$$
$$4 \longrightarrow 100 \text{ bills} = 400$$
$$1 \longrightarrow 10 \text{ bills} = 10$$
$$4 \longrightarrow 1 \text{ bills} = \underline{4}$$
$$\$3414$$

Numerals like 3414 are read *three thousand four hundred fourteen.*

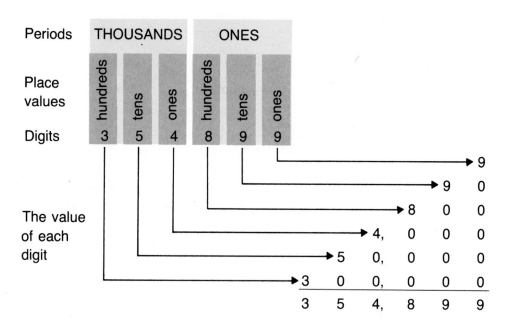

three hundred fifty-four thousand, eight hundred ninety-nine

Commas are used to separate the periods to make numerals easier to read.

Exercises

Copy. Put in commas.

1. 23948

2. 200008

3. 100100

4. 10010

5. 14260

6. 896544

7. 101001

8. 900010

Write the numeral.

9. fifty-six thousand, seven hundred seventy-three

10. four hundred thousand, sixteen

11. eleven thousand, eight hundred

12. thirty thousand, four hundred seventy-eight

Write in words.

13. 1000

14. 400,000

15. 624,911

16. 831,900

17. 748,938

18. 111,112

You are the teller. You have $1, $10, $100, $1000, and $10,000 bills. What is the fewest number of bills you would give a person withdrawing each of the following?

19. $6223

20. $5090

21. $63

22. $50,276

23. $68,414

24. $100,000

Write the *value* of the underlined digit.

25. 3̲62,469

26. 205,̲300

27. 30,46̲1

28. 2̲87,052

29. 75,0̲48

30. 98̲,321

31. 7̲04,925

32. 574,9̲00

15

Large Numbers

This is the estimated age of some moon rocks.

Periods	BILLIONS			MILLIONS			THOUSANDS			ONES		
Place values	hundreds	tens	ones	hundreds	tens	ones	hundreds	tens	ones	hundreds	tens	ones
Digits			4	2	6	0	0	0	0	0	0	0

4,260,000,000

four billion, two hundred sixty million

How would you name each of these as a numeral?

one million　　　　　*one billion*　　　　　*ten million*　　　　　*ten billion*

Read these numerals.

1,948,928,918　　　　　285,000,600　　　　　303,030,303,030

Exercises

Copy. Put in commas.

1. 274983046

2. 1234567890

3. 64788893000

Write the numeral.

4. seventy-three million, two hundred fifty-four thousand, three hundred ninety-eight

5. one hundred six billion, twenty-five million, one

6. six billion, nine hundred twenty-two thousand, sixty-three

7. one billion, seven hundred million

8. four billion, four million, four thousand, forty-four

9. nine billion, seventy-five million, six thousand, four hundred thirty

Write in words.

10. 6389

11. 246,020,900

12. 1,900,900,009

13. 3,204,306,200

14. 1,000,006,839

15. 189,000,000,002

Find each sum.

16. 10,000,000 + 200,000 + 400 + 50 + 1

17. 50,000,000,000 + 200,000,000 + 60,000 + 500 + 7

How Big Is a Billion?

Your heart beats about 76 times per minute. You will be 25 years old before it beats a billion times.

If you could spend $1.00 per minute, it would take about 2000 years to spend a billion dollars.

If this ring were a billion times bigger, it would fit around the earth.

Comparing Numbers

When shown on this number line, the greater of two numbers is always to the right.

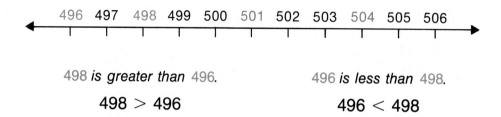

496 497 498 499 500 501 502 503 504 505 506

498 *is greater than* 496.

498 > 496

496 *is less than* 498.

496 < 498

The signs < and > always point to the smaller number.

504 *is greater than* 501.

504 > 501

501 *is less than* 504

501 < 504

Exercises

Copy. Replace the blank with > or <.

1. 56 ___ 65

2. 90 ___ 95

3. 100 ___ 95

4. 95 ___ 100

5. 106 ___ 109

6. 106 ___ 206

7. 206 ___ 107

8. 206 ___ 1007

9. 1005 ___ 206

10. 895 ___ 97

11. 80 ___ 800

12. 1001 ___ 1010

13. 909 ___ 99

14. 676 ___ 667

15. 480 ___ 479

16. 223 ___ 232

17. 2000 ___ 999

18. 434 ___ 343

19. 999 ___ 666

20. 99 ___ 888

21. Arrange the numbers from greatest to least.

35, 23, 11, 30, 2, 56, 90, 109, 0

22. In a recent marathon, Freda was ahead of 96 runners, while John was ahead of 106. Who was ahead of more runners?

23. In the same race, Kim was ahead of 457 runners, while Sherry was ahead of 475. Was Sherry ahead of Kim?

24. In a later race, Kim was the 191st finisher. Sherry finished 99th. Who ran faster?

25. Paul finished ahead of 399 runners, Brian finished ahead of 412, and Al finished ahead of 409. Of these three runners, who finished first? Second?

26. To run in the Boston Marathon, Tracy traveled 7888 miles, Julie traveled 2799 miles, and Juan traveled 999 miles. Who traveled farthest?

CHAPTER REVIEW

Find each result.

1. $\begin{array}{r} 52 \\ +27 \\ \hline \end{array}$

2. $\begin{array}{r} 96 \\ -51 \\ \hline \end{array}$

3. $\begin{array}{r} 87 \\ \times 9 \\ \hline \end{array}$

4. $64 \div 4$

Subtract and check.

5. $\begin{array}{r} 93 \\ -71 \\ \hline \end{array}$

6. $\begin{array}{r} 62 \\ -51 \\ \hline \end{array}$

7. $\begin{array}{r} 83 \\ -57 \\ \hline \end{array}$

8. $\begin{array}{r} 52 \\ -46 \\ \hline \end{array}$

Divide and check.

9. $3\overline{)87}$

10. $7\overline{)210}$

11. $4\overline{)160}$

12. $5\overline{)85}$

Write the numeral.

13. three hundred sixty-seven thousand, two hundred seventeen

14. five million, nine hundred thousand

15. one billion, six hundred ten million, three thousand, ten

What is the *value* of the underlined digit in each numeral?

16. 938,6_52,000

17. 4,567,8_90

18. 36,27_3,847,402

19. Dave is withdrawing $5680 from his savings account. How many $1, $10, $100, and $1000 bills should he get to have the fewest bills possible?

Copy. Replace the blanks with $>$ or $<$.

20. 385 ___ 358

21. 1967 ___ 1980

22. 99 ___ 900

23. 6 ___ 0

2 Addition and Subtraction

Fredrik D. Bodin

Addition

The sonar on a submarine detected a whale. How many feet underwater is the whale?

313 ft

To find the answer, add.

449 ft

Add the ones.	Add the tens.	Add the hundreds.

H	T	O
	1	
3	1	3
+4	4	9
		2

	O
	3
+	9
1	2

H	T	O
	1	
3	1	3
+4	4	9
	6	2

H	T	O
	1	
3	1	3
+4	4	9
7	6	2

The whale is 762 feet underwater.

22

Exercises

1. 237
 +392

2. 539
 + 80

3. 214
 +738

4. 279
 +159

5. 756
 + 34

6. 629
 +306

7. 719
 +174

8. 626
 +187

9. 492
 +493

10. 729
 + 52

11. 842
 +108

12. 425
 +146

13. 325
 +132

14. 266
 +382

15. 271
 +178

16. 86
 +423

17. 302
 +632

18. 828
 + 75

19. 529
 +295

20. 321
 +279

21. 444 + 26

22. 289 + 721

23. 33 + 77

24. 351 + 258

25. 109 + 209

26. 310 + 190

27. 890 + 109

28. 615 + 294

29. 555 + 55

30. 55 + 555

31. 666 + 44

32. 777 + 33

33. Last year Pat gained 625 yards for the Jefferson High School football team. He gained 796 yards this year. How many yards did he gain in the last two years?

34. Myra read 324 pages of a book one week and 176 pages another week. How many pages did she read in those two weeks?

35. Tom used his calculator to add 516 and 394 and got an answer of 900. Could Tom have pressed the wrong keys? Why?

36. Joan weighs 113 pounds, and David weighs 196 pounds. What is the sum of their weights?

Extra Practice—Set B, page 315

23

Addition

How many feet are between the highest point and the lowest point?

The highest point above sea level is 29,028 feet.

Sea Level

The lowest point below sea level is 36,198 feet.

Add the ones, tens, and hundreds.	Add the thousands.	Add the ten thousands.

Add the ones, tens, and hundreds.

TTh	Th	H	T	O
		1	1	
2	9	0	2	8
+3	6	1	9	8
		2	2	6

Add the thousands.

TTh	Th	H	T	O
1		1	1	
2	9	0	2	8
+3	6	1	9	8
	5	2	2	6

   9 Th
+ 6 Th
1 5 Th

Add the ten thousands.

TTh	Th	H	T	O
1		1	1	
2	9	0	2	8
+3	6	1	9	8
6	5	2	2	6

The answer is 65,226 feet.

Exercises

1. 11,293
    +12,113

2. 60,013
    +36,395

3. 26,839
    + 2,318

4. 13,293
    +82,831

5.	13,928 +12,839	**6.**	1930 +6923	**7.**	1,928 +12,132	**8.**	32,009 + 2,395

9.	14,293 + 1,473	**10.**	19,002 +24,757	**11.**	21,392 +55,466	**12.**	32,938 +60,380

13.	37,820 +47,590	**14.**	82,019 +16,478	**15.**	72,938 + 7,274	**16.**	37,920 +45,046

17.	54,928 +44,236	**18.**	62,891 +33,729	**19.**	50,093 +21,836	**20.**	39,928 +51,079

21. 50,926 + 20,944

22. 78,503 + 21,497

23. 66,666 + 44,444

24. 12,345 + 67,890

25. The distance around the moon is about 6786 miles. The distance around the earth, at the equator, is 18,116 miles more than that. Find the distance around the earth.

26. The altitude of Mount McKinley is 20,320 feet. Mount Everest is 8708 feet taller than that. What is the altitude of Mount Everest?

27. The Gulf coast of the United States is 17,141 miles long. The Atlantic coast is 11,532 miles longer than that. How long is the Atlantic coast?

28. The Pacific coast is 23,157 miles longer than the Gulf coast. How long is the Pacific coast?

NASA

Addition

State	Area (square miles)	Population
Montana	145,587	786,690
Idaho	82,677	943,935
Wyoming	97,203	470,816
Utah	82,096	1,461,037
Colorado	103,766	2,888,834

To find the combined population of Idaho and Utah, add.

Discuss the steps used to add the numbers. How would you read the sum?

M	HTh	TTh	Th	H	T	O
1	1				1	
1	4	6	1	0	3	7
+	9	4	3	9	3	5
2	4	0	4	9	7	2

Exercises

1. 1,238,483
    +3,429,526

2. 394,832
    +148,293

3. 600,205
    +203,406

4. 45,293
    +24,385

5. 1,283,392
    +4,606,608

6. 382,830
    +1,524,900

7. 623,830
    +230,482

8. 223,567
    +240,053

9. 1,024,028
    +   14,925

10. 2,903
     +9,683,007

11. 402,000
     + 29,000

12. 52,395
     +47,699

13.	26,370 +82,849	14.	37,605,208 + 396,602	15.	827 +3,416,903	16.	2,001 +18,999
17.	4,444,444 +6,666,666	18.	353,353 +464,464	19.	28,309 +28,309	20.	57,772 +57,772

Find the area and the population of these new states.

21.

22.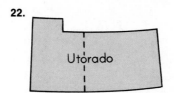

23.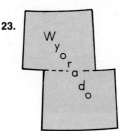

Make up a name for each new state below. Find the area and the population of each new state.

24.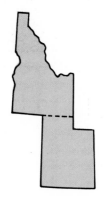

25.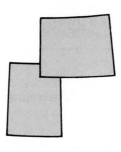

26.

27. Using the states shown on page 26, can you find another new state?

What would you name that new state?

What is its area? Its population?

Extra Practice—Set B, page 316   **27**

Rounding

Attendance

42,873 people
about 42,900 people
about 43,000 people

Artstreet

The number of people at the circus is shown in three ways. We can round numbers when we only need to know "about how many."

You could use a number line to round to the nearest thousand. Is 42,873 closer to 42,000 or 43,000?

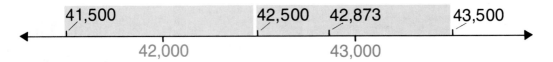

41,500   42,500   42,873   43,500

          42,000   43,000

Here is an easy way to round to the nearest thousand.

Look at the digit to the right of the thousands place (the hundreds digit).

42,315	42,515	42,815
Less than 5, so round down to	Equal to 5, so round up to	More than 5, so round up to
42,000	43,000	43,000

Here is an easy way to round to the nearest hundred.

Look at the digit to the right of the hundreds place (the tens digit).

42,8**1**5	42,9**5**0	42,8**7**3
↓	↓	↓
Less than 5, so round down to	Equal to 5, so round up to	More than 5, so round up to
42,800	43,000	42,900

In the second example above, why is 42,950 rounded to 43,000?

Exercises

Round to the nearest thousand.

1. 3500   2. 3499   3. 3501   4. 9527

5. 7205   6. 11,976   7. 19,500   8. 19,204

Round to the nearest hundred.

9. 361   10. 429   11. 750   12. 1091

13. 543   14. 907   15. 970   16. 1991

17. 5392   18. 7501   19. 11,050   20. 9950

Round to the nearest ten.

21. 34   22. 534   23. 1634   24. 285

Round to the nearest thousand, the nearest hundred, and the nearest ten.

25. 42,315   26. 6092   27. 692   28. 999

Estimating Sums

That can't be right. 5000+6000 is 11,000. What did I do wrong?

Connie and P. C. Peri

To estimate the answer, Juan rounded both numbers to the nearest thousand so he could add "in his head."

$$5246 \longrightarrow \text{is about} \longrightarrow 5,000$$
$$+6109 \longrightarrow \text{is about} \longrightarrow +6,000$$
$$\text{The sum is about} \longrightarrow 11,000$$

Here is how to estimate other sums.

$$
\begin{array}{ccc}
832 & \longrightarrow & 800 \\
+245 & \longrightarrow & +200 \\
\hline
 & & 1000
\end{array}
\qquad\qquad
\begin{array}{ccc}
37,676 & \longrightarrow & 38,000 \\
+\ 9,038 & \longrightarrow & +\ 9,000 \\
\hline
 & & 47,000
\end{array}
$$

Exercises

Estimate each sum.

1. 3921
    +1500

2. 1009
    +6293

3. 158
    +928

4. 12,919
    + 7,012

5. 61,032
    +19,866

6. 798
    +20,718

7. 4500
    +5500

8. 9900
    + 900

30

Far Out Galaxy

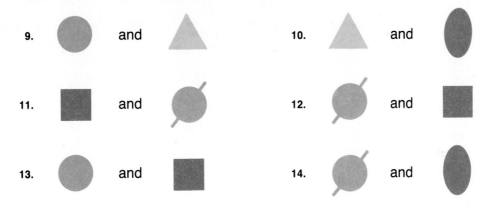

17,985 miles   16,279 miles   11,276 miles   9411 miles

Estimate the distance between

9. ⬤ and ▲

10. ▲ and ⬭

11. ◼ and ⬤

12. ⬤ and ◼

13. ⬤ and ◼

14. ⬤ and ⬭

Estimate each sum.

15. 32,938 + 26,920   16. 60,239 + 1992   17. 695 + 824

18. Chris traveled 2199 miles in June and 2613 miles in July. Estimate how many miles he traveled during those two months.

19. One of the pyramids of ancient Egypt was completed about the year 2560 B.C. Estimate how many years ago that was.

20. Kathy used her calculator to add 8495 and 1500. She got an answer of 13,995. Estimate the answer to see if her answer is reasonable.

21. An Alaskan brown bear weighs about twice as much as a grizzly bear. A grizzly weighs about 780 pounds. Estimate the weight of a brown bear.

Gunter Reitz/Leo de Wys Inc.

31

Several Addends

Discuss the steps Joe used to add the scores.

```
  H | T | O
    2 | 2 |
    1 | 0 | 3
    1 | 6 | 7
    1 | 5 | 9
  + |   | 8 | 7
    5 | 1 | 6
```

Mike Malyszko/Stock Boston

Exercises

1.
```
  8023
  1930
+ 3900
```

2.
```
  920
  139
  302
+ 138
```

3.
```
  5920
  1002
+ 2889
```

4.
```
   89
   70
  149
+  93
```

5.
```
  392
  194
+ 692
```

6.
```
  50,920
   8,849
   1,193
+ 13,928
```

7.
```
  103
  592
+ 206
```

8.
```
  306
   29
  492
+  95
```

9.
```
   200
    89
   701
  2335
+  264
```

10.
```
  40,561
   3,820
+ 51,675
```

11.
```
    21
     9
   362
    84
+ 9617
```

12.
```
     8
    88
   888
+ 8888
```

13. 27 + 5 + 68 + 80 + 32 + 10 + 64

14. 35,617 + 253,710 + 24,999 + 21 + 602

32

Bill's Trip

869 miles   598 miles   255 miles   269 miles

Los Angeles   Denver   Kansas City   St. Louis   Louisville

15. How far did Bill travel by plane?

16. How far did Bill travel by car?

17. How far would you travel if you went from Denver to St. Louis and back to Kansas City?

18. If you start at Louisville and stop at Denver, how far would you travel?

19. Leo goes bowling every Saturday. Last Saturday Leo bowled scores of 135, 167, and 224. What was his score for three games?

20. In her three years of basketball in junior high, Amy scored 197, 245, and 278 points. How many points did she score while in junior high school?

21. David's bowling scores were 119, 126, and 165. Jane's bowling scores were 135, 100, and 89. What was the total score for their six games?

22. To train for a bicycle race, Brett rode 25, 25, 30, 45, and 45 miles during the past five days. How many miles did he ride?

Challenge

Bowling Score Sheet				
	Game 1	Game 2	Game 3	Series Total
Brian	138	154	215	
Joan	96	104	135	
Janet	190	160	173	
Phil	172	65	181	
Game Total				

Add across.

Add down.   Check.

Subtraction

The Sears Tower is how many feet taller than the John Hancock Center?

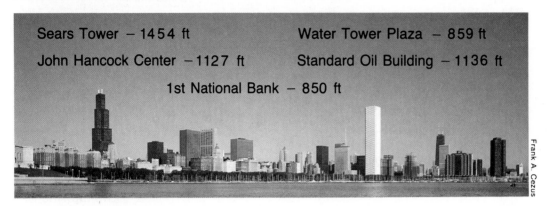

Sears Tower – 1454 ft   Water Tower Plaza – 859 ft

John Hancock Center – 1127 ft   Standard Oil Building – 1136 ft

1st National Bank – 850 ft

Frank A. Cezus

To find out, subtract.

Subtract the ones.	Subtract the tens.	Subtract the hundreds.	Check

Th	H	T	O
		4	14
1	4	5̶	4̶
−1	1	2	7
			7

Th	H	T	O
		4	14
1	4	5̶	4̶
−1	1	2	7
		2	7

Th	H	T	O
		4	14
1	4	5̶	4̶
−1	1	2	7
	3	2	7

Th	H	T	O
		1	
1	1	2	7
+	3	2	7
1	4	5	4

Rename 5 tens,
4 ones as
4 tens, 14 ones.

The Sears Tower is 327 feet taller than the John Hancock Center.

Discuss this example.

Why is 2007 renamed?

How is 2007 renamed?

$$\begin{array}{r} {}^{9}\;{}^{10} \\ 1\;\;\cancel{10} \\ \cancel{2}\;\cancel{0}\;\cancel{0}\;7 \\ -\;\;\;4\;6\;3 \\ \hline 1\;5\;4\;4 \end{array}$$

Exercises

For each problem, tell which building is taller and how much taller.

1. Water Tower Plaza or Standard Oil Building

2. Sears Tower or Water Tower Plaza

3. John Hancock Center or 1st National Bank

4.	5.	6.	7.	8.
4920	729	382	3294	1039
−2830	−460	−249	−1128	− 618

9.	10.	11.	12.	13.
5384	429	1039	928	1148
−2414	−248	− 648	−588	−1129

14.	15.	16.	17.	18.
1005	600	342	1028	1200
− 88	−509	−171	− 725	−1047

19. Find Kris's score for Game 1.

20. Find Peggy's score for Game 2.

21. Find the difference between Kris's best score and Peggy's best score.

SCORES	Kris	Peggy
Game 1		4602
Game 2	3873	
Total	7690	7920

22. The most skiers to start a race was 8755. There were 7565 skiers who finished the race. How many did not finish the race?

What Is Missing?

1.	2.	3.	4.
2 3 ▪	5 ▪ ▪ 1	4 9 2 7	▪ 7 8
−1 ▪ 5	−3 0 0 9	−3 ▪ 1 ▪	−1 ▪ 3
1 1 3	▪ 1 8 2	▪ 5 ▪ 9	4 9 ▪

Estimating Differences

Estimate the distance from Hong Kong to San Francisco.

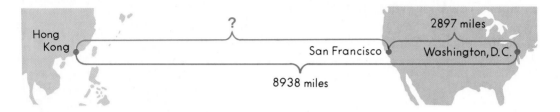

To estimate the distance, round both numbers to the nearest thousand and subtract "in your head."

$$8938 \longrightarrow \text{is about} \longrightarrow 9000$$
$$-2897 \longrightarrow \text{is about} \longrightarrow -3000$$
$$\text{Difference is about} \longrightarrow 6000$$

Discuss how you would estimate these differences.

6250	17,500	8463
−2907	− 9,489	−7920

Exercises

Estimate.

1.	7928	2.	42,935	3.	432,103	4.	803
	−4029		− 9,138		−127,920		−296
5.	43,928	6.	55,023	7.	161,902	8.	904
	−20,120		−32,932		− 89,003		−492
9.	83,000	10.	38,293	11.	928,038	12.	302
	−53,080		− 994		− 69,028		− 83

Solving Problems

1. There were 6,470,000 farms in the United States fifty years ago. Today there are only 2,798,000. How many fewer farms are there today?

2. Maria wants to buy a bike. It costs $103. She has $9. How much more does she need?

3. 26,832 people were at the game. Of these, 24,575 paid to get in. The rest were guests. How many guests were there?

4. There are 491 pupils in Field School. There are 238 boys. How many pupils are girls?

Camerique

The odometer in a car tells how many miles the car has traveled.

ODOMETER

Monday morning

ODOMETER

Monday night

ODOMETER

Friday night

5. Estimate how many miles were traveled on Monday.

6. Estimate how many miles were driven from Monday night to Friday night?

7. A service station had 6219 gallons of gasoline and sold 4913 gallons. Estimate the number of gallons that are left.

8. Rico used his calculator to subtract 5607 from 10,518 and got an answer of 8109. Estimate to see if his answer is reasonable.

Extra Practice—Set B, page 318

Do each of the following three times. If you know a result, can you find a way to tell the number you picked?

1. Pick a number between 20 and 30.
   Subtract 10.
   Multiply by 2.
   Subtract 20.
   Divide by 2.

2. Pick any number.
   Add it to the number that comes after it.
   Add 51. Divide by 2.
   Subtract 16.

Subtract and check.

3. 79
   -46

4. 37
   -21

5. 56
   -54

6. 40
   -18

7. 82
   -19

Divide and check.

8. $6\overline{)174}$

9. $7\overline{)224}$

10. $3\overline{)207}$

11. $4\overline{)96}$

Write the numeral.

12. seventeen thousand, six hundred thirty-two

13. two hundred fifty thousand

14. six million, two hundred thousand

15. nine million, nine hundred

Give the value of the underlined digit.

16. 32,456

17. 205,877,319

18. 10,724,300

19. 27

20. 246,770,354

21. 2,345,678,901

22. 376,009,825,881

Write in words.

23. 8,009,000

24. 396

25. 52,908

26. 360,002,070

Calculator Words

To add 2867 and 4241 on a calculator, push the keys in this order.

| 2 | 8 | 6 | 7 | + | 4 | 2 | 4 | 1 | = |

Do that on a calculator. What answer did you get?

Read the answer upside down. What word is it?

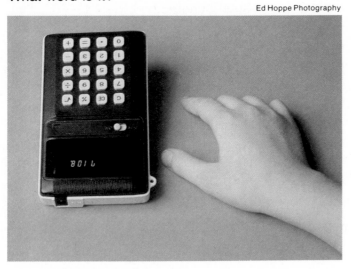

Other words can be found by doing these on a calculator. Find the word for each answer.

1. 100,004 − 22,659

2. 10,001 − 9291

3. 5981 + 2098

4. 11,004 − 3,899

5. 13,605 − 9096

6. 445 + 360

7. 1411 − 1066

8. 3059 + 645

9. 1235 − 428

10. 399,898 − 19,979

11. 377,999 + 199,346

12. 2725 + 3212

13. 26 + 87,321 − 8358 + 792 − 40,466

14. 10,125 + 2986 − 7898 + 6137 − 3275 + 37,000

39

CHAPTER REVIEW

Add.

1. 583
    +236

2. 291
    +327

3. 9284
    +1647

4. 1243
    +9928

5. 21,572
    +60,255

6. 300,809
    +296,280

7. 311,854
    +485,829

8. 2,467,009
    +   28,691

Round to the nearest thousand and the nearest hundred.

9. 3720

10. 2295

11. 8551

12. 62,449

13. 9509

14. Estimate the total points.

Game 1	132
Game 2	290
Game 3	219

15. Nancy bowled games of 201, 186, and 189. What was her three-game total?

16. Paul got scores of 75, 75, 25, and 100 by throwing four darts. What was his total score?

Subtract.

17. 6925
    −4132

18. 5210
    −1009

19. 7006
    −6123

20. 5278
    −1996

21. At a spook convention there were 13,928 witches and 8019 ghosts. Estimate how many more witches than ghosts were at the spook convention.

22. Ellen wants to buy a bike that costs $112. She has saved $18. How much more does she need?

23. Jane read two books. One had 183 pages. The other had 280 pages. How many pages were in both books?

3 Multiplication

Fredrik D. Bodin

41

Multiplication Facts

Mr. and Mrs. Wynn and their 2 children spent a vacation in Florida. Each person brought 2 rolls of film. How many rolls of film did they bring?

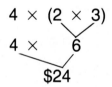

$$2 + 2 + 2 + 2 = 8$$

$$4 \times 2 = 8$$

factors ⌐↑___↑   ↑⌐ product

They brought 8 rolls of film.

Each roll of film costs $3. How much did the film cost? Here are two ways to find how much the film cost.

$(4 \times 2) \times 3$ Do what is in $4 \times (2 \times 3)$
the ( ) first.
8    $\times$ 3 $4 \times$ 6

$24 $24

Are both answers the same?

Exercises

Multiply.

1. 8×0 2. 3×4 3. 2×2 4. 4×9 5. 7×6

6. 7×3 7. 4×7 8. 0×1 9. 5×8 10. 6×6

11. 4×8 12. 9×5 13. 3×8 14. 8×3 15. 9×0

16. 8×9 **17.** 9×8 **18.** 3×9 **19.** 0×0 **20.** 1×1

21. $\begin{array}{r} 9 \\ \times 6 \\ \hline \end{array}$ **22.** $\begin{array}{r} 8 \\ \times 5 \\ \hline \end{array}$ **23.** $\begin{array}{r} 7 \\ \times 4 \\ \hline \end{array}$ **24.** $\begin{array}{r} 6 \\ \times 3 \\ \hline \end{array}$ **25.** $\begin{array}{r} 5 \\ \times 2 \\ \hline \end{array}$

26. $\begin{array}{r} 7 \\ \times 5 \\ \hline \end{array}$ **27.** $\begin{array}{r} 8 \\ \times 6 \\ \hline \end{array}$ **28.** $\begin{array}{r} 9 \\ \times 7 \\ \hline \end{array}$ **29.** $\begin{array}{r} 0 \\ \times 8 \\ \hline \end{array}$ **30.** $\begin{array}{r} 1 \\ \times 9 \\ \hline \end{array}$

31. $(2 \times 4) \times 2$ **32.** $2 \times (4 \times 2)$ **33.** $(3 \times 3) \times 3$ **34.** $4 \times (2 \times 3)$

35. $1 \times (3 \times 1)$ **36.** $(0 \times 9) \times 6$ **37.** $0 \times (4 \times 6)$ **38.** $(3 \times 3) \times 9$

39. 4×6 **40.** 6×4 **41.** Is $4 \times 6 = 6 \times 4$?

42. 3×9 **43.** 9×3 **44.** Is $3 \times 9 = 9 \times 3$?

45. The Wynns spent 3 weeks on vacation. How many days was that?

46. Paula bought each of her 4 closest friends a $5 gift. How much did she spend for the gifts?

47. The Wynns spent the first 4 days at Disney World. Tim went on the same ride 5 times each day. How many times did Tim go on that ride?

48. Each member of the Wynn family bought a $9 T-shirt at Disney World. How much did they spend for T-shirts?

Photri

49. During the second week Sam and Paula each took 2 pictures a day for 4 days. How many pictures did they take in those 4 days?

50. On the last day of vacation, each of the Wynns bought 2 gifts costing $3 each. How much did they spend for the gifts?

Multiples of Ten

The trainer feeds each porpoise 30 fish during the show. There are 4 porpoises. How many fish are needed?

James P. Rowan

Multiply the ones by 4.	**Multiply the tens by 4.**

T	O
3	0
×	4
	0

H	T	O
	3	0
	×	4
1	2	0

	3	T
×		4
1	2	T

120 fish are needed.

A maximum of 300 tickets can be sold for each show. How many tickets can be sold for 4 shows?

Multiply the ones by 4.	**Multiply the tens by 4.**	**Multiply the hundreds by 4.**

H	T	O
3	0	0
	×	4
		0

H	T	O
3	0	0
	×	4
	0	0

Th	H	T	O
	3	0	0
		×	4
1	2	0	0

1200 tickets can be sold.

Exercises

Multiply.

1. 7
   ×5

2. 70
   ×5

3. 700
   ×5

4. 50
   ×7

5. 500
   ×7

6.	8 ×4	7.	80 ×4	8.	800 ×4	9.	40 ×8	10.	400 ×8
11.	90 ×2	12.	20 ×9	13.	70 ×6	14.	60 ×8	15.	50 ×7
16.	50 ×4	17.	500 ×4	18.	600 ×7	19.	800 ×7	20.	900 ×8
21.	10 ×5	22.	50 ×9	23.	30 ×9	24.	70 ×2	25.	700 ×7

James P. Rowan

26. The seals get 30 fish during each show. How many fish will they get during 3 shows?

27. How many fish will the seals get during 5 shows?

28. An aquarium has 200 different kinds of fish. It has 6 fish of each kind. How many fish are there?

29. Dolphins can swim 40 feet in one second. How far can they swim in 9 seconds?

30. There are 3 porpoises. The trainer feeds each porpoise 30 fish per show. How many fish are needed for 6 shows?

31. 300 people attend each show. There are 2 shows each day. How many people attend the show in one week?

Multiplying 10's and 100's

Notice the pattern of 0's in these products.

30	300	30	300	300
×2	×2	×20	×20	×200
60	600	600	6000	60,000

The same pattern is shown in these products.

60	600	60	600	600
×8	×8	×80	×80	×800
480	4800	4800	48,000	480,000

Is the same pattern shown in these products?

5	50	50	500	500
×8	×8	×80	×80	×800
40	400	4000	40,000	400,000

Exercises

Multiply.

1. 30
    ×70

2. 300
    ×70

3. 300
    ×700

4. 700
    ×30

5. 400
    ×50

6. 40
    ×60

7. 400
    ×60

8. 400
    ×600

9. 600
    ×40

10. 200
    ×200

11. 40
    ×40

12. 400
    ×40

13. 90
    ×60

14. 60
    ×90

15. 900
    ×600

16. $\begin{array}{r} 30 \\ \times 90 \\ \hline \end{array}$	17. $\begin{array}{r} 70 \\ \times 20 \\ \hline \end{array}$	18. $\begin{array}{r} 700 \\ \times 40 \\ \hline \end{array}$	19. $\begin{array}{r} 50 \\ \times 20 \\ \hline \end{array}$	20. $\begin{array}{r} 500 \\ \times 20 \\ \hline \end{array}$
21. $\begin{array}{r} 50 \\ \times 40 \\ \hline \end{array}$	22. $\begin{array}{r} 600 \\ \times 50 \\ \hline \end{array}$	23. $\begin{array}{r} 800 \\ \times 100 \\ \hline \end{array}$	24. $\begin{array}{r} 600 \\ \times 30 \\ \hline \end{array}$	25. $\begin{array}{r} 500 \\ \times 600 \\ \hline \end{array}$
26. $\begin{array}{r} 900 \\ \times 800 \\ \hline \end{array}$	27. $\begin{array}{r} 900 \\ \times 900 \\ \hline \end{array}$	28. $\begin{array}{r} 100 \\ \times 100 \\ \hline \end{array}$	29. $\begin{array}{r} 200 \\ \times 50 \\ \hline \end{array}$	30. $\begin{array}{r} 900 \\ \times 100 \\ \hline \end{array}$

31. Pokey goes 2 centimeters each minute. How far will he go in 6 minutes?

32. Speedy goes 20 centimeters each minute. How far will he go in 6 minutes?

33. How far will Pokey go in 60 minutes?

34. How far will Speedy go in 1 hour?

Tricky Move

Lay 10 objects on your desk so that they look like this.

Now move *only 3 objects* to make them look like this.

Extra Practice—Set A, page 320

Tens, Hundreds, and Thousands

	TTh	Th	H	T	O
10 × 10 means 10 tens.			1	0	0
31 × 10 means 31 tens.			3	1	0
100 × 10 means 100 tens.		1	0	0	0
256 × 10 means 256 tens.		2	5	6	0
10 × 100 means 10 hundreds.		1	0	0	0
51 × 100 means 51 hundreds.		5	1	0	0
317 × 100 means 317 hundreds.	3	1	7	0	0

Exercises

Write a numeral for each of the following:

1. 16 tens
2. 16 hundreds
3. 95 tens
4. 86 hundreds

5. 524 tens
6. 502 tens
7. 87 tens
8. 25 hundreds

9. 5 tens
10. 9 hundreds
11. 395 hundreds
12. 23 tens

13. 60 hundreds
14. 20 tens
15. 340 tens
16. 300 tens

17. 23 thousands
18. 230 thousands
19. 1000 thousands

20. 1000 tens
21. 2304 tens
22. 2000 thousands

Hidden Fruit

What fruit gets its name by combining the name
of a tree and the name of another fruit?

Coded name: 64–1111–8–114–49–64–64–7383–114

167 −118	8004 − 801	13,938 + 6,158	169 +2831
A	**B**	**C**	**D**
933 −819	1239 − 884	10,083 +63,219	9911 −7890
E	**F**	**G**	**H**
418 +693	5094 +1200	7931 −5117	8032 − 649
I	**J**	**K**	**L**
999 + 9	801 −793	11,130 +17,930	1208 −1144
M	**N**	**O**	**P**

Estimating Products

Ivan used his calculator to multiply 37 and 28.

Then he estimated the product by rounding both numbers to the nearest ten and multiplying "in his head."

Ed Hoppe Photography

296 can't be right.
40 × 30 = 1200.
What did I
do wrong?

$$37 \xrightarrow{\text{is about}} 40$$
$$\times 28 \xrightarrow{\text{is about}} \times 30$$
$$\xrightarrow{\hspace{2cm}} 1200$$

The product
should be
about 1200.

Why did he think he did something wrong?

Here is how to estimate some other products.

595 —— Round to the nearest 100. ⟶ 600
×8 —— Leave a single digit as it is. ⟶ ×8
⎯⎯⎯⎯⎯⎯⎯
4800

396 — Round to the nearest 100. ⟶ 400
×72 — Round to the nearest 10. ⟶ ×70
⎯⎯⎯⎯⎯⎯⎯
28,000

485 — Round to the nearest 100. ⟶ 500
×750 — Round to the nearest 100. ⟶ ×800
⎯⎯⎯⎯⎯⎯⎯
400,000

Exercises

Estimate each product.

1. 47
   ×6

2. 39
   ×21

3. 198
   ×4

4. 402
   ×6

5. 51
   ×31

6. 302
   ×8

7. 91
   ×49

8. 99
   ×49

9. 397
   ×41

10. 208
    ×79

11. 402
    ×199

12. 797
    ×301

13. 349
    ×350

14. 550
    ×449

15. 126
    ×76

16. 890
    ×890

17. 555
    ×730

18. 650
    ×605

19. 777
    ×200

20. 930
    ×20

21. Jim tries to run 14 miles every week. Estimate how many miles a year that is.

22. Jim's dad tries to run 210 miles a month. Estimate how many miles a year that is.

23. Jim's dad usually runs 154 miles a month more than his son. Estimate how many miles a year that is.

John D. Brooks/Joan Kramer and Associates

Look Again

$$66 \times 94$$

Round both factors down.

$$60 \times 90$$

5400

Round both factors up.

$$70 \times 100$$

7000

The product is between the two estimates.

Use this method to give two estimates for each product.

$$54 \times 75 \qquad 64 \times 64 \qquad 28 \times 96 \qquad 250 \times 16$$

Multiplication (2-digit by 1-digit)

There are 50 pupils and 3 adults on each bus. Here is a way to find how many people are on all of the buses.

	on each bus		number of buses		on all buses
Pupils:	50	×	6	=	300
Adults:	3	×	6	=	18
People:					318	Add.

Here is another way to find how many.

Multiply the ones by 6.	**Multiply the tens by 6.**

In both ways, is 3 multiplied by 6? Is 50 multiplied by 6?

In the second way, why is the *1 ten* added to the *30 tens*?

52

Exercises

Multiply.

1. 8 ×4	2. 70 ×4	3. 78 ×4	4. 7 ×6	5. 30 ×6	6. 37 ×6
7. 5 ×3	8. 60 ×3	9. 65 ×3	10. 30 ×2	11. 35 ×1	12. 82 ×4
13. 22 ×4	14. 41 ×2	15. 51 ×0	16. 60 ×4	17. 36 ×3	18. 71 ×6
19. 29 ×7	20. 70 ×5	21. 50 ×6	22. 58 ×8	23. 83 ×0	24. 63 ×5
25. 89 ×6	26. 74 ×9	27. 69 ×7	28. 96 ×5	29. 85 ×9	30. 49 ×8
31. 59 ×8	32. 26 ×9	33. 98 ×5	34. 62 ×7	35. 88 ×8	36. 99 ×9

37. 4 buses took people to a basketball game. There were 48 pupils and 2 adults on each bus. How many people went to the game?

38. At Big Ben Elementary School there are 5 classes. There are 23 girls and 21 boys in each class. How many pupils are there?

Magic Square

Multiply across.

Multiply down.

Multiply on this diagonal.

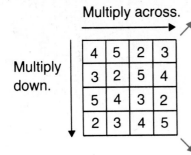

4	5	2	3
3	2	5	4
5	4	3	2
2	3	4	5

Multiply on this diagonal.

What did you discover about the ten answers?

Multiplication (3-digit by 1-digit)

Dominick has 4 albums of postcards. Each album has 264 postcards. You can multiply to find how many postcards he has.

Multiply the ones by 4.	Multiply the tens by 4.	Multiply the hundreds by 4.

Dominick has 1056 postcards.

Exercises

Multiply.

1. 121 $\times 2$	2. 239 $\times 6$	3. 193 $\times 5$	4. 381 $\times 4$	5. 475 $\times 8$
6. 306 $\times 7$	7. 412 $\times 4$	8. 736 $\times 3$	9. 517 $\times 1$	10. 693 $\times 8$
11. 281 $\times 4$	12. 173 $\times 7$	13. 492 $\times 8$	14. 508 $\times 6$	15. 914 $\times 5$
16. 391 $\times 3$	17. 907 $\times 7$	18. 693 $\times 4$	19. 782 $\times 8$	20. 891 $\times 5$

21. 509 ×3	22. 815 ×8	23. 649 ×9	24. 962 ×5	25. 789 ×9
26. 637 ×5	27. 908 ×1	28. 777 ×6	29. 259 ×8	30. 654 ×7

31. Simon has 3 boxes of football cards. Each box has 225 cards. How many cards does he have?

32. Each display case has 250 buttons. How many buttons are in 6 display cases?

33. Another display case has 138 buttons. How many buttons are in 9 of these cases?

34. Lucy collects coins. Each coin book contains 6 pages. Each page contains 30 coins. How many coins are needed to fill 7 books?

35. Renaldo has been saving a certain comic strip every day for the last 5 years (including 2 leap years). How many does he now have?

©(1978) United Features Syndicate Inc.

©(1980) United Features Syndicate Inc.

Extra Practice—Set A, page 321

Multiplication (2-digit)

50 ROWS

46 SEATS

7 more rows of seats are to be put at the back of this theater. How many seats will the theater have then?

Multiply by 6.			**Multiply by 40.**			**Add the products.**		

H	T	O
	5	7
×	4	6
3	4	2

```
  5 7
×   6
3 4 2
```

Th	H	T	O
		5	7
	×	4	6
	3	4	2
	2	8	0

```
  5 7
×  4 T
2 2 8 T
```

Th	H	T	O
		5	7
	×	4	6
	3	4	2
2	2	8	0
2	6	2	2

Estimate the product of 65 and 28. Then discuss each step in the multiplication below.

$$
\begin{array}{r}
65 \\
\times\,28 \\
\hline
520 \\
\end{array}
\qquad
\begin{array}{r}
65 \\
\times\,28 \\
\hline
520 \\
1300 \\
\end{array}
\qquad
\begin{array}{r}
65 \\
\times\,28 \\
\hline
520 \\
1300 \\
\hline
1820 \\
\end{array}
$$

How does the answer compare with your estimate?

Exercises

Multiply.

1. 34
   ×14

2. 17
   ×31

3. 59
   ×28

4. 61
   ×65

5. 74
   ×44

6. 27
   ×4

7. 27
   ×30

8. 27
   ×34

9. 38
   ×16

10. 43
    ×32

11. 65
    ×17

12. 52
    ×46

13. 78
    ×39

14. 90
    ×55

15. 49
    ×71

16. 81
    ×63

17. 97
    ×29

18. 60
    ×81

19. 58
    ×73

20. 86
    ×95

21. 68
    ×27

22. 71
    ×51

23. 93
    ×68

24. 48
    ×57

25. 98
    ×76

26. A theater shows a movie 19 times in one week. How many times will it be shown in 4 weeks?

27. Another theater shows a movie 79 times a month. How many times will it be shown in 3 months?

28. A theater shows a movie 3 times each day. How many times will it be shown in 4 weeks?

29. The play *Fiddler on the Roof* ran for 8 years on Broadway. There were 34 performances a month. How many performances were given?

Multiplication (3-digit by 2-digit)

To break the bowling record, you would have to average 213 pins for 28 games.

How many pins would you have to get?

Multiply by 8.	**Multiply by 20.**	**Add the products.**

Th	H	T	O
	2	1	3
	×	2	8
1	7	0	4

Th	H	T	O			2	1	3
	2	1	3			×	2	T
	×	2	8		4	2	6	T
1	7	0	4
4	2	6	0

Th	H	T	O
	2	1	3
	×	2	8
1	7	0	4
4	2	6	0
5	9	6	4

You would have to get 5964 pins.

Discuss each step in the multiplication below.

Th	H	T	O
	5	2	7
	×	3	9
4	7	4	3

TTh	Th	H	T	O
			6	
		5	2	7
		×	3	9
	4	7	4	3
1	5	8	1	0

TTh	Th	H	T	O
		5	2	7
		×	3	9
	4	7	4	3
1	5	8	1	0
2	0	5	5	3

58

Exercises

Multiply.

1. 128
    × 34

2. 206
    × 21

3. 281
    × 12

4. 198
    × 50

5. 329
    × 41

6. 382
    × 56

7. 492
    × 37

8. 509
    × 67

9. 827
    × 43

10. 628
    × 26

11. 730
    × 80

12. 938
    × 74

13. 837
    × 54

14. 971
    × 58

15. 683
    × 69

16. 650
    × 28

17. 881
    × 19

18. 705
    × 57

19. 399
    × 76

20. 482
    × 66

21. 733
    × 73

22. 625
    × 55

23. 948
    × 83

24. 592
    × 97

25. 927
    × 38

26. The leapfrog record is 739 leaps each hour for 23 hours. How many leaps set the record?

27. Picasso painted more pictures than did any other artist. He painted 173 paintings a year for 78 years. How many paintings is that?

What Is Missing?

1. 1 ▓
    ×   7
    ─────
    1 ▓ 3

2. ▓ 0 0
    ×   3
    ─────
    2 1 0 ▓

3. ▓ 1 ▓
    ×   3
    ─────
    ▓ 7 ▓ 1

4. 2 ▓
    × 1 7
    ─────
    ▓ 0 3
    2 ▓ 0
    ─────
    ▓ ▓ 3

Multiplication (3-digit)

Jerry and Kim had to do these multiplication exercises on a math test.

$$532 \times 126 \qquad 429 \times 308$$

Here is how Jerry multiplied 532 by 126.

Multiply by 6.	Multiply by 20.	Multiply by 100.	Add the products.

TTh	Th	H	T	O
		1	1	
	5	3	2	
×	1	2	6	
3	1	9	2	

TTh	Th	H	T	O
		5	3	2
	×	1	2	6
	3	1	9	2
1	0	6	4	0

TTh	Th	H	T	O
		5	3	2
	×	1	2	6
	3	1	9	2
1	0	6	4	0
5	3	2	0	0

TTh	Th	H	T	O
		5	3	2
	×	1	2	6
	3	1	9	2
1	0	6	4	0
5	3	2	0	0
6	7	0	3	2

Here is how Kim multiplied 429 by 308.

$$
\begin{array}{r}
429 \\
\times 308 \\
\hline
3432 \\
0000 \\
128700 \\
\hline
132{,}132
\end{array}
$$

Jerry had a different way of multiplying 429 by 308.

How do the two ways differ?

Which way do you prefer?

$$
\begin{array}{r}
429 \\
\times 308 \\
\hline
3432 \\
128700 \\
\hline
132{,}132
\end{array}
$$

60

Exercises

Multiply.

1. 251 ×107	2. 616 ×402	3. 354 ×803	4. 760 ×504	5. 859 ×609
6. 217 ×319	7. 509 ×282	8. 371 ×537	9. 488 ×716	10. 960 ×544
11. 300 ×104	12. 628 ×340	13. 590 ×175	14. 610 ×600	15. 700 ×940
16. 440 ×440	17. 475 ×386	18. 706 ×305	19. 909 ×310	20. 800 ×345

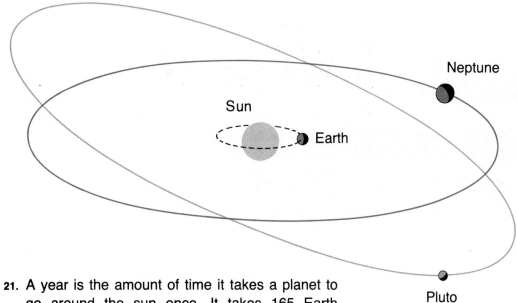

21. A year is the amount of time it takes a planet to go around the sun once. It takes 165 Earth years for Neptune to go around the sun once. How many Earth days is that?

22. It takes 249 Earth years for Pluto to go around the sun once. How many Earth days is that?

Multiplication (4-digit by 1-digit)

Two elephants get 2650 pounds of hay each week. How many pounds of hay will they get in 4 weeks?

To find out, multiply 2650 by 4.

Multiply the ones by 4.	Multiply the tens by 4.	Multiply the hundreds by 4.	Multiply the thousands by 4.

Th	H	T	O
2	6	5	0
		×	4
			0

Th	H	T	O
		2	
2	6	5	0
		×	4
		0	0

Th	H	T	O
	2	2	
2	6	5	0
		×	4
	6	0	0

TTh	Th	H	T	O
		2	2	
	2	6	5	0
			×	4
1	0	6	0	0

4 elephants will get 10,600 pounds of hay in a week.

Exercises

Multiply.

1. 2404
   ×5

2. 3351
   ×2

3. 5370
   ×4

4. 2761
   ×7

5. 4283
   ×3

6. 1506
   ×6

7. 2814
   ×3

8. 6875
   ×2

9. 4651
   ×7

10. 7280
    ×5

11. 3570
    ×7

12. 4134
    ×6

13. 5203
    ×2

14. 6195
    ×1

15. 2708
    ×8

16. 2478
    ×6

17. 5310
    ×9

18. 7876
    ×2

19. 6971
    ×6

20. 5180
    ×4

21. 9476
    ×8

22. 5963
    ×3

23. 6825
    ×5

24. 7249
    ×6

25. 9983
    ×9

26. A train travels 3700 miles a week. How many miles will it travel in 8 weeks?

27. Another train travels 3809 miles a month. How many miles will it travel in 7 months?

28. There are 1760 yards in a mile. How many feet is that?

29. How many yards are there in 5 miles?

30. Each elephant gets 1325 pounds of hay each week. How many pounds of hay will 8 elephants get in a week?

31. Each elephant gets 1325 pounds of hay each week. How many pounds of hay will 1 elephant get in 5 weeks?

William E. Remark/Cyr Color Photo Agency

32. Each of these hippopotamuses is fed 1250 pounds of food a week. How many pounds of food are they fed in 8 weeks?

Try This

Follow these steps to multiply 12 by 37.

1. Divide by 2. Forget the remainders. Do that until you get to 1.

```
12 ÷ 2
 6 ÷ 2
 3 ÷ 2
 1
```

```
 37 × 2
 74 × 2
148 × 2
296
```

2. Multiply by 2. Do that until the columns are the same length.

3. If a number in this column is even, cross out both numbers like this.

```
12        37
 6        74
 3       148
 1       296
        ─────
         444
```

4. Add the rest of the numbers in this column. This is the product.

Now try this method to multiply 17 by 45.

SKILLS REVIEW

Group A

1. 83
   −12

2. 139
   − 17

3. 70
   −48

4. 132
   − 60

5. 590
   −418

6. 382
   −119

7. 709
   − 69

8. 421
   −158

9. 902
   −517

10. 82
   −78

11. 1005
   − 999

12. 273
   −198

Group C

Watch the signs!

1. 593
   + 11

2. 1003
   − 601

3. 821
   − 90

4. 492
   − 16

5. 4927
   +1587

6. 908
   −719

7. 182
   +928

8. 4293
   −1382

9. 1058
   − 839

10. 600
   −515

11. 5060
   + 444

12. 7100
   +2990

Group B

1. 63
   14
   +18

2. 17
   38
   40
   +64

3. 16
   +92

4. 152
   421
   +2140

5. 100
   312
   611
   +138

6. 4219
   +5781

7. 991
   130
   +700

8. 492
   420
   +520

9. 6
   60
   600
   +6000

10. 4293
   1320
   4300
   +9000

11. 143,928
   + 75,938

12. 36,299
   +64,901

13. 63,319
   +952,839

14. 406,124
   +392,908

Solving Problems

1. A piano has 88 keys. There are 52 white keys. The rest are black. How many keys are black?

2. The earliest piano in existence was built in 1720. How many years ago was that piano built?

3. A pipe organ has 18,000 pipes. One of the largest organs in the world has 12,067 more pipes than that. How many pipes does that organ have?

4. An upright piano is 60 inches tall. A spinet piano is 39 inches tall. How much taller is an upright piano than a spinet piano?

5. A piano string can be as short as 5 centimeters. Other piano strings can be 40 times that long. How long can the piano strings be?

6. Beethoven was born in the year 1770. Mozart died in the year 1791. How old was Beethoven when Mozart died?

7. Some concert pianos are 9 feet long. How many inches long are they?

8. Beethoven lived from 1770 to 1827. How old was he when he died?

9. Mozart was born in the year 1756. Five years later he started composing. What year was that?

10. Chopin was born 40 years after Beethoven was born. In what year was Chopin born?

The Bettmann Archive

The Bettmann Archive

CHAPTER REVIEW

Multiply.

1. 5×9 2. 2×7 3. 4×1 4. 7×7 5. 8×8

6. 6×9 7. 5×0 8. 9×2 9. 0×1 10. 9×9

Write a numeral for each of the following:

11. 12 tens   12. 45 hundreds   13. 36 tens

14. 243 hundreds   15. 72 thousands   16. 20 thousands

Estimate each product.

17. 25   18.   23   19. 675   20. 875   21.   749
    $\times 6$ $\times 45$ $\times 9$ $\times 94$ $\times 894$

Multiply.

22. 30   23. 40   24. 40   25. 80   26. 800
    $\times 8$ $\times 6$ $\times 60$ $\times 90$ $\times 90$

27. 800   28. 300   29. 500   30. 37   31. 59
    $\times 5$ $\times 400$ $\times 700$ $\times 7$ $\times 5$

32. 348   33. 896   34. 67   35. 59   36. 601
    $\times 6$ $\times 4$ $\times 45$ $\times 78$ $\times 27$

37. 316   38. 532   39. 486   40. 4378   41. 3291
    $\times 59$ $\times 678$ $\times 593$ $\times 6$ $\times 4$

42. Pat has 6 albums of postcards. Each album has 118 postcards. How many postcards does Pat have?

43. A theater has 36 rows of seats with 46 seats in each row. How many seats are there in the theater?

4 Division

Grant Heilman

Division

Here are two ways to show "12 divided by 4."

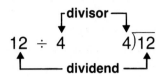

To find each **quotient,** you can use multiplication.

How many 4's in 12?

$$4\overline{)12} \longrightarrow \square \times 4 = 12 \longrightarrow 3 \times 4 = 12 \longrightarrow \quad \text{quotient} \longrightarrow \overset{3}{4\overline{)12}}$$

Exercises

Use multiplication to find each quotient.

1. $6\overline{)18}$ $\square \times 6 = 18$ 2. $5\overline{)35}$ $\square \times 5 = 35$

3. $4\overline{)32}$ 4. $7\overline{)42}$ 5. $8\overline{)16}$ 6. $9\overline{)54}$ 7. $7\overline{)63}$ 8. $9\overline{)72}$

9. $7\overline{)21}$ 10. $6\overline{)24}$ 11. $9\overline{)36}$ 12. $9\overline{)45}$ 13. $8\overline{)56}$ 14. $4\overline{)36}$

John is not next to Joe or Tom.
Ted is not next to Joe or Tom.
Jim is not next to Joe or Ted.
Tom is just to the right of Jim.

For a clue to who's where, use Code I from page
69 like this.

		Write on
Divide.	Use the code.	your paper.

15. $18 \div 9 = 2 \longrightarrow$ *J* is code letter for 2. $\longrightarrow$ 15. *J*

16. $20 \div 4 = 5 \longrightarrow$ *I* is code letter for 5. $\longrightarrow$ 16. *I*

17. 56 ÷ 7   24. 0 ÷ 8

18. 45 ÷ 9   25. 48 ÷ 6

19. 72 ÷ 8   26. 40 ÷ 8

20. 5 ÷ 1   27. 36 ÷ 6

21. 6 ÷ 6   28. 24 ÷ 4

22. 28 ÷ 7   29. 63 ÷ 9

23. 15 ÷ 5   30. 0 ÷ 7

Code I

quotient	letter	quotient	letter
0	E	5	I
1	N	6	D
2	J	7	L
3	H	8	M
4	T	9	S

Read the answers for exercises 15—30 for a clue to who's where.

Do you need more help to tell who's where?

Use Code II to do exercises 31—46. Read answers to tell who's where.

31. 16 ÷ 2   39. 3 ÷ 3

32. 25 ÷ 5   40. 16 ÷ 4

33. 14 ÷ 7   41. 24 ÷ 3

34. 42 ÷ 6   42. 30 ÷ 5

35. 48 ÷ 8   43. 32 ÷ 8

36. 0 ÷ 2   44. 7 ÷ 1

37. 45 ÷ 5   45. 6 ÷ 1

38. 49 ÷ 7   46. 30 ÷ 6

Code II

quotient	letter	quotient	letter
0	H	5	E
1	I	6	O
2	D	7	J
3	Y	8	T
4	M	9	N

Finding Quotients

The Millers gave their 3 children $75 to spend on vacation. They are to share the money equally. How much will each child get?

Estimate the tens digit.	Multiply and subtract.	Bring down the ones. Estimate the ones digit.	Multiply and subtract.

$3\overline{)75}$

$3\overline{)7}$ is about 2.
Try 2 as the tens digit.

Each child will get $25.

```
  T|O
  2 |
3)7|5
  6 |
  1
```

```
  T|O
  2 |
3)7|5
  6|↓
  1|5
```

$3\overline{)15}$ is 5.
Use 5 as the ones digit.

```
  T|O
  2|5
3)7|5
  6|↓
  1|5
  1|5
   |0
```

Tell how to estimate each digit in the quotient.

$$4\overline{)9\ 6} \longrightarrow \begin{array}{r} 2\ \ \\ 4\overline{)9\ 6} \\ 8\ \ \\ \hline 1\ 6 \end{array} \longrightarrow \begin{array}{r} 24 \\ 4\overline{)96} \\ 8\ \ \\ \hline 16 \\ 16 \\ \hline 0 \end{array}$$

Exercises

Divide.

1. $8\overline{)96}$ 2. $7\overline{)91}$ 3. $9\overline{)99}$ 4. $6\overline{)96}$

5. $7\overline{)84}$ 6. $5\overline{)90}$ 7. $4\overline{)88}$ 8. $5\overline{)85}$

9. $6\overline{)78}$ 10. $4\overline{)72}$ 11. $3\overline{)87}$ 12. $4\overline{)92}$

13. $2\overline{)78}$ 14. $2\overline{)90}$ 15. $5\overline{)70}$ 16. $3\overline{)99}$

17. $4\overline{)56}$ 18. $4\overline{)96}$ 19. $3\overline{)84}$ 20. $2\overline{)98}$

21. $6\overline{)90}$ 22. $6\overline{)72}$ 23. $3\overline{)78}$ 24. $6\overline{)84}$

25. Janet had 57 hours of ballet lessons last month. Each lesson was 3 hours long. How many lessons did she have?

26. Four boys have to share 76 baseball cards evenly. How many should each boy get?

27. Frank earns $5 an hour. How many hours must he work to earn $95?

Frank Siteman/Taurus

Tom McGuire

28. Five girls hiked 84 miles in 4 days. They hiked the same number of miles each day. How many miles did they hike each day?

29. Mrs. Jones spent $60 on sleds for each of her 2 sons and 2 daughters. How much did each sled cost?

Finding Quotients

Bohdan Hrynewych/Picture Group

Anyone buying a bicycle from Mr. Martin gets 3 free reflectors. Mr. Martin has 423 reflectors. How many customers will get free reflectors?

Estimate the hundreds digit.	Multiply and subtract.	Estimate the tens digit. Multiply and subtract.	Estimate the ones digit. Multiply and subtract.
$3)\overline{423}$ 3)4 is about 1. Try 1 as the hundreds digit.	H T O 1 3)4 2 3 3 ̄ 1	H T O 1 4 3)4 2 3 3 ↓ ̄ 1 2 1 2 ̄ 0	H T O 1 4 1 3)4 2 3 3 ̄ 1 2 ↓ 1 2 ̄ 0 3 3 ̄ 0

141 customers will get free reflectors.

Tell how to estimate each digit in the quotient below.

$8\overline{)2608}$ $\longrightarrow$ $8\overline{)2\ 6\ 0\ 8}$ $\longrightarrow$ $\begin{array}{r} 3 \\ 8\overline{)2\ 6\ 0\ 8} \\ \underline{2\ 4} \\ 2\ 0 \end{array}$ $\longrightarrow$ $\begin{array}{r} 3\ 2 \\ 8\overline{)2\ 6\ 0\ 8} \\ \underline{2\ 4} \\ 2\ 0 \\ \underline{1\ 6} \\ 4\ 8 \end{array}$

$8\overline{)2}$ 8 > 2,
so the first
digit is not
in the thou-
sands place.

Exercises

Divide.

1. $2\overline{)374}$
2. $4\overline{)304}$
3. $6\overline{)294}$
4. $3\overline{)477}$

5. $7\overline{)847}$
6. $5\overline{)145}$
7. $8\overline{)520}$
8. $9\overline{)486}$

9. $3\overline{)369}$
10. $2\overline{)982}$
11. $5\overline{)680}$
12. $4\overline{)872}$

13. $6\overline{)750}$
14. $2\overline{)858}$
15. $5\overline{)785}$
16. $4\overline{)996}$

17. $9\overline{)2979}$
18. $7\overline{)1792}$
19. $9\overline{)1341}$
20. $4\overline{)4852}$

21. $4\overline{)2084}$
22. $8\overline{)9688}$
23. $2\overline{)3968}$
24. $6\overline{)1872}$

25. Cowgirl Pearl put a shoe on each hoof of some horses. If she used 368 horseshoes, how many horses did she shoe?

26. Sue needs to earn $375 this summer. How many yards will she have to mow if she charges $5 a yard?

27. A camp director is expecting 207 children to attend camp this summer. He needs 1 counselor for every 9 children. How many counselors are needed?

28. 2 brothers and 3 sisters received 875 stamps through the mail. How many stamps will each child get if the stamps are shared equally?

Remainders in Division

Margo opened a box of 675 paper cups. She put the same number of paper cups in each of 6 vending machines. How many cups were put in each vending machine? How many cups were left over?

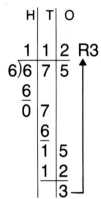

Record the remainder 3 like this.

112 cups were put in each machine.

3 cups were left over.

Exercises

Divide.

1. 3)647

2. 4)329

3. 6)897

4. 4)330

5. 7)320

6. 3)5000

7. 2)7233

8. 9)1099

9. 6)366

10. 5)8188

11. 7)1000

12. 8)3007

13. 5)2056

14. 8)4360

15. 6)6770

16. 9)2004

17. 3)1499

18. 5)827

19. 4)2222

20. 7)9999

Extra Practice—Set A, page 324

21. 9)$\overline{4019}$ 22. 8)$\overline{2760}$ 23. 4)$\overline{1714}$ 24. 5)$\overline{8271}$

25. 6)$\overline{6686}$ 26. 7)$\overline{3632}$ 27. 8)$\overline{9059}$ 28. 9)$\overline{2676}$

Complete each exercise.

29. 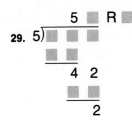 30. 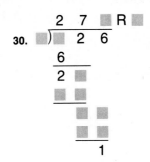 31.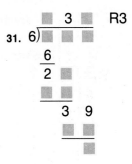

32. 8 people netted 1005 smelt. They shared them equally and threw the rest back. How many smelt did each person get? How many were thrown back?

33. A company has 279 wagon wheels. That is enough for how many wagons? How many wheels will be left over?

34. Bill and four of his friends shared 138 baseball cards equally, except that Bill got the extra cards. How many cards did each friend get? How many did Bill get?

Too Big for Commas?

A googol is a very LARGE number. To name a googol, write 1 followed by one hundred 0's. Which of these shows where the commas belong?

1,000,000,···,000
100 zeros

10,000,···,000
100 zeros

100,000,···,000
100 zeros

Checking Division

Here are two examples of how to check division.

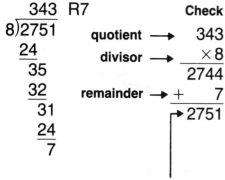

```
  343 R7                  Check
8)2751      quotient  →     343
  24        divisor   →     ×8
  35                      2744
  32        remainder →  +   7
  31                      →2751
  24
   7
```

This should be the dividend.

```
  312                           Check
6)1872                            312
  18      When the                ×6
   7      remainder             1872
   6      is 0, you
  12      need not
  12      write R0
   0      here.
```

Is it necessary to add
the remainder of zero?

Exercises

Check each division. Is the answer correct? Write *Yes* or *No* for each exercise.

1. 6)977   162 R2

2. 5)3289   657 R4

3. 8)239   31 R1

4. 3)3335   1111 R2

5. 9)2000   222 R2

6. 8)4736   592

7. 3)1000   333 R3

8. 7)2080   297 R1

9. 5)1099   219 R4

10. 8)9   1 R1

11. 1)2536   2536

12. 9)8279   919 R9

Divide and check.

13. 7)2744

14. 6)3759

15. 4)3815

16. 2)966

17. 5)6759

18. 3)9557

19. 8)9696

20. 7)8925

21. To check division, multiply the ___ by the ___
and add the ___. The answer should be the ___.

SKILLS REVIEW

Add.

1. $\quad$ 25 $\quad +69$	2. $\quad$ 59 $\quad +91$	3. $\quad$ 56 $\quad +40$	4. $\quad$ 34 $\quad +20$	5. $\quad$ 68 $\quad +40$
6. $\quad$ 57 $\quad$ 605 $\quad + \ 28$	7. $\quad$ 8 $\quad$ 37 $\quad +960$	8. $\quad$ 205 $\quad$ 38 $\quad +602$	9. $\quad$ 286 $\quad$ 4509 $\quad + \ 509$	10. $\quad$ 56 $\quad$ 56 $\quad$ 56 $\quad +56$

Subtract.

11. $\quad$ 509 $\quad -392$	12. $\quad$ 777 $\quad -325$	13. $\quad$ 5432 $\quad -5000$	14. $\quad$ 6021 $\quad -5700$	15. $\quad$ 3817 $\quad -2900$
16. $\quad$ 3090 $\quad -2196$	17. $\quad$ 5066 $\quad -3092$	18. $\quad$ 8091 $\quad -7192$	19. $\quad$ 2783 $\quad -1784$	20. $\quad$ 8472 $\quad -2695$

Multiply.

21. $\quad$ 76 $\quad \times 8$	22. $\quad$ 58 $\quad \times 5$	23. $\quad$ 30 $\quad \times 9$	24. $\quad$ 30 $\quad \times 90$	25. $\quad$ 60 $\quad \times 40$
26. $\quad$ 26 $\quad \times 80$	27. $\quad$ 92 $\quad \times 60$	28. $\quad$ 90 $\quad \times 18$	29. $\quad$ 76 $\quad \times 93$	30. $\quad$ 15 $\quad \times 87$

31. Lil has 5 hats. Jill has 9 hats. How many more hats does Jill have?

32. Gil has 4509 stamps. Bill has 591 stamps. How many stamps are there in all?

33. Loril is 2 inches taller than Robin. Loril is 51 inches tall. How tall is Robin?

34. Will has 73 marbles. Phil has 5 times as many. How many marbles does Phil have?

Divisibility Rules

A number is divisible by another number if the remainder is 0 when you divide.

$$\begin{array}{r} 22 \\ 7\overline{)154} \end{array}$$

154 is
divisible by 7.

$$\begin{array}{r} 51 \text{ R4} \\ 6\overline{)310} \end{array}$$

310 is **not**
divisible by 6.

$$\begin{array}{r} 214 \\ 9\overline{)1926} \end{array}$$

1926 is
divisible by 9.

A number is divisible by 2 if its last digit is even.

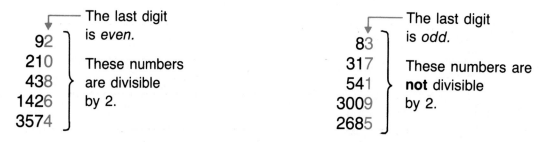

The last digit
is *even.*

92
210
438
1426
3574

These numbers
are divisible
by 2.

The last digit
is *odd.*

83
317
541
3009
2685

These numbers are
not divisible
by 2.

A number is divisible by 2 if its ones digit is ___0___ ,
___, ___, ___, or ___.

A number is divisible by 5 if its last digit is 0 or 5.

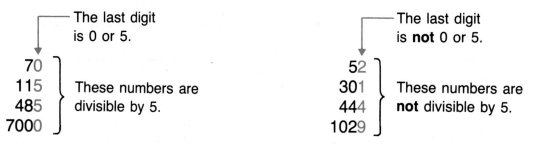

The last digit
is 0 or 5.

70
115
485
7000

These numbers are
divisible by 5.

The last digit
is **not** 0 or 5.

52
301
444
1029

These numbers are
not divisible by 5.

If you multiply any number by 10, what will the last digit of the product be?

A number is divisible by 10 if its last digit is ___.

Exercises

Is the first number divisible by the second number? Write *Yes* or *No*.

1. 432; 8   2. 4568; 7   3. 4000; 3   4. 711; 9

5. 135; 6   6. 3260; 9   7. 2145; 3   8. 111; 3

Complete the chart below.

	Number	Divisible by 2?	Divisible by 5?	Divisible by 10?
9.	426			
10.	305			
11.	800			
12.	123			
13.	390			
14.	538			
15.	1245			
16.	1007			
17.	3332			
18.	5554			
19.	1000			

How Can This Happen?

2 fathers and their 2 sons caught 3 fish of the same size. They shared the fish equally without cutting them.

Dividing by Multiples of Ten

Frank and Tony are planning a 920-mile trip on their bicycles this summer. If they travel 40 miles each day, how long will the trip take?

Think: How many 40's in 920?

$$40\overline{)920}$$

Estimate the quotient to decide how many digits it will have.

$$100 \times 40 = 4000$$
$$? \times 40 = 920$$
$$10 \times 40 = 400$$

The quotient is between 10 and 100.

The quotient has two digits. The first digit will be in the *tens* place.

Estimate the tens digit.	Multiply and subtract.	Estimate the ones digit.	Multiply and subtract.

$40\overline{)920}$	H T O
	    2
	 $40\overline{)9\ 2\ 0}$
	    8 0
	    1 2
		H T O
		    2 3
		 $40\overline{)9\ 2\ 0}$
		    8 0 ↓
		    1 2 0
			H T O
			    2 3
			 $40\overline{)9\ 2\ 0}$
			    8 0
			    1 2 0
			    1 2 0
			       0

$4\overline{)9}$ is about 2. Try 2 as the tens digit.		$4\overline{)12}$ is 3. Try 3 as the ones digit.	

The trip will take 23 days.

80

Exercises

Divide.

1. $6\overline{)42}$ 2. $6\overline{)420}$ 3. $60\overline{)420}$ 4. $60\overline{)4200}$

5. $20\overline{)280}$ 6. $60\overline{)540}$ 7. $30\overline{)720}$ 8. $50\overline{)750}$

9. $40\overline{)960}$ 10. $80\overline{)480}$ 11. $10\overline{)790}$ 12. $70\overline{)420}$

13. $50\overline{)950}$ 14. $30\overline{)960}$ 15. $40\overline{)840}$ 16. $40\overline{)8120}$

17. $50\overline{)2600}$ 18. $20\overline{)1360}$ 19. $90\overline{)2340}$ 20. $30\overline{)2760}$

21. $80\overline{)6320}$ 22. $40\overline{)8640}$ 23. $70\overline{)7910}$ 24. $60\overline{)9240}$

25. A family collected $210 in pledges after finishing a 30-mile bike-a-thon. How much did they collect for each mile traveled?

26. How many hours are there in 1440 minutes?

27. How many scores of years are there in 1980 years?
    (A *score* is a group of 20.)

Difference of 3

Arrange the numbers so that any two adjoining numbers have a difference of 3 or more.

Example:

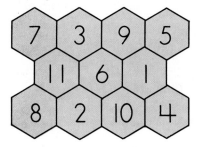

Use 1 though 11.

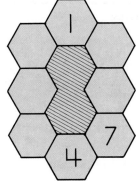

Use 1 through 8.

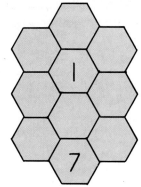

Use 1 through 10.

81

2-Digit Divisors

The International Pen Pal Club of Detroit wrote 819 letters in one year. Each of the 63 members wrote the same number of letters.

How many letters did each member write?

$63\overline{)819}$ Estimate the quotient to decide how many digits it will have.

$100 \times 63 = 6300$
$? \times 63 = 819$
$10 \times 63 = 630$

The quotient is between 10 and 100.

The first digit will be in the *tens* place.

Estimate the tens digit.	Multiply and subtract.	Estimate the ones digit.	Multiply and subtract.

60

↑
$63\overline{)819}$

Round 63 to 60.

$6\overline{)8}$ is about 1.
Try 1 as the
tens digit.

	H	T	O
		1	
63)8	1	9
	6	3
	1	8

	H	T	O
		1	
63)8	1	9
	6	3
	1	8	9

$6\overline{)18}$ is 3.
Try 3 as the
ones digit.

	H	T	O
		1	3
63)8	1	9
	6	3
	1	8	9
	1	8	9
			0

Each member wrote 13 letters.

Answer the following for $59\overline{)376}$:

$100 \times 59 = 5900$ What is your estimate of the quotient?

$10 \times 59 = 590$ How many digits will the quotient have?

$1 \times 59 = 59$ What would you try as the ones digit?

Exercises

Divide.

1. $12\overline{)372}$ 2. $27\overline{)400}$ 3. $19\overline{)645}$ 4. $38\overline{)303}$

5. $28\overline{)950}$ 6. $45\overline{)943}$ 7. $37\overline{)999}$ 8. $49\overline{)590}$

9. $11\overline{)562}$ 10. $36\overline{)884}$ 11. $39\overline{)819}$ 12. $95\overline{)871}$

13. $62\overline{)868}$ 14. $17\overline{)646}$ 15. $85\overline{)320}$ 16. $63\overline{)945}$

17. $81\overline{)783}$ 18. $39\overline{)838}$ 19. $78\overline{)936}$ 20. $94\overline{)752}$

21. $59\overline{)904}$ 22. $35\overline{)809}$ 23. $83\overline{)913}$ 24. $57\overline{)987}$

The Thomas Gilcrease Institute of American History and Art, Tulsa, Okla.

25. The pony express could cover as much as 252 miles a day, changing horses every 12 miles. How many horses were used each day?

26. A pony-express trip of 1968 miles took 8 days. How many miles were traveled each day?

27. The Overland Stage took 24 days to go the same distance. To go 1968 miles, how many miles were traveled each day?

Fascinating Fact

Did you know that the pony express was used for only $1\frac{1}{2}$ years?
Do some research and find out what ruined the pony express.

Extra Practice—Set C, page 324   **83**

37 is more than 25.
What should I do now?

25)873   Estimate the quotient $100 \times 25 = 2500$ The quotient is
         to decide how many $? \times 25 = 873$ between 10 and 100.
         digits it will have. $10 \times 25 = 250$

The first digit will be in the tens place.

Estimate the tens digit.	Multiply and subtract.	Multiply and subtract.	Estimate the ones digit. Multiply and subtract.

30
↑
25)873
	2
	25)873
	  50
	  37
		3
		25)873
		  75
		  12
			34 R23
			25)873
			  75
			 123
			 100
			  23

Round 25 to 30. 3)8 is about 2. Try 2 as the tens digit.	STOP! 37 > 25 2 is too small for the tens digit. Try 3.	12 < 25 3 is the correct tens digit.	23 < 25 4 is the correct ones digit.

Exercises

There is an error in each division below. Find the error and correct it.

1.
```
     5  R46
87)715
   679
    46
```

2.
```
     6  R50
37)272
   222
    50
```

3.
```
    46  R6
17)888
   68
   108
   102
     6
```

4.
```
   131  R16
45)646
   45
   196
   135
    61
    45
    16
```

Five numbers were divided by 24. These are the answers. In which exercises are the remainders too large?

5. 6 R20   6. 2 R29   7. 18 R5   8. 46 R30   9. 345 R24

Divide.

10. 55)463   11. 57)856   12. 38)530   13. 87)980

14. 85)429   15. 76)915   16. 94)126   17. 18)397

18. 35)249   19. 27)405   20. 19)668   21. 69)969

22. 35)136   23. 48)432   24. 26)183   25. 38)304

26. 77)620   27. 15)794   28. 46)980   29. 15)645.

30. 765 pupils went on a field trip. Each bus held 45 pupils. How many buses were needed?

31. Pete can type 45 words per minute. How long will it take him to type 405 words?

32. Fran's class needs 53 pounds of wax for a class project. Her class has collected 800 ounces. How many more ounces are needed?

33. Sport socks are packed 24 pairs per box. A store ordered 250 pairs. How many full boxes were ordered? How many extra pairs were ordered?

Extra Practice—Set A, page 325

2-Digit Divisors

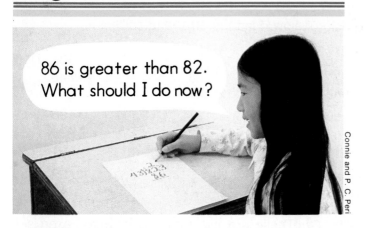

86 is greater than 82. What should I do now?

Connie and P. C. Peri

43)823   Estimate the quotient   100 × 43 = 4300   The quotient is
          to decide how many   ? × 43 = 823   between 10 and 100.
          digits it will have.   10 × 43 = 430

The first digit will be in the tens place.

Estimate the tens digit.	Multiply and subtract.	Multiply and subtract.	Estimate the ones digit. Multiply and subtract.
40 ↳43)823 Round 43 to 40. 4)8 is 2. Try 2 as the tens digit.	2 43)823 86 STOP! 86 > 82 2 is too big for the tens digit. Try 1.	1 43)823 43 39 39 < 43 1 is the correct tens digit.	19 R6 43)823 43 393 387 6 6 < 43 9 is the correct ones digit.

Exercises

Divide.

1. 64)563

2. 43)165

3. 52)831

4. 92)730

5. 83)570 6. 74)295 7. 63)939 8. 44)329

9. 31)680 10. 22)867 11. 34)793 12. 92)180

13. 73)210 14. 27)862 15. 53)688 16. 42)882

17. 12)284 18. 32)950 19. 83)992 20. 23)715

21. How many feet long is the right arm of the Statue of Liberty?

22. Each train car can hold 12 automobiles. How many train cars are needed to haul 324 automobiles?

23. Mrs. Washington drove 288 miles on 18 gallons of gasoline. How far did she go on 1 gallon of gasoline?

24. Zena is 64 months old. How many more months is it until her next birthday?

25. Thad packs 24 apples in each box. He has 618 apples. How many boxes can he fill? How many more apples does he need to fill another box?

504 in

Artstreet

Pogo Pete

In two jumps Pogo Pete always jumps 5 feet forward and then 2 feet backward. If he makes one jump each second, how long will it take him to finish a 20-foot race?

Zeros in the Quotient

Estimate the hundreds digit. Multiply and subtract.	Estimate the tens digit. Multiply and subtract.	Estimate the ones digit. Multiply and subtract.
$$\begin{array}{r} 5 \\ 6\overline{)3046} \\ 30 \\ \hline 0 \end{array}$$	$$\begin{array}{r} 50 \\ 6\overline{)3046} \\ 30\downarrow \\ \hline 04 \end{array}$$	$$\begin{array}{r} 507 \quad R4 \\ 6\overline{)3046} \\ 30\downarrow \\ \hline 046 \\ 42 \\ \hline 4 \end{array}$$
	$6\overline{)4}$ $6 > 4$, so write 0 as the tens digit.	

Explain how to do this division.

$$\begin{array}{r} 4 \\ 23\overline{)920} \\ 92 \\ \hline 0 \end{array}$$

$$\begin{array}{r} 40 \\ 23\overline{)920} \\ 92 \\ \hline 00 \end{array}$$

How many 23's in 0?
Why is the ones digit 0?

Exercises

Divide.

1. $4\overline{)80}$
2. $3\overline{)90}$
3. $4\overline{)20}$
4. $5\overline{)100}$

5. $3\overline{)150}$
6. $2\overline{)100}$
7. $7\overline{)140}$
8. $9\overline{)270}$

9. $3\overline{)720}$
10. $6\overline{)543}$
11. $4\overline{)121}$
12. $9\overline{)963}$

13. $34\overline{)680}$
14. $48\overline{)960}$
15. $40\overline{)800}$
16. $20\overline{)600}$

17. $82\overline{)820}$
18. $96\overline{)963}$
19. $52\overline{)531}$
20. $72\overline{)790}$

21. $4\overline{)8012}$
22. $3\overline{)6012}$
23. $3\overline{)6102}$
24. $8\overline{)9601}$

25. $30\overline{)601}$
26. $50\overline{)526}$
27. $9\overline{)9018}$
28. $8\overline{)4006}$

Extra Practice—Set C, page 325

Solving Problems

1. The world's largest Ferris wheel was built for the World's Columbian Exposition in Chicago in 1893. How many years ago was that?

2. 11 years later it was moved to the St. Louis Exhibition. In what year was it moved to St. Louis?

3. Each of the 36 cars could hold 60 people. How many people could the Ferris wheel hold?

4. The Ferris wheel of today is pictured below. How many inches high is it?

Culver Pictures

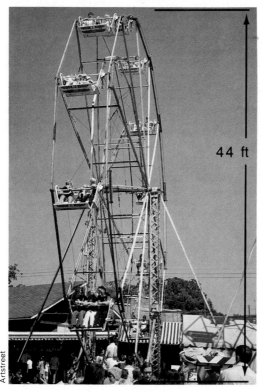

44 ft

Artstreet

5. Today's Ferris wheel has 14 seats, each holding 2 people. How many times will the wheel be filled to give 700 people a ride?

6. The Ferris wheel of 1893 had 36 sixty-person cars. How many more people could it hold than the Ferris wheel of today?

7. You and a friend get on different seats. As the Ferris wheel goes around once, how many times will you and your friend be the same distance above the ground?

Division (4-digit by 2-digit)

Tom Stack

A person threw the discus 1970 inches in a decathlon. How would you give that distance in feet and inches?

$12\overline{)1970}$

Estimate the quotient to decide how many digits it will have.

$$1000 \times 12 = 12,000$$
$$? \times 12 = 1,970$$
$$100 \times 12 = 1,200$$

The quotient is between 100 and 1000.

The first digit will be in the hundreds place.

Estimate the hundreds digit.	Multiply and subtract.	Divide the tens and ones.
10 ↑ └─ $12\overline{)1970}$ Round 12 to 10. $1\overline{)1}$ is 1. Try 1 as the hundreds digit.	$\begin{array}{r} 1 \\ 12\overline{)1970} \\ 12 \\ \hline 7 \end{array}$	$\begin{array}{r} 164 \text{ R2} \\ 12\overline{)1970} \\ 12\downarrow \\ \hline 77 \\ 72\downarrow \\ \hline 50 \\ 48 \\ \hline 2 \end{array}$

1970 inches is 164 feet 2 inches.

Check to see if the answer is correct.

How many inches short of 165 feet was the throw?

Extra Practice—Set A, page 326

Exercises

How many digits will be in each quotient?

1. 25)2416   2. 37)3400   3. 89)1005   4. 20)4020

Divide and check.

5. 35)7350   6. 41)4036   7. 39)5002   8. 34)3610

9. 25)5162   10. 67)7073   11. 57)6840   12. 11)9982

Divide.

13. 78)3042   14. 39)3042   15. 13)7841   16. 13)1820

17. 84)3108   18. 68)1919   19. 28)7009   20. 73)7323

21. 12)9660   22. 55)8965   23. 33)7600   24. 28)5419

25. 18)6000   26. 16)7000   27. 28)2766   28. 34)6830

29. 33)5555   30. 25)1001   31. 72)7271   32. 60)1260

33. A bakery made 6480 loaves of bread in 16 hours. How many loaves were made in 1 hour?

34. Mr. Wagner needs 4920 wall tiles to decorate his kitchen. The tiles are packed 48 to a carton. How many cartons should he buy? How many tiles will be left over?

35. A person threw the javelin 2698 inches in an Olympic decathlon. How far is that in yards, feet, and inches?

Finding Averages

Pupil	Test scores			
Jane	90	78	47	81
Tom	86	100	0	74
Jim	65	65	65	65

Miss Riggins found the average score for each pupil.

average = (sum of the scores) ÷ (number of scores)

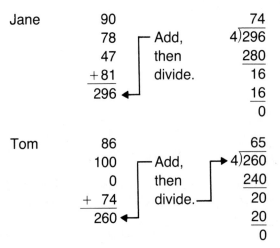

Jane

$$\begin{array}{r} 90 \\ 78 \\ 47 \\ +81 \\ \hline 296 \end{array}$$ Add, then divide.

$$\begin{array}{r} 74 \\ 4\overline{)296} \\ \underline{280} \\ 16 \\ \underline{16} \\ 0 \end{array}$$

Tom

$$\begin{array}{r} 86 \\ 100 \\ 0 \\ +\ 74 \\ \hline 260 \end{array}$$ Add, then divide.

$$\begin{array}{r} 65 \\ 4\overline{)260} \\ \underline{240} \\ 20 \\ \underline{20} \\ 0 \end{array}$$

Suppose Jane had scored 74 on each test. How would the sum of those scores compare with her present sum?

Can you tell Jim's average without adding and dividing? How?

Exercises

Find the average of each set of numbers.

1. 34 + 56 + 9 + 17

2. 5 + 2 + 4 + 6 + 3

3. 28 + 500 + 25 + 7

4. 600 + 29 + 7

5. Find Kurt's average score.

6. Find Ollie's average score.

7. Find Polly's average score.

8. Find Molly's average score.

Pupil	Scores				
Kurt	97	85	99	68	81
Ollie	62	87	100	71	0
Polly	100	83	95	26	86
Molly	76	76	77	75	76

	Ken	Sven	Len	Ben
Height (inches)	64	58	67	51
Weight (pounds)	79	61	86	62

9. Find the average height (in inches) for the group of children.

10. Find the average weight for the group of children.

11. During 5 days Betsy rode her bike 25 miles. Find the average number of miles she rode each day.

12. Wanda rode 16 miles in 2 hours. Find her average speed in miles per hour.

13. Which is a higher average—4 scores that total 388 or 5 scores that total 480?

14. During the month of July, Juan rode his bicycle 465 miles. How many miles did he average a day?

15. In one season Matt bowled 84 games. His total score was 8988. What was his average score for each game?

16. Larry averages 1 hit for every 4 times at bat. How many hits is that for 1000 times at bat? (This is his batting average.)

Challenge

The average depth of a lake is 9 feet. Is it safe to dive in anywhere from the shore? Why?

Using a Calculator

Maria bowled 5 games. These were her scores.

Game 1   Game 2   Game 3   Game 4   Game 5

137   141   121   175   131

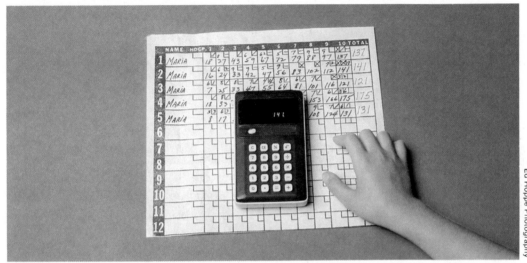

Maria used her calculator to find her bowling average by pressing the keys in this order.

1 3 7 + 1 4 1 + 1 2 1 + 1 7 5 + 1 3 1 = ÷ 5 =

Use a calculator to find the average of each set of numbers.

1. 86, 80

2. 6, 7, 10, 8,
   12, 14, 20

3. 216, 320, 492,
   500

4. 32, 64, 28,
   95, 41

5. 34, 18, 209, 2,
   36, 10, 159, 20,
   7, 8, 38, 59

6. 2461, 18, 193, 6,
   250, 8220

7. 6, 7, 12, 18,
   24, 18, 29, 38

8. 336, 875, 29,
   36, 129

9. 32, 56, 41, 309,
   27, 8, 72, 100, 21,
   3204

What Are They?

They are

31–82–57–2–48–82–79–57–11–57–48–2

11–98–67–57–82–21

55–1–63–48–5–79–92.

Use the answers to find the letter for each number.

0×9	$8 \div 8$	$34 - 29$	$28 \div 14$	6×8
A	**B**	**C**	**D**	**E**

A	B	C	D	E
129 −118	110 − 89	87 − 9	308 −251	618 −555
F	**G**	**H**	**I**	**J**

F	G	H	I	J
19 28 +13	60 11 +28	12 +52	77 + 5	55 + 0
K	**L**	**M**	**N**	**O**

K	L	M	N	O
47 ×2	130 ×0	14 ×7	23 ×4	79 ×1
P	**Q**	**R**	**S**	**T**

P	Q	R	S	T
4)124	30)120	13)351	61)1220	48)3216
U	**V**	**W**	**X**	**Y**

CHAPTER REVIEW

Divide.

1. $8\overline{)72}$ 2. $6\overline{)54}$ 3. $3\overline{)69}$ 4. $4\overline{)76}$

5. $7\overline{)175}$ 6. $8\overline{)352}$ 7. $6\overline{)7050}$ 8. $4\overline{)2872}$

9. $8\overline{)125}$ 10. $7\overline{)2349}$ 11. $6\overline{)1339}$ 12. $9\overline{)4789}$

13. $20\overline{)80}$ 14. $50\overline{)1200}$ 15. $90\overline{)1890}$ 16. $60\overline{)720}$

17. $12\overline{)372}$ 18. $29\overline{)962}$ 19. $67\overline{)999}$ 20. $21\overline{)4444}$

21. $18\overline{)741}$ 22. $29\overline{)239}$ 23. $47\overline{)297}$ 24. $35\overline{)7812}$

Divide and check.

25. $54\overline{)160}$ 26. $32\overline{)943}$ 27. $23\overline{)227}$ 28. $44\overline{)8523}$

29. $7\overline{)712}$ 30. $6\overline{)2405}$ 31. $62\overline{)6262}$ 32. $25\overline{)7523}$

33. Find the average score for the red darts.

34. Find the average score for the green darts.

35. Find the average score for all the darts.

36. Bob's Cycle Shop has 3000 spokes. Bob uses 36 spokes to repair one wheel. How many wheels can he repair with those spokes? How many more spokes does he need to repair one more wheel?

5 Problem Solving

Jacqueline Durand

97

Reading Problems

There are four main steps for solving a problem. This lesson deals with the first step.

Terry has 80 baseball cards. He is going to buy 15 more baseball cards. How many baseball cards will he have then?

What do you know?

    Terry has 80 cards.
He is buying 15 more.

What are you to find?

    How many cards will he have?

Read each of the following. Tell what you know, and tell what you are to find.

a. John had 15 model cars. He lost 3 of them. How many does he have left?

b. Gerard is 7 years old. Gerri is twice as old as Gerard. How old is Gerri?

c. There are 25 boys and 22 girls in Jamie's class. How many children are in her class?

d. Bill has 56 postcards. He put 4 postcards in each row. How many rows did he make?

Exercises

For each problem, write what you know and what you are to find.

1. Jack is 5 years older than his sister. His sister is 12 years old. How old is Jack?

2. Miss Jones's classroom has 6 rows of seats. There are 7 seats in each row. How many seats are in her classroom?

3. Sue ran 3 miles each day last week. How many miles did she run last week?

4. There are 10 teams. There are 12 girls on each team. How many girls are there?

98

5. Janice bought 3 packages of balloons. How many balloons did she buy?

6. Hal bought a package of paper plates and 2 rolls of streamers. How much did he spend?

7. How many feet of streamers can Lulu get for $1?

8. How many paper plates can Harold get for $5?

9. The company that Bill works for is having a picnic. They need 450 paper plates. How much will they cost?

10. Some people need 250 feet of streamers for a party. How many rolls of streamers will they need?

11. How many horns can Richard get for $8?

12. How many balloons can Wayne get for 70¢?

13. Margaret invited 12 people to a surprise birthday party for her sister. She bought 6 packages of balloons. How many balloons will each person get?

14. Dan has a $10 bill. What will be his change if he buys 6 horns, 4 rolls of streamers, and a package of paper plates?

Planning to Solve Problems

Terry has 80 baseball cards. He is going to buy 15 more baseball cards. How many baseball cards will he have then?

Know: Terry has 80 cards.
He is buying 15 more.

Find: How many cards will he have?

How can you solve the problem?   Add 80 and 15.

To plan how to solve a problem, you must decide which operation to use and which numbers to use.

The following will help you decide which operation to use:

Add when joining sets of any size.

Subtract when comparing sets or when separating a set into sets of different sizes.

Multiply when joining sets of the same size.

Divide when separating a set into sets of the same size.

Terry is going to put his 95 baseball cards into stacks of 5 each. How would you plan to solve this problem?

Exercises

Tell how you would solve each problem.

1. Sally found 9 stones. Later she found 7 more stones. How many does she have now?

2. Ann worked 7 months. She earned $400 each month. How much did she earn?

3. Mary won 5 games. Deb won 6 games more than Mary. How many games did Deb win?

4. George has 3 more books than Sam. George has 56 books. How many does Sam have?

5. Fay drove for 5 hours. She drove 50 miles each hour. How many miles did she drive?

6. Simon is 60 inches tall. How many feet tall is he?

7. Jon had $25. After buying a baseball glove, he had $5. How much did the glove cost?

8. Julia is 6 feet tall. How many inches tall is she?

Tell which operation you would use to solve each problem.

9. A company sold several swimming pools. Each pool held the same amount of water. How much water is needed to fill all of them?

10. Al kept track of how many miles he drove and how many gallons of gasoline he used. How far did he travel on each gallon?

11. You knew the Tigers score at halftime. Later, you heard the final score. How many points did the Tigers score in the second half?

12. Felicia has some dogs. Al has a dog and some gerbils. Sol has a few parakeets. How many pets are there?

13. Ken and Jim shared some money equally. How much did each boy get?

14. Brad is twice as old as Bev. You know Bev's age. How old is Brad?

15. Patricia is taller than Phil. You know Patricia's height. How tall is Phil?

16. Mrs. Johnson's fifth-grade class separated into teams. The same number of pupils were on each team. How many teams were there?

Lambert Studios

<inline_image description="Black and white photograph of a football game with players in a pile, one player wearing number 34." />

Computing Answers to Problems

A marching band has 15 rows. Each row has 5 members. How many members are in the band?

Use all four steps to solve the problem.

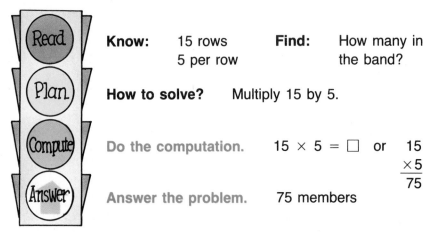

Know: 15 rows   **Find:**   How many in
                 5 per row   the band?

How to solve?   Multiply 15 by 5.

Do the computation. $15 \times 5 = \square$ or

$$\begin{array}{r} 15 \\ \times 5 \\ \hline 75 \end{array}$$

Answer the problem.   75 members

Explain how you would solve this problem.

Mr. Hoffman began conducting the marching band 19 years ago today. What year was that?

Exercises

Use the four steps to solve each problem.

1. There are 23 bands. Five bands have no cymbals. How many have cymbals?

2. There are 9 pupils on each team. One class has 198 pupils. How many teams can the class have?

3. A state park has 528 trees. There are only 49 pine trees. How many are not pine trees?

4. It takes 15 minutes to paint a model plane. How long will it take to paint 5 model planes?

5. Laura is 8 years older than Sid. Sid is 16. How old is Laura?

6. Jim is 7 years younger than Michelle. Michelle is 14. How old is Jim?

7. Larry's 4 dogs eat 832 pounds of dog food each year. What is the average amount each dog eats per year?

8. Bill has 6 spools of fishing line. Each spool has 175 yards of line. How many yards of line are on 5 spools?

9. The test has 100 problems. There are 25 problems on each part of the test. How many parts are there?

10. John has 437 more baseball cards than Lon. John has 1438 baseball cards. How many cards does Lon have?

11. Frank delivers 28 papers each morning. How many papers does he deliver each week?

12. Sue is 5 years younger than Delores. Sue is 10 years old. How old is Delores?

13. Pete has 35 goldfish. This is 7 times as many fish as Jody has. How many fish does Jody have?

14. Gina is 6 inches shorter than Link. Link is 72 inches tall. How tall is Gina?

Take a Gander at These!

1. It takes 20 minutes to hard-boil 1 goose egg. How long does it take to hard-boil 4 goose eggs?

2. Some geese are swimming in a line so that one of them is ahead of 3 geese, and one of them is behind 3 geese. What is the least number of geese possible?

Writing Questions

There are 18 golf balls and 6 tennis balls.

You can write many questions to make a problem.
Some questions use all the information in the problem.

How many balls are there?

How many more golf balls than tennis balls are there?

Some questions do not use all the information in the problem.

How many golf balls are in each box?

Some questions use numbers not given in the problem.

If each can of tennis balls costs $3, how much will 2 cans of tennis balls cost?

Exercises

Write a question to make a problem.

1.

2.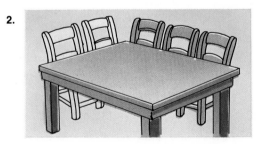

3. The children found 36 empty cans and 12 empty bottles.

4. Max won 9 blue ribbons and 6 red ribbons.

5. The girl ran 6 blocks in 6 minutes.

6. There are 28 horses. There are 5 saddles.

7. Each case holds 24 bottles. There are 15 cases.

8.

9.

10.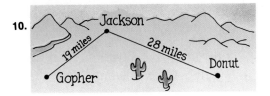

11.

12. They have 40 red stamps and 8 orange stamps.

13. There are 48 squares and 6 circles.

14.

15.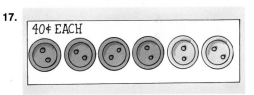

16.

17.

18. Write a question that does not use all the information.
Then write a question that uses a number not given in the problem.

Making Up Problems

For each math sentence, you can make up many problems.

$$\square + 5 = 21$$

Eva had some golf balls. She found 5 more. Now she has 21. How many did she have in the beginning?

Fran is 5 years older than Bob. Fran is 21. How old is Bob?

$$184 \div 8 = \square$$

184 boys are at camp. Each cabin sleeps 8 boys. How many cabins are they using?

There are 184 flowers in a box. Each girl gets 8 flowers. How many girls are there?

Exercises

For each math sentence, make up a problem.

1. $7 - \square = 3$

2. $12 \times 18 = \square$

3. $108 \div 9 = \square$

4. $\square \times 12 = 96$

5. $16 + 93 = \square$

6. $36 \div 4 = \square$

7. $18 - 7 = \square$

8. $24 \times 8 = \square$

9. $8 + \square = 19$

Use the picture to write a problem.

10.

11. *Before*   *After*

Don't Get Fooled

1. Does England have a fourth of July?

2. How far can a dog run into the forest?

3. If you took 6 oranges from 9 oranges, how many would you have?

4. How much dirt is there in a hole that is 10 inches deep and 12 inches square?

5. Someone left the cage door open. All but 7 of the gerbils got away. How many are left in the cage?

6. A doctor gave Kevin 6 pills and told him to take 1 pill every half hour. How long will they last?

7. Two men played 5 games of checkers. Each man won the same number of games. There were no ties. How can that be?

8. An animal went 1 mile south, 1 mile east, and 1 mile north and was back where it started. Was it a lion or a bear?

Extra Information

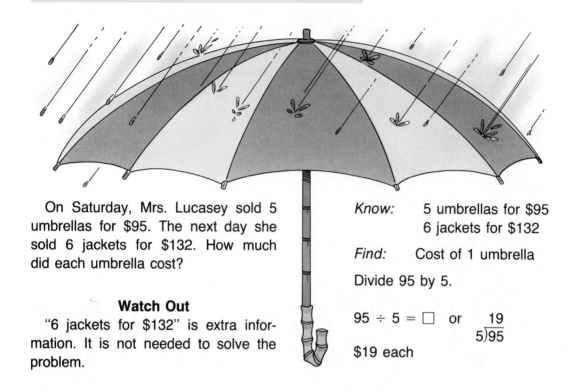

On Saturday, Mrs. Lucasey sold 5 umbrellas for $95. The next day she sold 6 jackets for $132. How much did each umbrella cost?

Watch Out

"6 jackets for $132" is extra information. It is not needed to solve the problem.

Know: 5 umbrellas for $95
            6 jackets for $132

Find: Cost of 1 umbrella

Divide 95 by 5.

$95 \div 5 = \square$ or $\begin{array}{r} 19 \\ 5\overline{)95} \end{array}$

$19 each

Exercises

Solve each problem. Watch out for extra information.

1. Carlos earned 60¢. He spent 50¢ on 2 books. How much did he pay for each book?

2. Paula walked 11 blocks and ran 9 blocks in 30 minutes. How many blocks did she go?

3. Raul bought 2 erasers at 25¢ each. How much would 3 erasers cost?

4. 6 pencils cost 54¢, 2 erasers cost 44¢, and 3 pens cost $6. How much do 4 erasers cost?

5. Elizabeth sold 4 jackets for $108. The next day she sold 9 umbrellas for $162. How much did each umbrella cost?

6. John and Frida each bought 3 shirts. John spent $45 and Frida spent $48. What is the average price of the shirts Frida bought?

7. Each wallet uses 3 pieces of leather, 48 inches of black lacing, and 15 inches of brown lacing. How much lacing is needed to make one wallet?

8. Each comb case uses 2 pieces of leather and 24 inches of lacing. How many pieces of leather are needed to make 16 comb cases?

9. It costs 50¢ for children and $1 for adults to ride the train at the zoo. How much will it cost for 6 adults to ride the train?

Brent Jones

10. One day the train traveled 80 miles and carried 1088 people. The train made 16 trips that day. How many miles long is a trip?

11. In 5 days 3592 children and 2840 adults rode the train. What was the average number of adults riding the train each day?

12. The train runs twice each hour. The zoo is open 9 hours each day. How many trips does the train make in 18 hours?

13. The train pulls 5 cars. Each car has 7 seats. Each seat holds 5 people. How many seats does the train have? How many people can the train hold?

Missing Information

A doubles tennis court is how much longer than it is wide?

Know: 78 feet long
          36 feet wide

Find: How much longer?

Subtract 36 from 78.

$78 - 36 = \square$ or $\begin{array}{r} 78 \\ -36 \\ \hline 42 \end{array}$

42 feet

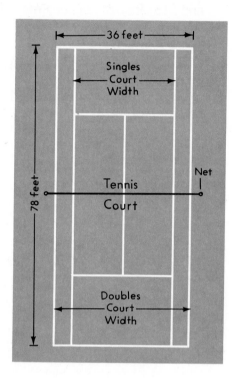

How many feet wider is the doubles court than the singles court?

Know: Doubles court is 36 feet wide.

Find: How much wider is the doubles court?

Cannot solve the problem.
Width of the singles court is missing.

Exercises

Solve each problem. If a problem cannot be solved, tell what is missing.

1. Len jogs 15 minutes a day. How many blocks will he jog in 5 days?

2. A girl jogs 6 blocks each day. How many blocks will she jog in 14 days?

110

3. The children need some boards for the walls and 43 more for the floor and the roof. How many boards do they need in all?

4. It took the children 6 hours to build the clubhouse and clean up. If it took 5 hours to build, how long did it take to clean up?

Tom McGuire

5. They cut a 45-inch board into 2 pieces. One piece was 26 inches long. How long was the other piece?

6. They sawed another board into 3 pieces. How long was each piece?

7. Nails cost 3¢ each. Find the cost of 27 nails.

8. Which holds more paint, 1 big can or 2 little cans?

9. Each child agreed to pay an equal part of the cost. How much should each child pay?

10. They gave the clerk 90¢ for paint. It costs 82¢. How much change should they get back?

11. The children figure they can use the clubhouse 8 months out of the year. How many months a year won't they use it?

12. How many months will the children be able to use the clubhouse in 2 years? In a decade?

Extra Practice—Set A, page 328

SKILLS REVIEW

Add.

1. $\begin{array}{r} 15,938 \\ +23,141 \\ \hline \end{array}$

2. $\begin{array}{r} 109,928 \\ +\ 62,160 \\ \hline \end{array}$

3. $\begin{array}{r} 938 \\ 192 \\ 693 \\ +328 \\ \hline \end{array}$

4. $\begin{array}{r} 3928 \\ 67 \\ 93 \\ +\ 183 \\ \hline \end{array}$

Subtract.

5. $\begin{array}{r} 17,005 \\ -16,002 \\ \hline \end{array}$

6. $\begin{array}{r} 128,920 \\ -\ 50,739 \\ \hline \end{array}$

7. $\begin{array}{r} 837 \\ -799 \\ \hline \end{array}$

8. $\begin{array}{r} 1000 \\ -\ 128 \\ \hline \end{array}$

Multiply.

9. $\begin{array}{r} 39 \\ \times 13 \\ \hline \end{array}$

10. $\begin{array}{r} 729 \\ \times 62 \\ \hline \end{array}$

11. $\begin{array}{r} 308 \\ \times 251 \\ \hline \end{array}$

12. $\begin{array}{r} 320 \\ \times 204 \\ \hline \end{array}$

Divide.

13. $34\overline{)794}$

14. $27\overline{)1104}$

15. $89\overline{)9080}$

Watch the signs!

16. $\begin{array}{r} 173,921 \\ -\ \ \ 9,148 \\ \hline \end{array}$

17. $\begin{array}{r} 12,837 \\ +\ \ \ 179 \\ \hline \end{array}$

18. $18\overline{)3284}$

19. $\begin{array}{r} 293,921 \\ +\ 15,938 \\ \hline \end{array}$

20. $\begin{array}{r} 938 \\ \times 29 \\ \hline \end{array}$

21. $\begin{array}{r} 19,938 \\ 6,938 \\ +98,927 \\ \hline \end{array}$

22. $\begin{array}{r} 352 \\ \times 209 \\ \hline \end{array}$

23. $57\overline{)2290}$

24. $\begin{array}{r} 81,920 \\ -\ 9,039 \\ \hline \end{array}$

Problems Without Computation

1. Kerry, Larry, and Mary each ate something different for dinner. One had chicken, one had steak, and one had soup. Larry did not have meat. Mary did not have steak. What did each person eat?

2. Todd compared the price per pound for hamburger, turkey, chicken, and steak. Steak cost the most. Chicken cost the least. Poultry cost less than beef. List the meats according to cost, starting with the most expensive.

3. Dave, Tom, Jane, and Mary each found their height. Jane is not the shortest. Tom and Mary are taller than Jane. A boy is the tallest of the four. List their names in order of height, starting with the tallest.

4. Ramon is older, but shorter, than Sally and Joan. Sally is older, but shorter, than Joan and Telly. Telly is taller but older than Joan. List their names in order of their ages, starting with the oldest.

Jacqueline Durand

Two-Step Problems

9 girls and 7 boys formed 2 volleyball teams. Each team had the same number of players. How many players were on each team?

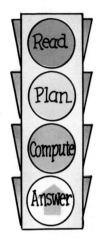

Know: 9 girls, 7 boys
       2 teams, same size

Find: Number on each team

Add 9 and 7, then divide the sum by 2.

9 + 7 = 16   or   9   8
                      +7   2)16
16 ÷ 2 = 8   16

8 players

Exercises

1. 18 boys and 12 girls formed teams of 5 players each. How many teams were formed?

2. 3 children shared 36¢ equally. Then each child spent 5¢. How much does each child have left?

3. 15 children each made 3 sandwiches. They ate 7 sandwiches. How many sandwiches are left?

4. Each pupil wrote 2 long poems and 4 short poems. There were 18 pupils. How many poems were written?

5. On each team there are 3 boys and 3 girls. How many players are on 3 teams?

Free throws—1 point
Field goals—2 points

6. One basketball team made 13 field goals and scored 8 points on free throws. How many points did the team score?

7. In a contest each player shoots 10 free throws. Tim made 3 and then missed 4. How many free throws does he have left to shoot?

8. Pedro scored 136 points this year. That is 45 more points than he scored last year. How many points did he score in the last 2 years?

Dale Moyer/Photo Trends

Taurus

9. During 4 years of Little League baseball, Lyle hit 64 home runs. Lyle's brother averaged 18 home runs a year in Little League. Who averaged more home runs? How many more?

10. Ben is 6 feet tall. Lisa is 4 feet tall. How many inches taller is Ben than Lisa?

11. Frank is 80 inches tall. Gina is 60 inches tall. How much taller is Frank than Gina, in feet and inches?

CHAPTER REVIEW

Write what you know, what you are to find, and how you would solve each problem.

1. Kyla threw a softball 12 yards farther than Joan did. Joan threw it 29 yards. How far did Kyla throw the softball?

2. There are 180 doodads. There are 12 doodads in each box. How many boxes of doodads are there?

Solve each problem. If a problem cannot be solved, tell what information is missing.

3. One day, 35 sausages were sold at Bob's Farm Stand. How many pounds of sausage were sold?

4. Janice bought a bushel of apples and a pound of cheese. How much did she spend?

5. Mr. Phillips bought a pound of cheese and a bushel of apples. How much change should he receive?

6. Tom spent $6 for cheese, $15 for apples, and $8 for sausage. How much more did he spend for sausage than for cheese?

7. Sally spent $56 at Bob's Farm Stand. She spent $36 for sausage. How many sausages did she buy?

8. Mary bought 5 pounds of sausage. How much did she spend for sausage?

6 Geometry

Space Figures

Each face of the box shown at the right is a rectangle. The box has the shape of a **rectangular prism.**

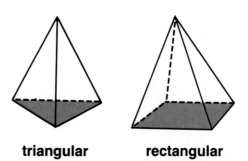

faces

edges
(where faces meet)

vertices
(where edges meet)

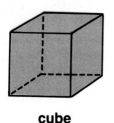

cube

(Each face is a square.)

The base of each **pyramid** at the right is shown in red.

A pyramid is named by the shape of its base. All other faces of a pyramid are triangles.

triangular pyramid

rectangular pyramid

These figures have no straight edges.

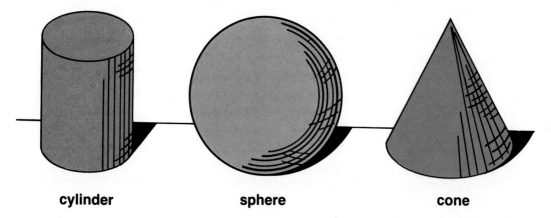

cylinder

sphere

cone

Exercises

Name a figure for the shape of each object.

1.

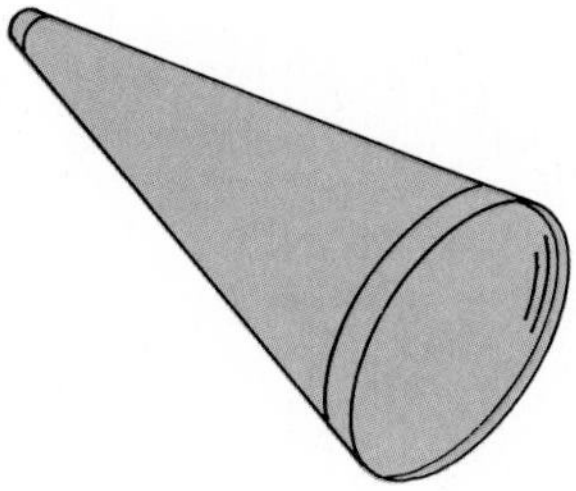

2.

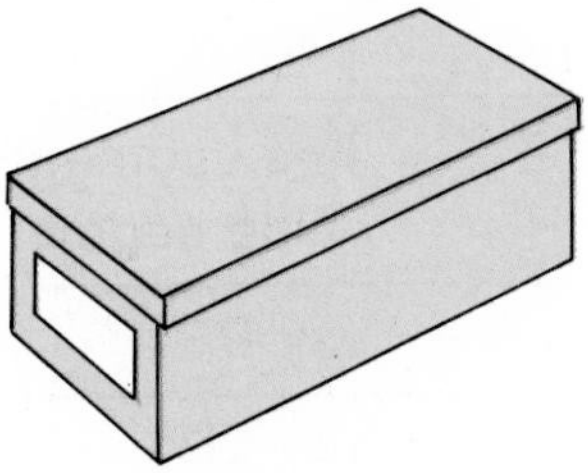

3.

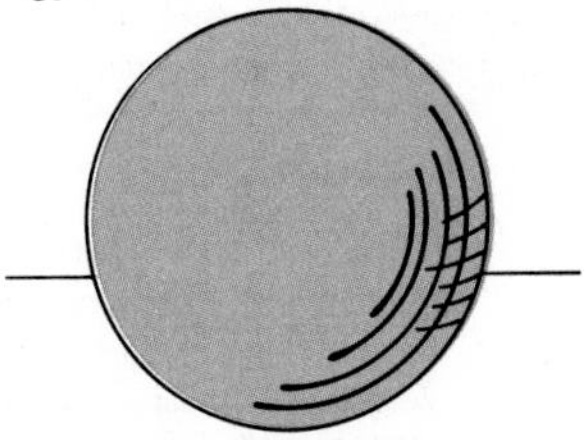

4.

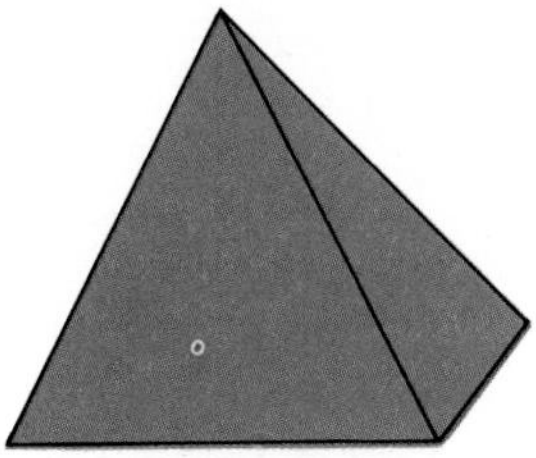

5.

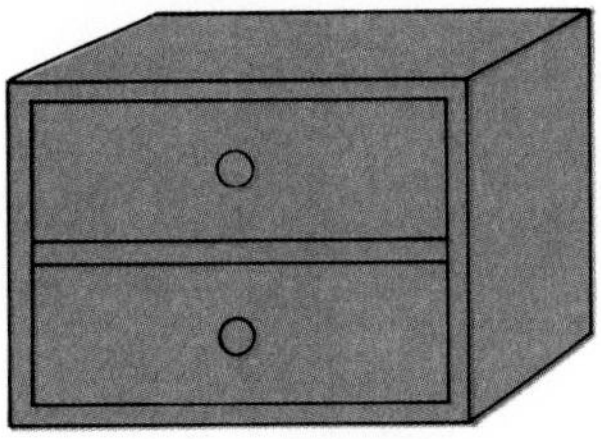

6.

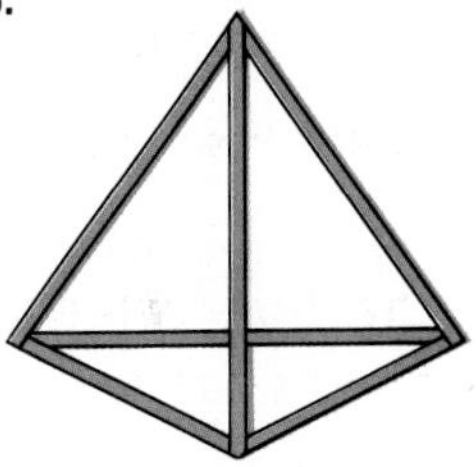

7.

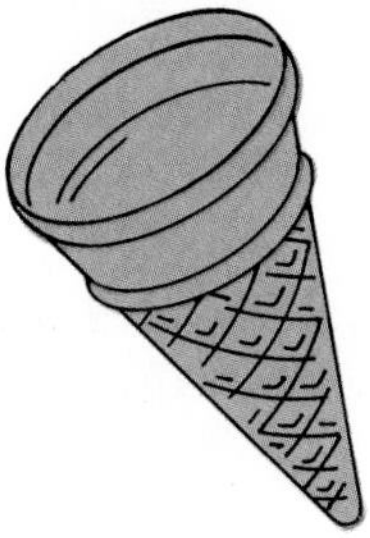

8.

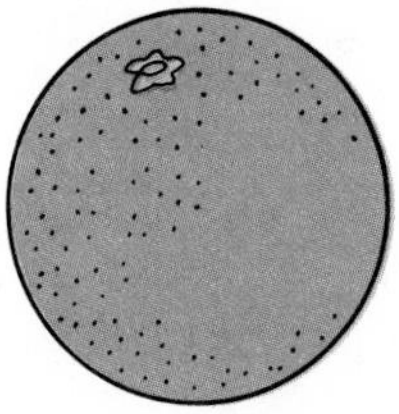

9.

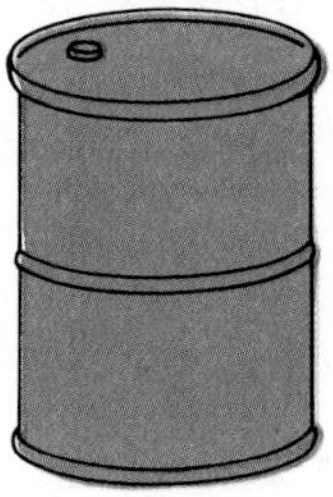

Figure	Number of Faces	Number of Edges	Number of Vertices
10. rectangular prism			
11. triangular pyramid			
12. rectangular pyramid			

Extra Practice—Set B, page 329

Lines, Line Segments, Rays

Figure	Endpoints	Name
 D E	none	**line DE** or **line ED**
D E	D and E	**line segment DE** or **line segment ED**
D E	D	**ray DE**
D E	E	**ray ED**

Do ray DE and ray ED name the same ray?

Is the endpoint named first or last when naming a ray?

Exercises

Name each figure.

1.

2.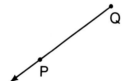

3.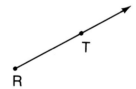

4.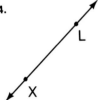

5.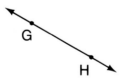

6.

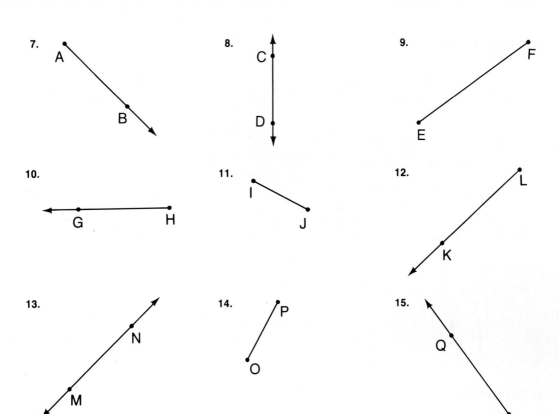

16. Two examples of line segments are given below. Give three others.

an edge of this book

the red rule on a sheet of notebook paper

Two figures are named in each exercise. If you joined them, what figure would you get?

17. line segment AB and line segment BC

18. line segment AB and ray BC

19. line segment BC and ray BA

20. ray BA and ray BC

Line Segments

Trace line segment AB.

Move the tracing onto line segment CD.

Are the two line segments the same length?

We say the two line segments are **congruent.**

Line segments having the same length are congruent.

Exercises

Trace one of the line segments. Place the tracing on the other line segment. If they are congruent, write *Yes.* If not, write *No.*

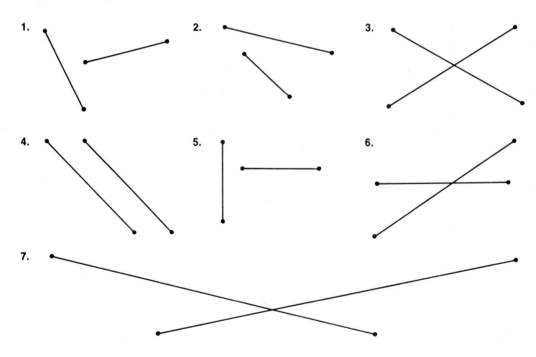

1.

2.

3.

4.

5.

6.

7.

8. Compare the lengths of sides AB and CD. Are sides AB and CD congruent?

9. Compare the lengths of sides AD and BC. Are sides AD and BC congruent?

10. Opposite sides of a rectangle are ___.

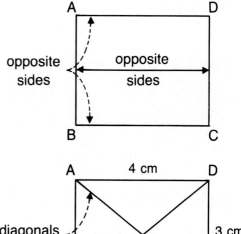

11. Compare the lengths of diagonals AC and BD. Are they the same length?

12. Diagonals of a rectangle are ___.

Some measurements are given for rectangle ABCD.

13. How long is side AB?

14. How long is side BC?

15. If diagonal AC is 5 centimeters long, how long is diagonal BD?

Be Careful!

Which line segment is longer, the red one or the blue one?

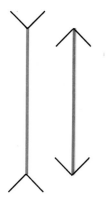
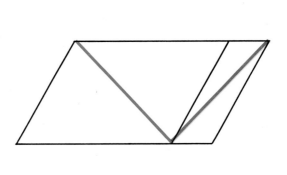
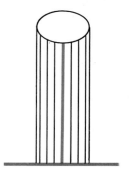

Angles

An **angle** is formed by two rays with the same endpoint.

When naming an angle, the middle letter names the **vertex.**

Here are two names for the angle.

angle MRT   or   angle TRM

You can use the symbol ∠ for "angle."

∠MRT   or   ∠TRM

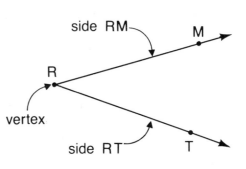

side RM
M
R
vertex
side RT
T

Name each angle shown below.

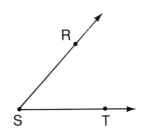

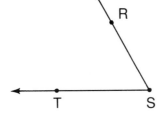

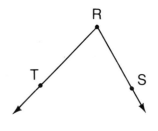

Exercises

Write a name for each angle.

1.

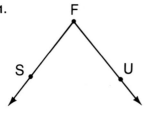

2.

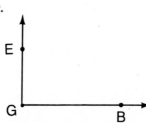

3.

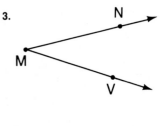

Name the red angle. Then name the black angle.

4.

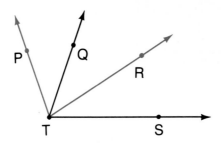

5.

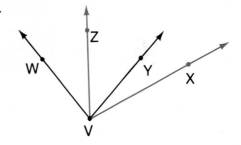

Two sides of a triangle form an angle. Name each angle in the triangle.

6.

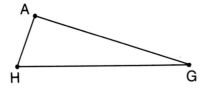

7.

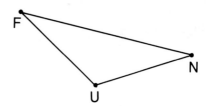

8. A pentagon has 5 sides and 5 angles. Name the five angles.

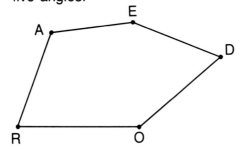

Measuring Angles

Angles can be measured in **degrees** with a protractor.

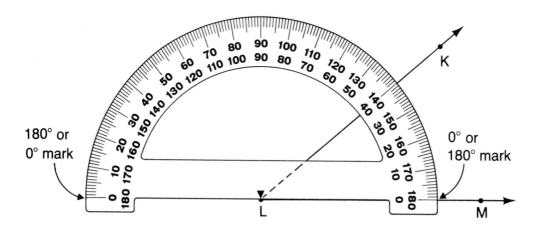

180° or
0° mark

0° or
180° mark

L   M

The measurement of angle KLM is 40 degrees, or 40°.

To measure an angle, how do you place the protractor?

How do you decide when to use the inside scale or the outside scale?

Exercises

Give the measurement of each angle.

1. ∠BRF
2. ∠KRF
3. ∠DRF
4. ∠ERF
5. ∠CRA
6. ∠KRA
7. ∠DRA
8. ∠ERA
9. ∠FRA

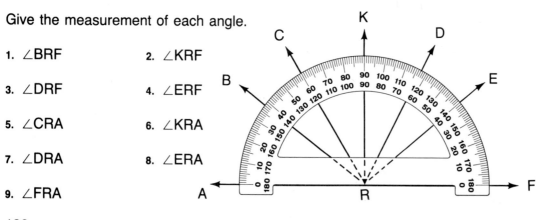

Find the measurement of each angle.

10.

11.

12.

13.

14.

15.

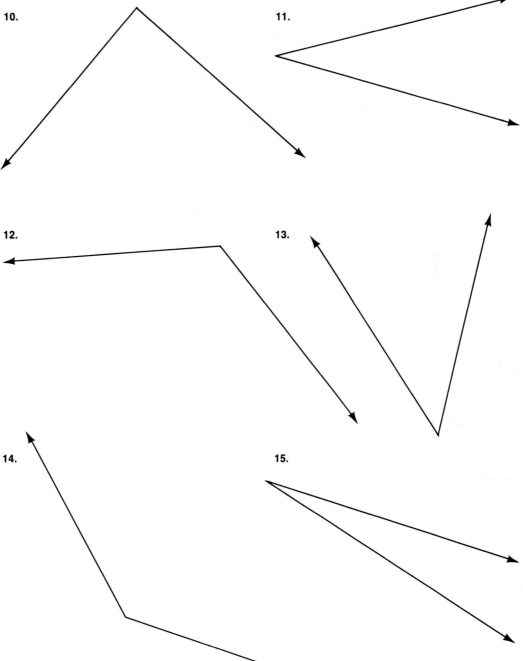

Kinds of Angles

Angles can be grouped according to their measurements.

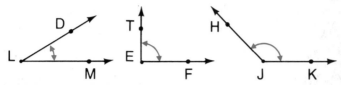

Angle	Measurement	Kind of Angle
∠DIM	between 0° and 90°	**acute angle**
∠TEF	90°	**right angle**
∠HJK	between 90° and 180°	**obtuse angle**

Exercises

Find the measurement of each angle. Tell what kind of angle it is.

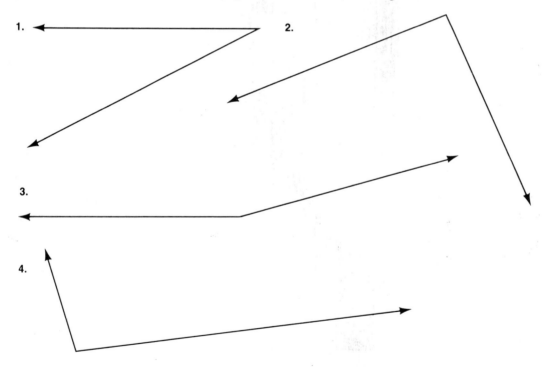

1.

2.

3.

4.

Tell if each angle is an acute angle, an obtuse angle, or a right angle.

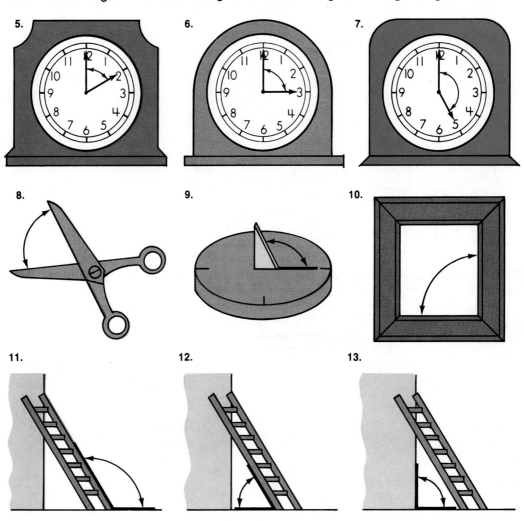

5.

6.

7.

8.

9.

10.

11.

12.

13.

14. There are 3 acute angles in the figure at the right. Name each acute angle.

15. There are 2 obtuse angles in the figure. Name each obtuse angle.

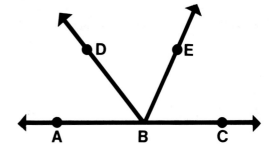

Drawing Angles

You can draw an angle with a measurement of 45° as shown below.

Step 1:

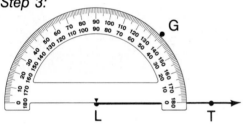

Draw ray LT.

Step 2:

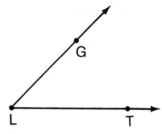

Place the center mark of the protractor at L.

Step 3:

Mark point G at 45.

Step 4:

Draw ray LG.

Exercises

Draw angles with these measurements.

1. 75°

2. 130°

3. 12°

4. 90°

5. 35°

6. 160°

7. 64°

8. 100°

9. 60°

10. 120°

11. 99°

12. 50°

13. 25°

14. 150°

15. 110°

16. 180°

17. Measure the angle below. Then draw an angle having the same measurement.

SKILLS REVIEW

Group A

Add.

1. 847
    +614

2. 938,837
    +121,318

3. 9387
    +1131

4. 18,928
    +148,037

5. 9327
    +6324

6. 121,827
    +113,820

7. 938,283
    + 63,829

8. 23,842
    + 7,839

Group B

Subtract.

1. 9360
    −6109

2. 900,845
    −150,482

3. 920
    −140

4. 342,938
    −138,829

5. 17,293
    − 417

6. 13,827
    − 2,824

7. 82,904
    −61,487

8. 100,829
    − 89,937

Group C

Multiply.

1. 21
    ×5

2. 36
    ×7

3. 856
    ×7

4. 209
    ×8

5. 25
    ×30

6. 82
    ×19

7. 326
    ×70

8. 289
    ×45

Group D

Divide.

1. 7)98

2. 5)37

3. 8)409

4. 6)362

5. 4)920

6. 34)658

7. 56)2938

8. 73)7373

131

Congruent Angles

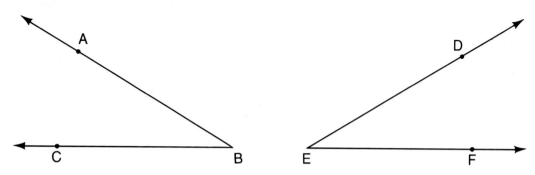

Measure ∠ABC and ∠DEF. Do they have the same measurement?

We say the two angles are *congruent.*

Angles having the same measurement are congruent.

Find the measurement of each angle below.

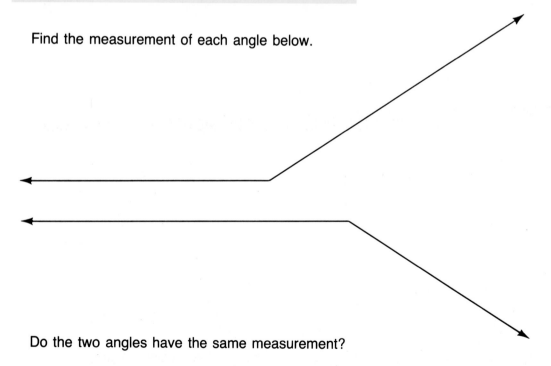

Do the two angles have the same measurement?

Are they congruent?

Exercises

Find the measurements of the angles in each pair. Are the angles congruent?

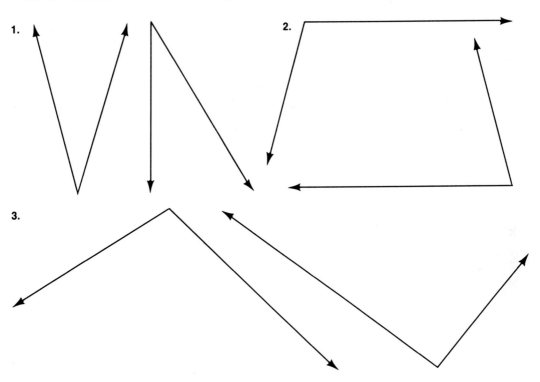

1.
2.
3.

The two angles in each exercise below are congruent. What is the measurement of the red angle?

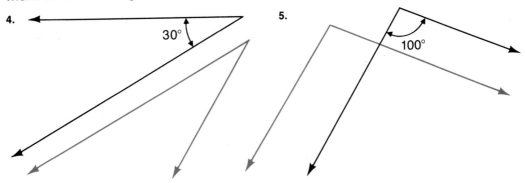

4.
30°
5.
100°

6. Draw an acute angle.
   Draw an angle congruent to it.

7. Draw an obtuse angle.
   Draw an angle congruent to it.

Circles

A **circle** is shown below in red. Point K is the same distance from each point on the circle. Point K is the **center** of the circle.

Point K is *inside* the circle. Points A, B, and C are *on* the circle.

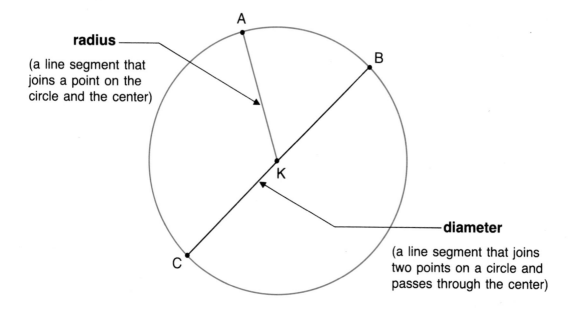

radius ─

(a line segment that joins a point on the circle and the center)

diameter

(a line segment that joins two points on a circle and passes through the center)

Line segments KA, KB, and KC are **radii** (plural of *radius*). Compare the lengths of these radii. What did you discover?

All radii of a circle are congruent.

Compare the lengths of a radius and a diameter. What did you discover?

A diameter is twice as long as a radius.

Exercises

Tell whether each point is on, inside, or outside the circle.

1. A   2. T   3. D

Name the following:

4. two radii   5. a diameter

Answer these questions.

6. Why is line segment BC not a radius?

7. Why is it not a diameter?

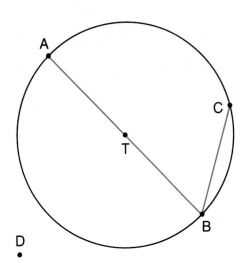

Use the circle below to complete the following.

8. If $d = 12$, then $r =$ ___.

9. If $r = 12$, then $d =$ ___.

10. If $d = 1$, then $r =$ ___.

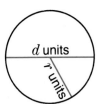

d units

r units

Use the two circles below to answer the following:

11. Which circle has the longer diameter? How long is it?

12. Which circle has the longer radius? How long is it?

13. You are to make a wire ring the size of each circle. For which circle will you need more wire?

14. Bonnie used 24 feet of fence to make a circular pen. Dave used 20 feet of fence to make a circular pen. Whose pen has the longer diameter?

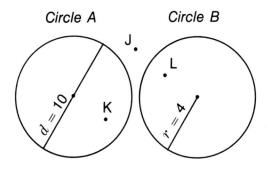

Circle A   Circle B

J

L

$d = 10$

K

$r = 4$

Polygons

Triangle	Quadrilateral	Pentagon	Hexagon	Octagon
		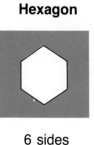	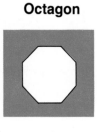	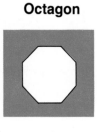
3 sides	4 sides	5 sides	6 sides	8 sides
How many angles?	How many angles?	How many angles?	How many angles?	How many angles?

What did you discover about the number of sides and the number of angles of a polygon?

Exercises

Give the name for each shape.

1.

2.

3.

4.

5.

6.

7.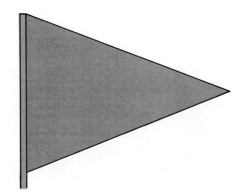

8.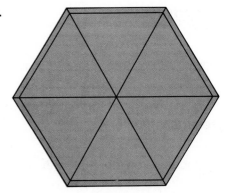

9.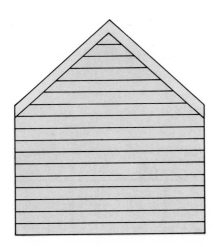

10.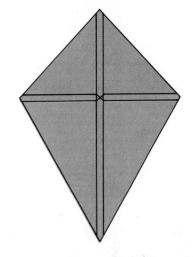

11. A polygon has 9 sides. How many angles does it have?

12. A polygon has 100 sides. How many angles does it have?

Toothpick Trick

Place 12 sticks like this to form 4 small squares.

Now change the position of **only 3 sticks** so that you have 3 squares the same size as the original 4 squares.

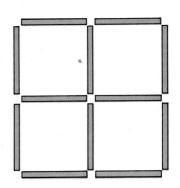

Extra Practice—Set B, page 332

Parallel Lines

Draw along both edges of a ruler.

Do the two line segments **intersect** (cross) each other?

Suppose you do that with a longer ruler. Would the two line segments intersect?

Suppose you do that with a still longer ruler. Would the two line segments intersect?

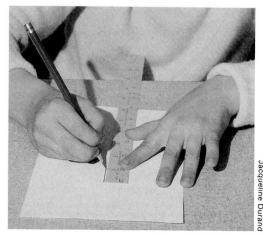

Jacqueline Durand

You have drawn two **parallel line segments.** They are parts of **parallel lines.**

Line AB *is parallel to* line CD.

Are the red line segments all the same length?

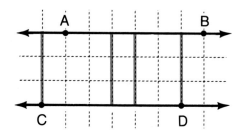

Parallel lines never intersect. The distance between them is always the same.

Line EF is parallel to line GH. Line segments EF and GH are parts of parallel lines. So *line segment EF is parallel to line segment GH.*

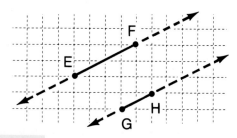

Parallel line segments are parts of parallel lines.

Exercises

Tell whether the lines or line segments are parallel.

1. 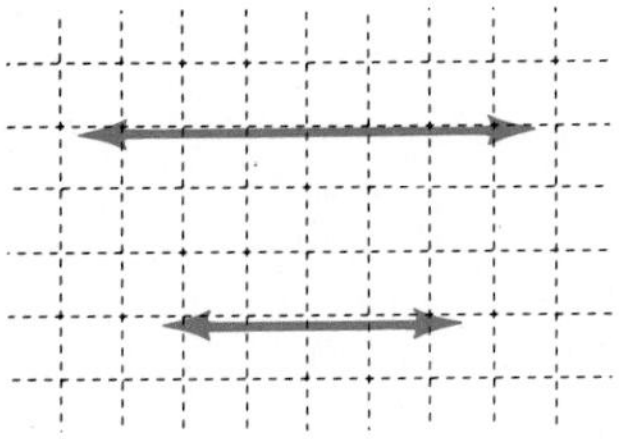 **2.** 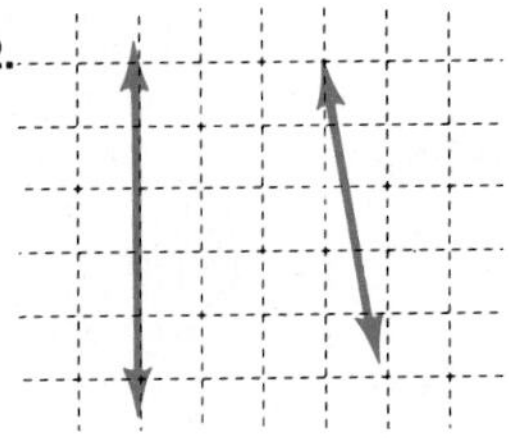 **3.**

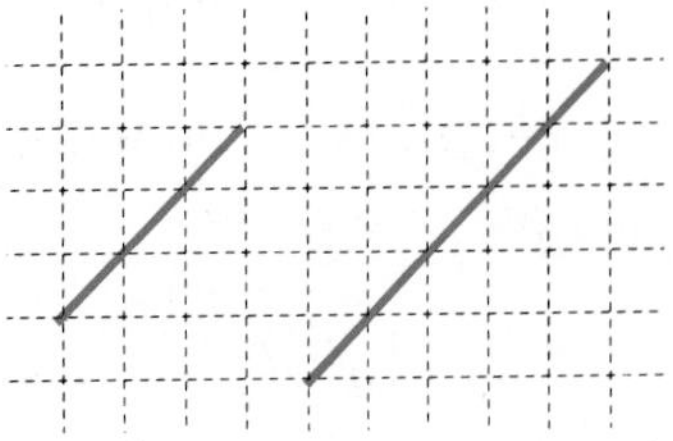

Copy each line and point A on grid paper. Then draw a line through Point A that is parallel to the given line.

4. 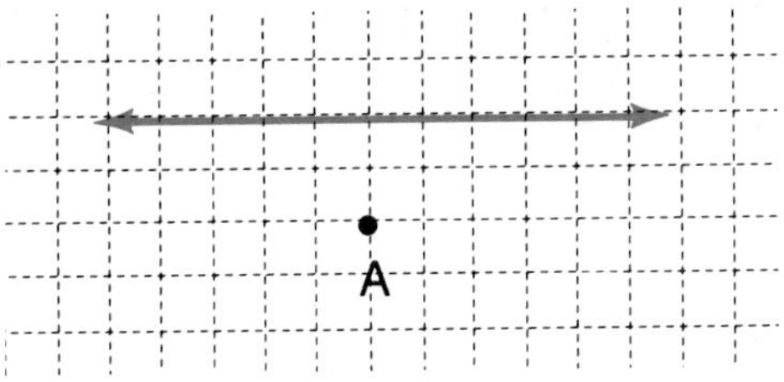 **5.**

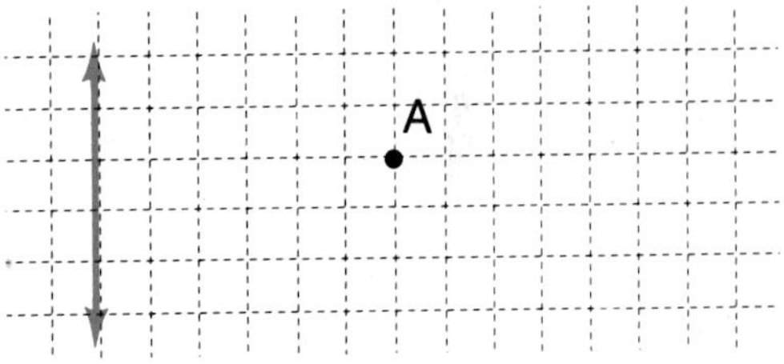

6. 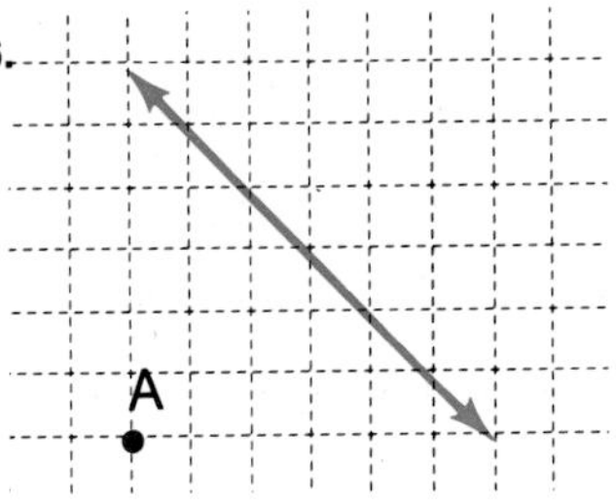 **7.** 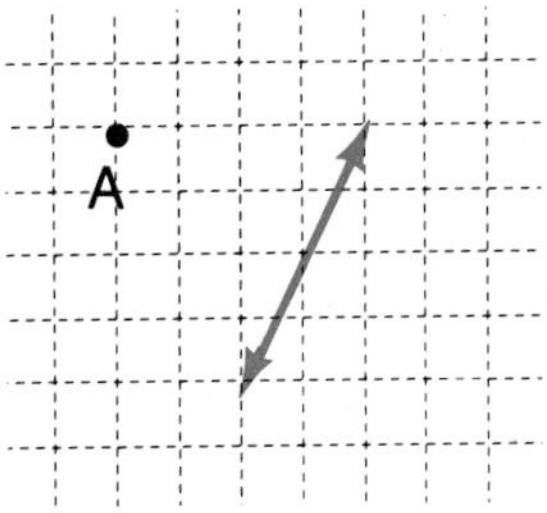 **8.**

Skew Lines

Each edge of a rectangular prism is part of a line.

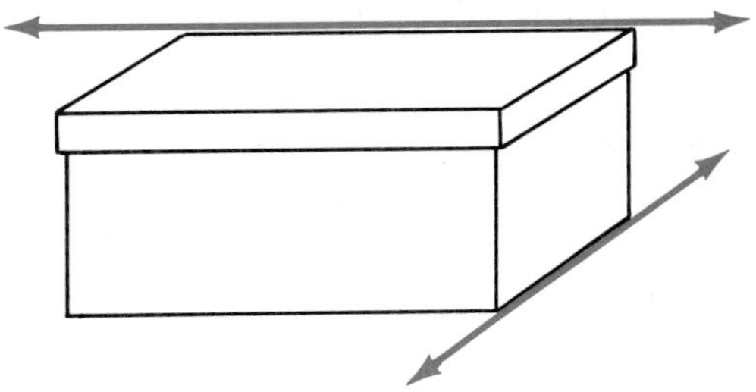

The blue lines do not intersect. The blue lines are not parallel.

The blue lines are **skew lines.**

Give examples of skew lines in the classroom.

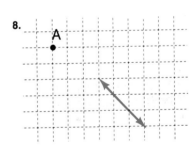

139

Perpendicular Lines

Measure each angle in the figure.

What kind of angles are they?

When two lines form right angles, the lines are **perpendicular.**

Line AD is *perpendicular* to line BC.

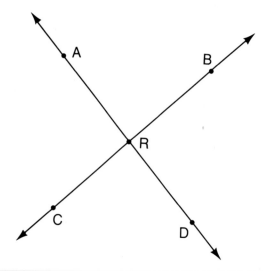

When two line segments form right angles, the line segments are perpendicular.

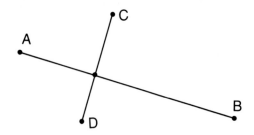

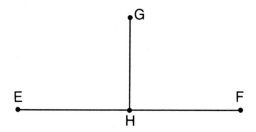

Line segments AB and CD are perpendicular.

Line segments EF and GH are perpendicular.

What is the measurement of ∠CLA?

What is the measurement of ∠FHG?

140

Exercises

Write *Yes* if the hands of the clock are perpendicular. Write *No* if they are not.

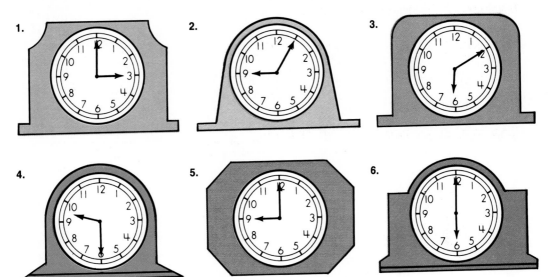

1.
2.
3.
4.
5.
6.

7. Would the hands of a clock be perpendicular at 3:30?

8. Are a flagpole and its shadow perpendicular?

9. Draw two line segments that are perpendicular.

10. Give three examples of two perpendicular line segments.

Can You Do This?

Draw a square and place 8 coins on it as shown. Move 4 coins—and only 4 coins—so that each side of the square will have 4 coins.

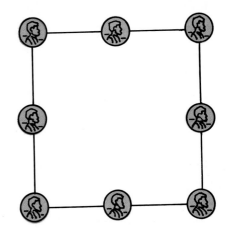

Extra Practice—Set A, page 333

CHAPTER REVIEW

Write a name for the shape of each object.

1.   2.   3.   4.

Write a name for each figure.

5.
B ——————————————— A

6. <—————————————————>
   F   G

Use the angle at the right to answer the following:

7. Name the angle.

8. Name the sides.

9. Find the measurement of the angle.

10. Tell whether the angle is acute, obtuse, or right.

11. Are the sides perpendicular?

12. Draw an angle that is congruent to this angle.

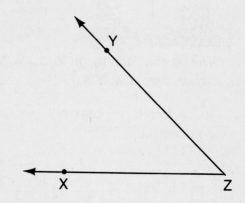

Use the circle at the right to answer the following:

13. Name a diameter.

14. Name a radius.

15. If line segment BD is 5 units long, how long is line segment AC?

16. Are line segments BC and BD parallel?

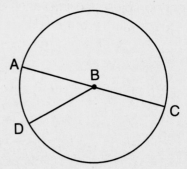

7 Fractions (×)

Lou Jones

Fractions

This rectangle is separated into parts of the same size.

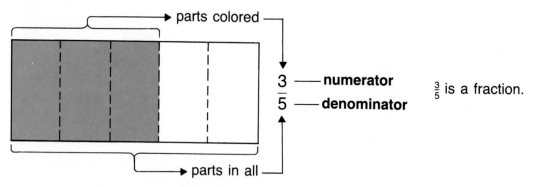

$\frac{3}{5}$ ——— **numerator**

$\frac{3}{5}$ is a fraction.

——— **denominator**

$\frac{3}{5}$ or *three fifths* of the rectangle is blue.

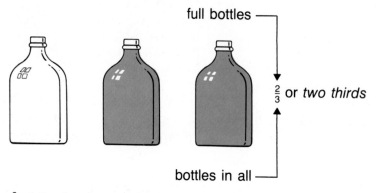

full bottles

$\frac{2}{3}$ or *two thirds*

bottles in all

$\frac{2}{3}$ of the bottles are full.

As you go from 0 to 1, match a fraction with each letter to tell how far you have gone.

$$\frac{1}{8} \quad \frac{3}{8} \quad \frac{5}{8} \quad \frac{7}{8} \quad \frac{1}{4} \quad \frac{2}{4} \quad \frac{3}{4}$$

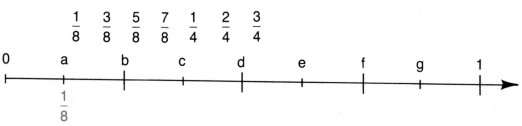

Exercises

Write a fraction to tell how much is blue.

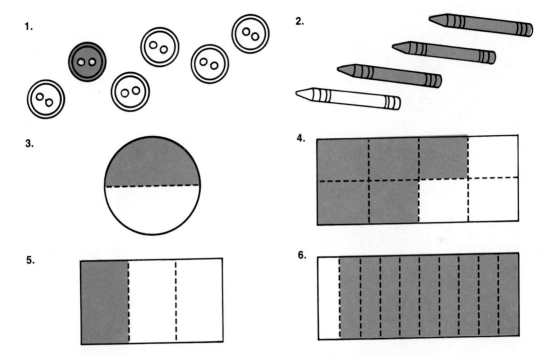

1.

2.

3.

4.

5.

6.

7. Len lives 7 blocks from school. He ran 4 blocks and walked the rest. Write a fraction for the part of the way that he ran.

8. Beth has 8 checkers. Five of them are black. Write a fraction for the part of the checkers that are black.

9. There are 6 books on a desk. Five of them are new books. Write a fraction for the part of the books that are new.

10. 3 out of 5 children are girls. Write a fraction for the part of the children who are boys.

Is $\frac{1}{4}$ of the figure shaded red? Answer *Yes* or *No* for each.

11.

12.

13.

14.

145

Equivalent Fractions

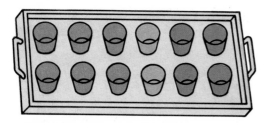

You can group the cups in several ways. Each way shows a different fraction for the red cups.

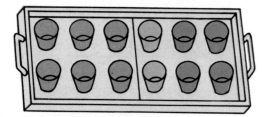

$\frac{1}{2}$ are red.

$\frac{2}{4}$ are red.

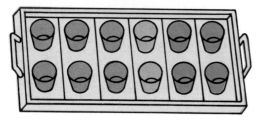

$\frac{3}{6}$ are red.

$\frac{6}{12}$ are red.

$\frac{1}{2}$, $\frac{2}{4}$, $\frac{3}{6}$, and $\frac{6}{12}$ are **equivalent fractions.**

Equivalent fractions name the same number.

$$\frac{1}{2} = \frac{2}{4} = \frac{3}{6} = \frac{6}{12}$$

Exercises

1. Write two equivalent fractions for the green cups.

2. Write two equivalent fractions for the blue cups.

146

3. Write two equivalent fractions for the red hats.

4. Write two equivalent fractions for the blue hats.

Write two equivalent fractions to tell how much of the rectangle is

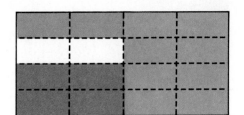

5. red

6. green

7. blue

8. white

Write two equivalent fractions to tell how much of the rectangle is

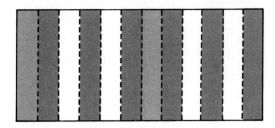

9. blue

10. white

11. green

12. red

Quick Trick

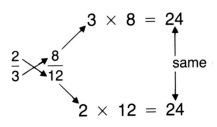

$3 \times 8 = 24$

$\dfrac{2}{3} \times \dfrac{8}{12}$

same

$2 \times 12 = 24$

$\frac{2}{3}$ and $\frac{8}{12}$ are equivalent.

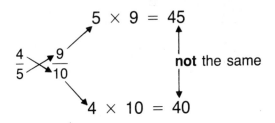

$5 \times 9 = 45$

$\dfrac{4}{5} \times \dfrac{9}{10}$

not the same

$4 \times 10 = 40$

$\frac{4}{5}$ and $\frac{9}{10}$ *are not* equivalent.

Tell whether the fractions are equivalent.

1. $\frac{3}{6}$ and $\frac{9}{12}$

2. $\frac{2}{5}$ and $\frac{8}{20}$

3. $\frac{6}{10}$ and $\frac{16}{24}$

Renaming Fractions

This rectangle is separated into parts of the same size.

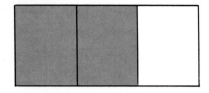

$$\frac{2}{3}$$

2 of the 3 parts are brown.

Two thirds of the rectangle is brown.

You can draw one dashed line so there are twice as many parts of the same size.

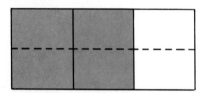

There are twice as many brown parts.

$$\frac{2}{3} = \frac{2 \times 2}{3 \times 2} = \frac{4}{6}$$

There are twice as many parts.

Or you can draw two dashed lines so there are three times as many parts of the same size.

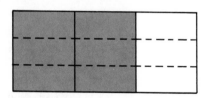

There are 3 times as many brown parts.

$$\frac{2}{3} = \frac{2 \times 3}{3 \times 3} = \frac{6}{9}$$

There are 3 times as many parts.

Are $\frac{2}{3}$, $\frac{4}{6}$, and $\frac{6}{9}$ equivalent?

You can multiply both the numerator and the denominator by the same number, but not by zero.

How can you find the number for each □?

$\frac{2}{3} = \frac{\square}{18}$

$\times\ 6$

$\frac{4}{5} = \frac{\square}{10}$

$\times\ 2$

$\frac{3}{4} = \frac{\square}{12}$

$\times\ ?$

$\frac{5}{6} = \frac{\square}{24}$

$\times\ ?$

Exercises

Find a number for each □.

1. $\frac{5 \times 4}{6 \times 4} = \frac{\square}{24}$ $\frac{5}{6} = \frac{\square}{24}$

2. $\frac{7}{8} = \frac{\square}{16}$

3. $\frac{1}{5} = \frac{\square}{20}$

4. $\frac{2}{5} = \frac{\square}{15}$

5. $\frac{1}{8} = \frac{\square}{16}$

6. $\frac{1}{3} = \frac{\square}{15}$

7. $\frac{5}{6} = \frac{\square}{12}$

8. $\frac{7}{12} = \frac{\square}{24}$

9. $\frac{3}{4} = \frac{\square}{32}$

10. $\frac{3}{16} = \frac{\square}{48}$

11. $\frac{4}{9} = \frac{\square}{45}$

12. $\frac{5}{8} = \frac{\square}{32}$

13. $\frac{4}{5} = \frac{\square}{100}$

14. $\frac{3}{10} = \frac{\square}{100}$

15. $\frac{1}{6} = \frac{\square}{60}$

Find three equivalent fractions for each fraction below.

16. $\frac{1}{3}$

17. $\frac{3}{8}$

18. $\frac{1}{5}$

19. $\frac{7}{10}$

20. $\frac{4}{5}$

21. $\frac{2}{8}$

Find a number for each □.

22. $\frac{4}{5} = \frac{16}{\square}$

23. $\frac{3}{4} = \frac{12}{\square}$

24. $\frac{1}{5} = \frac{2}{\square}$

25. $\frac{2}{7} = \frac{8}{\square}$

26. $\frac{5}{7} = \frac{10}{\square}$

27. $\frac{4}{5} = \frac{12}{\square}$

28. $\frac{1}{8} = \frac{8}{\square}$

29. $\frac{3}{9} = \frac{6}{\square}$

30. $\frac{1}{\square} = \frac{2}{12}$

31. $\frac{2}{\square} = \frac{8}{12}$

32. $\frac{\square}{2} = \frac{0}{12}$

33. $\frac{4}{\square} = \frac{12}{3}$

34. $\frac{3}{\square} = \frac{9}{15}$

35. $\frac{5}{\square} = \frac{15}{18}$

36. $\frac{4}{\square} = \frac{8}{18}$

37. $\frac{7}{\square} = \frac{21}{24}$

38. $\frac{\square}{5} = \frac{8}{20}$

39. $\frac{\square}{10} = \frac{21}{30}$

40. $\frac{\square}{5} = \frac{4}{20}$

41. $\frac{\square}{8} = \frac{15}{24}$

42. $\frac{\square}{16} = \frac{3}{48}$

43. $\frac{\square}{12} = \frac{10}{24}$

44. $\frac{\square}{20} = \frac{14}{40}$

45. $\frac{\square}{16} = \frac{20}{64}$

Renaming Fractions

These fractions are equivalent fractions.

$$\frac{1}{2} = \frac{2}{4} = \frac{3}{6} = \frac{4}{8} = \frac{5}{10} = \frac{6}{12} = \frac{7}{14} = \frac{8}{16}$$

You can multiply both the numerator and the denominator of $\frac{1}{2}$ by 5 to get $\frac{5}{10}$.

To "undo" this, divide both the numerator and the denominator of $\frac{5}{10}$ by 5 to get $\frac{1}{2}$.

$$\frac{5}{10} = \frac{5 \div 5}{10 \div 5} = \frac{1}{2}$$

You can divide both the numerator and the denominator by the same number, but not by zero.

$$\frac{7}{14} = \frac{7 \div 7}{14 \div 7} = \frac{1}{2} \qquad\qquad \frac{12}{15} = \frac{12 \div 3}{15 \div 3} = \frac{4}{5}$$

By what number would you divide both the numerator and the denominator of $\frac{12}{20}$ to get $\frac{6}{10}$? To get $\frac{3}{5}$?

How can you find the number for each □?

$\frac{8}{12} = \frac{\square}{6}$

$\div 2$

$\frac{10}{15} = \frac{\square}{3}$

$\div 5$

$\frac{6}{8} = \frac{\square}{4}$

$\div\ ?$

$\frac{18}{24} = \frac{\square}{4}$

$\div\ ?$

150

Exercises

Find a number for each $\square$.

1. $\frac{15 \div 3}{18 \div 3} = \frac{\square}{6}$

2. $\frac{6}{9} = \frac{\square}{3}$

3. $\frac{5}{15} = \frac{\square}{3}$

4. $\frac{4}{6} = \frac{\square}{3}$

5. $\frac{3}{9} = \frac{\square}{3}$

6. $\frac{6}{8} = \frac{\square}{4}$

7. $\frac{8}{10} = \frac{\square}{5}$

8. $\frac{10}{12} = \frac{\square}{6}$

9. $\frac{9}{24} = \frac{\square}{8}$

10. $\frac{8}{12} = \frac{\square}{3}$

11. $\frac{16}{20} = \frac{\square}{5}$

12. $\frac{15}{18} = \frac{\square}{6}$

13. $\frac{12}{18} = \frac{\square}{3}$

14. $\frac{14}{16} = \frac{\square}{8}$

15. $\frac{18}{24} = \frac{\square}{4}$

16. $\frac{9}{12} = \frac{\square}{4}$

Find three equivalent fractions for each fraction below. Divide both the numerator and the denominator by any number you choose, except zero.

17. $\frac{18}{24}$

18. $\frac{8}{32}$

19. $\frac{6}{30}$

20. $\frac{10}{20}$

21. $\frac{12}{24}$

22. $\frac{15}{30}$

23. $\frac{12}{36}$

24. $\frac{30}{45}$

25. $\frac{10}{30}$

26. $\frac{20}{30}$

27. $\frac{15}{45}$

28. $\frac{12}{30}$

Find a number for each $\square$.

29. $\frac{4}{12} = \frac{1}{\square}$

30. $\frac{8}{20} = \frac{2}{\square}$

31. $\frac{14}{21} = \frac{2}{\square}$

32. $\frac{8}{28} = \frac{2}{\square}$

33. $\frac{10}{\square} = \frac{5}{8}$

34. $\frac{16}{\square} = \frac{4}{9}$

35. $\frac{16}{\square} = \frac{8}{9}$

36. $\frac{24}{\square} = \frac{3}{8}$

37. $\frac{\square}{14} = \frac{5}{7}$

38. $\frac{\square}{24} = \frac{3}{8}$

39. $\frac{16}{\square} = \frac{1}{4}$

40. $\frac{\square}{32} = \frac{1}{4}$

Find three equivalent fractions for each fraction below.

41. $\frac{8}{12}$

42. $\frac{6}{9}$

43. $\frac{2}{6}$

44. $\frac{6}{24}$

45. $\frac{9}{12}$

46. $\frac{10}{20}$

47. $\frac{9}{15}$

48. $\frac{6}{10}$

49. $\frac{2}{3}$

50. $\frac{4}{10}$

51. $\frac{6}{8}$

52. $\frac{12}{16}$

Greatest Common Factor

Here is a way to find the factors of a number.

5	8	9	12
1×5	1×8	1×9	1×12
5×1	2×4	3×3	2×6
factors of 5	4×2	9×1	3×4
	8×1	factors of 9	4×3
	factors of 8		6×2
			12×1
			factors of 12

Numbers	Factors of each number	Common factors	Greatest common factor
8 and 12	1, 2, 4, 8 ——————— 1, 2, 3, 4, 6, 12	1, 2, 4	4
5 and 9	1, 5 ——— 1, 3, 9	1	1

How do you find the common factors of two numbers?

How do you find the greatest common factor of two numbers?

What is the greatest common factor of 5 and 8?

What is the greatest common factor of 9 and 12?

152

Exercises

1. List the factors of 4.

2. List the factors of 6.

3. What are the common factors of 4 and 6?

4. What is the greatest common factor of 4 and 6?

Copy and complete.

	Numbers	Factors of each number	Common factors	Greatest common factor
5.	8 and 10	————		
6.	6 and 9	————		
7.	8 and 4	————		
8.	10 and 12	————		

Find the greatest common factor of the two numbers.

9. 8, 16   10. 12, 16   11. 7, 21   12. 5, 9   13. 12, 14

14. 20, 25   15. 16, 18   16. 18, 36   17. 16, 20   18. 16, 24

19. 24, 32   20. 18, 54   21. 36, 45   22. 25, 50   23. 17, 21

Find the greatest common factor of the three numbers.

24. 12, 18, 36   25. 9, 12, 18   26. 12, 18, 32

Simplest Form

Equivalent fractions:		$\dfrac{2}{3}$	$=$	$\dfrac{4}{6}$	$=$	$\dfrac{6}{9}$	$=$	$\dfrac{8}{12}$

Name the greatest
common factor of: 2 and 3 4 and 6 6 and 9 8 and 12

For the fractions shown above, $\frac{2}{3}$ is in **simplest form.**

A fraction is in simplest form if the greatest common factor of the numerator and the denominator is 1.

The greatest common factor of 8 and 12 is 4. So you can change $\frac{8}{12}$ to simplest form.

$$\frac{8}{12} = \frac{8 \div 4}{12 \div 4} = \frac{2}{3}$$ Divide the numerator and
the denominator by their
greatest common factor.

To change $\frac{32}{48}$ to simplest form, Myra divided the numerator and denominator by 8.

$$\frac{32}{48} = \frac{32 \div 8}{48 \div 8} = \frac{4}{6}$$

What is the greatest common factor of 4 and 6?

Is $\frac{4}{6}$ in simplest form?

If not, how would you change it to simplest form?

To change a fraction to simplest form, do you have to start by dividing by the greatest common factor?

154

Exercises

Find a number for each □.

1. $\frac{9}{12} = \frac{\square}{4}$

2. $\frac{8}{28} = \frac{\square}{7}$

3. $\frac{6}{20} = \frac{\square}{10}$

4. $\frac{10}{12} = \frac{\square}{6}$

5. $\frac{4}{16} = \frac{\square}{4}$

6. $\frac{16}{36} = \frac{\square}{9}$

7. $\frac{16}{24} = \frac{\square}{3}$

8. $\frac{12}{15} = \frac{\square}{5}$

Change each fraction to simplest form.

9. $\frac{6}{8}$

10. $\frac{6}{9}$

11. $\frac{4}{6}$

12. $\frac{2}{8}$

13. $\frac{2}{6}$

14. $\frac{8}{12}$

15. $\frac{9}{12}$

16. $\frac{6}{12}$

17. $\frac{15}{18}$

18. $\frac{16}{40}$

19. $\frac{18}{27}$

20. $\frac{25}{40}$

21. $\frac{36}{48}$

22. $\frac{24}{40}$

23. $\frac{16}{24}$

24. $\frac{5}{15}$

25. $\frac{32}{56}$

26. $\frac{14}{18}$

27. $\frac{30}{50}$

28. $\frac{27}{36}$

29. $\frac{18}{45}$

30. $\frac{15}{21}$

31. $\frac{20}{30}$

32. $\frac{18}{20}$

33. $\frac{16}{20}$

34. $\frac{15}{30}$

35. $\frac{24}{30}$

36. $\frac{18}{81}$

37. $\frac{70}{80}$

38. $\frac{27}{30}$

39. $\frac{33}{99}$

40. $\frac{24}{64}$

41. $\frac{27}{72}$

42. $\frac{18}{54}$

43. $\frac{9}{90}$

44. $\frac{10}{100}$

45. $\frac{40}{100}$

46. $\frac{50}{100}$

47. $\frac{12}{144}$

48. $\frac{11}{121}$

∩ot Simple!

Myra divided the numerator and the denominator of a fraction by 3. Then she divided the numerator and denominator of her result by 2 and got $\frac{3}{4}$. What fraction did she start with?

Multiplying Fractions

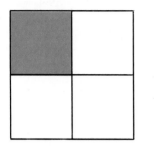

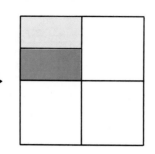

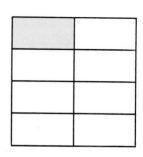

Mr. Gray gave $\frac{1}{4}$ of his farm to his son.

The son planted corn on $\frac{1}{2}$ of his $\frac{1}{4}$ of the farm.

The son planted corn on $\frac{1}{8}$ of the farm.

$\frac{1}{2}$ of $\frac{1}{4}$ is equal to $\frac{1}{8}$.

$$\frac{1}{2} \times \frac{1}{4} = \frac{1}{8}$$

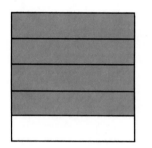

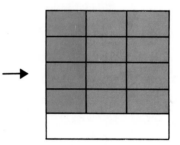

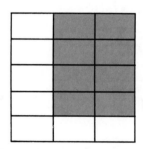

Mr. Brown decided to use $\frac{4}{5}$ of his yard for a garden.

$\frac{2}{3}$ of the garden will be used for tomatoes.

$\frac{8}{15}$ of his yard will be used for tomatoes.

$\frac{2}{3}$ of $\frac{4}{5}$ is equal to $\frac{8}{15}$.

$$\frac{2}{3} \times \frac{4}{5} = \frac{8}{15}$$

Here is an easy way to multiply fractions.

Multiply the numerators.

$$\frac{1}{2} \times \frac{1}{4} = \frac{1 \times 1}{2 \times 4} = \frac{1}{8}$$

Multiply the denominators.

Multiply the numerators.

$$\frac{2}{3} \times \frac{4}{5} = \frac{2 \times 4}{3 \times 5} = \frac{8}{15}$$

Multiply the denominators.

156

Exercises

Multiply.

1.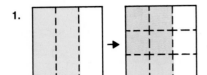

$$\frac{2}{3} \times \frac{2}{3}$$

2.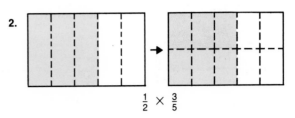

$$\frac{1}{2} \times \frac{3}{5}$$

3. $\frac{3}{4} \times \frac{3}{5}$ **4.** $\frac{4}{10} \times \frac{1}{10}$ **5.** $\frac{5}{6} \times \frac{1}{2}$ **6.** $\frac{1}{2} \times \frac{1}{10}$

7. $\frac{3}{5} \times \frac{1}{4}$ **8.** $\frac{1}{2} \times \frac{3}{4}$ **9.** $\frac{3}{5} \times \frac{1}{5}$ **10.** $\frac{1}{3} \times \frac{1}{4}$

11. $\frac{1}{6} \times \frac{1}{2}$ **12.** $\frac{2}{3} \times \frac{1}{7}$ **13.** $\frac{3}{4} \times \frac{1}{4}$ **14.** $\frac{7}{8} \times \frac{1}{5}$

15. $\frac{1}{4} \times \frac{3}{5}$ **16.** $\frac{1}{3} \times \frac{1}{3}$ **17.** $\frac{1}{10} \times \frac{1}{10}$ **18.** $\frac{1}{4} \times \frac{3}{8}$

19. $\frac{7}{9} \times \frac{2}{3}$ **20.** $\frac{4}{5} \times \frac{3}{7}$ **21.** $\frac{5}{6} \times \frac{5}{8}$ **22.** $\frac{7}{8} \times \frac{1}{9}$

23. When Mary got to the party there was only $\frac{1}{2}$ of a pizza left. She ate $\frac{3}{4}$ of what was left. Write a fraction for how much of the pizza she ate.

24. Olaf ate $\frac{3}{4}$ of a pizza. Horace ate $\frac{1}{3}$ as much pizza as Olaf. How much of the pizza did Horace eat?

Think About It

Which would you rather have? Why?

$\frac{1}{2}$ of $\frac{3}{4}$ of a pizza

or

$\frac{3}{4}$ of $\frac{1}{2}$ of a pizza

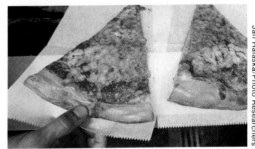

Jan Halaska/Photo Researchers

Products in Simplest Form

Lisa filled $\frac{2}{3}$ of the carton with hard-boiled eggs.

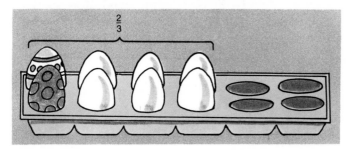

$\frac{1}{4}$ of the hard-boiled eggs are decorated. How much of the carton contains decorated eggs?

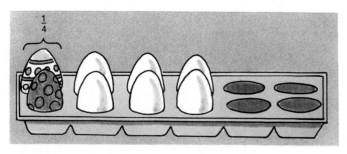

To find the answer, you can find $\frac{1}{4}$ of $\frac{2}{3}$ and change the answer to simplest form.

greatest common factor

$$\frac{1}{4} \times \frac{2}{3} = \frac{1 \times 2}{4 \times 3} = \frac{2}{12} = \frac{2 \div 2}{12 \div 2} = \frac{1}{6}$$

$\frac{1}{6}$ of the carton contains decorated eggs.

You could divide by the greatest common factor *before* you multiply.

$$\frac{1}{4} \times \frac{2}{3} = \frac{1 \times \overset{1}{\cancel{2}}}{\underset{2}{\cancel{4}} \times 3} = \frac{1}{6}$$

158

Explain what is done in each example.

$$\frac{2}{3} \times \frac{9}{16} = \frac{2 \times \overset{3}{\cancel{9}}}{\underset{8}{\cancel{16}} \times \underset{1}{\cancel{3}}} = \frac{3}{8}$$

$$\frac{3}{5} \times \frac{5}{6} = \frac{\overset{1}{\cancel{3}} \times \overset{1}{\cancel{5}}}{\underset{1}{\cancel{5}} \times \underset{2}{\cancel{6}}} = \frac{1}{2}$$

Exercises

Find each product in simplest form.

1. $\frac{1}{3} \times \frac{3}{10}$ 2. $\frac{2}{5} \times \frac{3}{4}$ 3. $\frac{1}{10} \times \frac{2}{3}$ 4. $\frac{1}{4} \times \frac{2}{3}$

5. $\frac{2}{3} \times \frac{3}{8}$ 6. $\frac{3}{5} \times \frac{5}{9}$ 7. $\frac{5}{6} \times \frac{7}{10}$ 8. $\frac{2}{5} \times \frac{5}{6}$

9. $\frac{2}{9} \times \frac{3}{4}$ 10. $\frac{3}{8} \times \frac{8}{9}$ 11. $\frac{2}{7} \times \frac{7}{16}$ 12. $\frac{4}{5} \times \frac{5}{8}$

13. $\frac{4}{5} \times \frac{5}{6}$ 14. $\frac{3}{4} \times \frac{5}{8}$ 15. $\frac{7}{8} \times \frac{2}{14}$ 16. $\frac{8}{9} \times \frac{15}{16}$

17. Mary has $\frac{2}{3}$ gallon of paint. She poured $\frac{1}{4}$ of it into a smaller can. How much paint is in the smaller can?

18. Peggy has $\frac{1}{2}$ gallon of paint. Sherman has $\frac{1}{2}$ as much paint as Peggy. How much paint does Sherman have?

19. Todd had $\frac{3}{4}$ gallon of paint. He poured $\frac{1}{6}$ of it into a smaller can. How much paint was in the smaller can?

20. Josie has $\frac{5}{8}$ gallon of paint. Phillip has $\frac{2}{5}$ gallon of paint. Phillip says he has $\frac{1}{2}$ as much paint as Josie. Is Phillip right?

How Are They Related?

Jane told her brother, "That man's mother is our mother's mother-in-law."

How are that man and Jane related?

He is

200-437-375   7-9-500-275-437

8-375   125-400-4-200-437-375.

Use the answers to find the letter for each number.

1. ▮▮▮ +235 635 **A**	2. 722 +▮▮▮ 830 **B**	3. ▮▮▮ +360 860 **C**	4. 418 +▮▮▮ 716 **D**	5. 120 +317 ▮▮▮ **E**
6. 678 −▮▮▮ 553 **F**	7. ▮▮▮ −248 627 **G**	8. ▮▮▮ −134 66 **H**	9. 527 − 18 ▮▮▮ **I**	10. 892 −647 ▮▮▮ **J**
11. ▮▮▮ ×2 1750 **K**	12. ▮▮▮ ×4 1100 **L**	13. 46 ×▮ 138 **M**	14. 79 ×▮ 711 **N**	15. 316 ×▮ 2528 **O**
16. $12\overline{)}$ 25 **P**	17. $3\overline{)1125}$ ▮▮▮ **R**	18. $▮\overline{)222}$ 37 **S**	19. $\frac{\Box}{5} = \frac{20}{25}$ **T**	20. $\frac{2}{\Box} = \frac{8}{28}$ **U**

160

Fractions for Whole Numbers

Two halves are equal to one.

$$\frac{2}{2} = 1$$

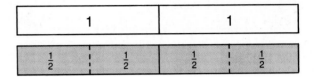

Four halves are equal to two.

$$\frac{4}{2} = 2$$

Fractions also indicate division.

$$\frac{10}{2} = 10 \div 2 = 5$$

$$\frac{4}{2} = 4 \div 2 = 2$$

$$\frac{24}{3} = 24 \div 3 = 8$$

$$\frac{8}{1} = 8 \div 1 = 8$$

Exercises

Find the whole number named by each fraction.

1. $\dfrac{12}{4}$

2. $\dfrac{18}{9}$

3. $\dfrac{24}{6}$

4. $\dfrac{32}{8}$

5. $\dfrac{32}{32}$

6. $\dfrac{8}{1}$

7. $\dfrac{36}{12}$

8. $\dfrac{56}{8}$

9. $\dfrac{48}{12}$

10. $\dfrac{9}{9}$

11. $\dfrac{72}{6}$

12. $\dfrac{42}{14}$

13. $\dfrac{144}{4}$

14. $\dfrac{144}{8}$

15. $\dfrac{144}{12}$

16. $\dfrac{11}{11}$

Fractions to Mixed Numerals

three halves

$$\frac{3}{2} = 1 + \frac{1}{2} \text{ or } 1\frac{1}{2}$$

1	1

$\frac{1}{2}$	$\frac{1}{2}$	$\frac{1}{2}$	$\frac{1}{2}$

five halves

$$\frac{5}{2} = 2 + \frac{1}{2} \text{ or } 2\frac{1}{2}$$

1	1	1	1

$\frac{1}{2}$	$\frac{1}{2}$	$\frac{1}{2}$	$\frac{1}{2}$	$\frac{1}{2}$	$\frac{1}{2}$	$\frac{1}{2}$	$\frac{1}{2}$

Numerals like $1\frac{1}{2}$ and $2\frac{1}{2}$ are called **mixed numerals.**

To change $\frac{7}{2}$ to a mixed numeral, divide like this.

$$\frac{7}{2} \longrightarrow \begin{array}{r} 3\frac{1}{2} \\ 2\overline{)7} \\ \underline{6} \\ 1 \end{array} \qquad 1 \div 2 = \frac{1}{2} \qquad \frac{7}{2} = 3\frac{1}{2}$$

Exercises

Complete to change each fraction to a mixed numeral.

1. $\frac{10}{3} = 3\frac{\square}{3}$

2. $\frac{14}{3} = 4\frac{\square}{3}$

3. $\frac{17}{6} = 2\frac{\square}{6}$

4. $\frac{23}{9} = 2\frac{\square}{9}$

5. $\frac{47}{8} = 5\frac{\square}{8}$

6. $\frac{39}{7} = 5\frac{\square}{7}$

7. $\frac{37}{4} = 9\frac{\square}{4}$

8. $\frac{43}{5} = 8\frac{\square}{5}$

9. $\frac{27}{8} = 3\frac{3}{\square}$

10. $\frac{19}{5} = 3\frac{4}{\square}$

11. $\frac{88}{9} = 9\frac{\square}{9}$

12. $\frac{77}{8} = 9\frac{\square}{\square}$

13. $\frac{49}{6} = 8\frac{1}{\square}$ **14.** $\frac{35}{4} = 8\frac{\square}{\square}$ **15.** $\frac{61}{9} = 6\frac{\square}{\square}$ **16.** $\frac{37}{5} = \square\frac{2}{5}$

17. $\frac{47}{6} = \square\frac{5}{6}$ **18.** $\frac{59}{7} = \square\frac{3}{7}$ **19.** $\frac{23}{3} = \square\frac{2}{3}$ **20.** $\frac{84}{9} = \square\frac{3}{9}$

Change each fraction to a mixed numeral.

21. $\frac{14}{5}$ **22.** $\frac{19}{7}$ **23.** $\frac{79}{8}$ **24.** $\frac{53}{6}$ **25.** $\frac{27}{4}$

26. $\frac{17}{12}$ **27.** $\frac{35}{11}$ **28.** $\frac{67}{22}$ **29.** $\frac{54}{13}$ **30.** $\frac{49}{11}$

31. $\frac{29}{10}$ **32.** $\frac{89}{6}$ **33.** $\frac{93}{4}$ **34.** $\frac{37}{2}$ **35.** $\frac{46}{12}$

36. $\frac{49}{15}$ **37.** $\frac{53}{3}$ **38.** $\frac{55}{4}$ **39.** $\frac{97}{10}$ **40.** $\frac{100}{30}$

Another Way

Study how $\frac{11}{8}$ is changed to a mixed numeral.

$$\frac{11}{8} = \frac{8}{8} + \frac{3}{8} = 1 + \frac{3}{8} = 1\frac{3}{8}$$

Study how $\frac{10}{3}$ is changed to a mixed numeral.

$$\frac{10}{3} = \frac{9}{3} + \frac{1}{3} = 3 + \frac{1}{3} = 3\frac{1}{3}$$

Change to a mixed numeral.

1. $\frac{13}{6}$ **2.** $\frac{4}{3}$ **3.** $\frac{9}{5}$ **4.** $\frac{11}{4}$ **5.** $\frac{7}{2}$

Mixed Numerals to Fractions

You can change a mixed numeral to a fraction like this.

$$2\frac{3}{4} = \frac{(4 \times 2) + 3}{4} = \frac{8 + 3}{4} = \frac{11}{4}$$

Use the same denominator.

Exercises

Complete to change each mixed numeral to a fraction.

1. $3\frac{2}{5} = \frac{(5 \times 3) + \blacksquare}{5}$

2. $2\frac{1}{6} = \frac{(6 \times 2) + \blacksquare}{6}$

3. $5\frac{3}{4} = \frac{(4 \times 5) + \blacksquare}{4}$

4. $6\frac{3}{7} = \frac{(7 \times 6) + \blacksquare}{7}$

5. $2\frac{5}{8} = \frac{(8 \times 2) + \blacksquare}{8}$

6. $5\frac{2}{3} = \frac{(3 \times 5) + \blacksquare}{3}$

7. $2\frac{3}{8} = \frac{(8 \times \blacksquare) + \blacksquare}{8}$

8. $3\frac{7}{9} = \frac{(9 \times \blacksquare) + \blacksquare}{\blacksquare}$

9. $8\frac{3}{4} = \frac{(\blacksquare \times \blacksquare) + \blacksquare}{\blacksquare}$

Change each mixed numeral to a fraction.

10. $2\frac{3}{4}$ 11. $3\frac{4}{5}$ 12. $3\frac{1}{8}$ 13. $4\frac{1}{6}$ 14. $7\frac{1}{2}$ 15. $8\frac{2}{3}$

16. $4\frac{4}{5}$ 17. $5\frac{2}{9}$ 18. $3\frac{3}{7}$ 19. $6\frac{7}{8}$ 20. $7\frac{5}{7}$ 21. $9\frac{2}{9}$

22. $4\frac{5}{6}$ 23. $3\frac{7}{10}$ 24. $2\frac{2}{9}$ 25. $1\frac{1}{2}$ 26. $10\frac{2}{3}$ 27. $1\frac{7}{8}$

28. $8\frac{8}{9}$ 29. $7\frac{3}{5}$ 30. $6\frac{3}{10}$ 31. $9\frac{4}{5}$ 32. $6\frac{1}{9}$ 33. $1\frac{5}{9}$

34. $10\frac{1}{4}$ 35. $100\frac{1}{4}$ 36. $25\frac{3}{4}$ 37. $33\frac{1}{3}$ 38. $333\frac{1}{3}$ 39. $66\frac{2}{3}$

Extra Practice—Set A, page 336

Practice

Write two fractions to tell how much of each figure is blue.

1.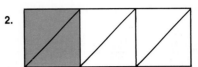

2.

Write three equivalent fractions for each fraction below.

3. $\dfrac{1}{4}$ 4. $\dfrac{3}{5}$ 5. $\dfrac{2}{6}$ 6. $\dfrac{1}{2}$ 7. $\dfrac{2}{9}$

Find the greatest common factor for each pair of numbers.

8. 18, 24   9. 6, 9   10. 12, 15   11. 5, 7

Change each fraction to a whole number or a mixed numeral.

12. $\dfrac{13}{12}$ 13. $\dfrac{28}{18}$ 14. $\dfrac{18}{7}$ 15. $\dfrac{13}{5}$

16. $\dfrac{25}{5}$ 17. $\dfrac{21}{12}$ 18. $\dfrac{39}{13}$ 19. $\dfrac{100}{20}$

20. $\dfrac{17}{5}$ 21. $\dfrac{29}{7}$ 22. $\dfrac{27}{12}$ 23. $\dfrac{28}{14}$

Change each mixed numeral to a fraction.

24. $1\frac{4}{5}$ 25. $4\frac{3}{7}$ 26. $1\frac{1}{9}$ 27. $10\frac{1}{10}$

Find each product.

28. $\frac{2}{3} \times \frac{4}{5}$ 29. $\frac{1}{4} \times \frac{2}{5}$ 30. $\frac{3}{8} \times \frac{5}{6}$

31. $\frac{3}{10} \times \frac{5}{12}$ 32. $\frac{7}{8} \times \frac{2}{3}$ 33. $\frac{5}{16} \times \frac{8}{15}$

Mixed Numerals in Multiplication

$\frac{1}{2}$ cup of lemon juice is needed for 1 gallon of lemonade. How much lemon juice is needed for $2\frac{1}{4}$ gallons of lemonade?

You can multiply $2\frac{1}{4}$ and $\frac{1}{2}$ like this.

$$2\frac{1}{4} \times \frac{1}{2} \qquad \text{Change } 2\frac{1}{4} \text{ to a fraction.} \qquad \frac{9}{4} \times \frac{1}{2} = \frac{9}{8} \quad \text{or} \quad 1\frac{1}{8}$$

$$2\frac{1}{4} = \frac{(4 \times 2) + 1}{4} = \frac{9}{4}$$

$1\frac{1}{8}$ cups of lemon juice are needed.

The mixed numeral $1\frac{1}{8}$ is in simplest form.

A mixed numeral is in simplest form when the fraction is less than 1 *and* in simplest form.

Explain how to find each product in simplest form.

$$1\frac{2}{3} \times 2\frac{1}{4} = \frac{5}{3} \times \frac{9}{4} = \frac{5 \times \cancel{9}}{\cancel{3} \times 4} = \frac{15}{4} = \boxed{} \frac{\boxed{}}{4}$$

$$4\frac{1}{6} \times 4 = \frac{25}{6} \times \frac{4}{1} = \frac{25 \times \cancel{4}}{\cancel{6} \times 1} = \frac{50}{3} = \boxed{}\frac{\boxed{}}{\boxed{}}$$

Read This

A direction like "Find each product in simplest form" means to give the answer as a whole number or as a mixed numeral in simplest form.

Exercises

Is the mixed numeral in simplest form? Answer *Yes* or *No*. If not, change it to simplest form.

1. $1\frac{8}{8}$

2. $6\frac{1}{2}$

3. $2\frac{5}{4}$

4. $7\frac{3}{8}$

5. $3\frac{3}{2}$

6. $3\frac{6}{8}$

Find each product in simplest form.

7. $\frac{1}{2} \times 1\frac{1}{4}$

8. $2\frac{2}{5} \times \frac{3}{4}$

9. $\frac{3}{10} \times 1\frac{5}{8}$

10. $8 \times \frac{1}{4}$

11. $1\frac{2}{3} \times \frac{2}{5}$

12. $1\frac{1}{4} \times 1\frac{1}{3}$

13. $\frac{1}{3} \times 7$

14. $10 \times \frac{7}{8}$

15. $2\frac{3}{4} \times 1\frac{1}{2}$

16. $3 \times \frac{5}{6}$

17. $2\frac{1}{4} \times \frac{1}{3}$

18. $3\frac{1}{3} \times 1\frac{3}{5}$

19. $\frac{5}{12} \times 24$

20. $2\frac{2}{5} \times \frac{5}{6}$

21. $1\frac{5}{8} \times 2\frac{2}{5}$

22. $\frac{9}{10} \times 3\frac{1}{3}$

23. $5\frac{1}{4} \times \frac{6}{7}$

24. $3\frac{3}{4} \times 1\frac{1}{5}$

25. $\frac{7}{10} \times 1\frac{3}{7}$

26. $3\frac{3}{8} \times \frac{14}{15}$

27. Peggy ran $5\frac{1}{4}$ miles. Sue ran $\frac{1}{4}$ of that distance. How far did Sue run?

28. Roscoe ran the marathon in $4\frac{2}{3}$ hours. Sasha ran it in $\frac{3}{4}$ that amount of time. How long did it take Sasha?

29. Meggan is $7\frac{1}{2}$ years old. Chad is twice as old as Meggan. How old is Chad?

30. Kurt is $3\frac{3}{4}$ feet tall. How many inches tall is Kurt?

31. How many minutes are there in $3\frac{5}{6}$ hours?

Victoria Beller-Smith/Photo Trends

Solving Problems

Solve each problem. If there is not enough information, tell what is missing.

1. After 3 hours of racing, one driver went 136 laps. Another driver went 7 fewer laps. How many laps had the second driver gone?

2. In one race, a driver went the first 50 laps in 1 hour, and the next 50 laps in 50 minutes. How many minutes did it take for the 100 laps?

3. One driver left the race after 3 hours. He went 450 miles. What was his average speed?

4. Another driver left the race after 2 hours. What was his average speed?

5. Once around the track at the Indianapolis Motor Speedway is $2\frac{1}{2}$ miles. How far would you travel in 6 laps?

6. How long would it take you to travel 2 laps at the Indianapolis Motor Speedway?

7. A driver made 4 pit stops during a race. The times for the stops were 28, 31, 33, and 24 seconds. Find the average time for each pit stop.

8. Another driver made 4 pit stops. He averaged $18\frac{1}{2}$ seconds each stop. How many seconds did he spend in the pit area?

9. One driver had trouble with his car and made a $3\frac{1}{2}$-minute pit stop. How many seconds was that?

10. At the Indianapolis Motor Speedway, the winner finished $1\frac{1}{2}$ laps ahead of the second-place driver. How many miles ahead was he?

11. During the first lap of the race a driver had engine trouble $\frac{3}{4}$ of the way around the $2\frac{1}{2}$-mile track. How far had he driven?

12. The winner of the first Indianapolis 500 averaged 75 miles per hour. How much faster was this year's average winning speed?

Lou Jones/Mind's Eye

Richard L. Capps

169

Add.

1.	6703 + 89	**2.**	45,092 + 2,919	**3.**	99,025 + 986	**4.**	3025 + 86

5.	370 25 486 + 9	**6.**	293 20,609 46 + 3,295	**7.**	3,718 29,001 967 +45,444	**8.**	9 25,414 30,092 + 785

Subtract.

9.	692 − 68	**10.**	1392 −1195	**11.**	5090 −3091	**12.**	7184 −1268

13.	3756 − 657	**14.**	5200 −2222	**15.**	25,000 −15,011	**16.**	31,916 −20,997

Multiply.

17.	67 ×7	**18.**	99 ×9	**19.**	348 ×6	**20.**	518 ×5

21.	79 ×42	**22.**	38 ×54	**23.**	8251 ×6	**24.**	906 ×75

25.	729 ×13	**26.**	6218 ×6	**27.**	538 ×108	**28.**	603 ×324

Divide.

29. 5)105 **30.** 8)116 **31.** 15)529 **32.** 27)138

33. 7)145 **34.** 4)812 **35.** 8)1382 **36.** 5)3142

37. 9)3601 **38.** 42)8029 **39.** 36)7790 **40.** 27)5699

41. Babe Ruth was born in 1895. At the age of 19 he hit his first major-league homerun. In what year did that happen?

42. Babe Ruth hit his 714th homerun in 1935. Hank Aaron did the same thing 39 years later. In what year did that happen?

43. Melinda has 568 baseball cards. She put the same number of cards into each of 4 stacks. How many cards were in each stack?

44. Andrea has 18 cards from each of 12 teams and 22 extra cards. How many cards does she have?

45. Kim is 5 years older than Keri. Keri is 6 years younger than Ned. Ned is 12 years old. How old is Keri? How old is Kim?

46. Fred is 4 years older than Jim. Fred is 10 years old. How many years old is Jim?

47. Francesco has scores of 86, 85, 73, 80, and 91 on his tests. What is his average score?

The Bettmann Archive

48. Jill ran 3 miles on Monday and 4 miles on Tuesday. On those two days she rode her bicycle twice as far as she ran. How far did she ride her bicycle?

49. Gina ran 5 miles on Wednesday and 5 miles on Thursday. On those two days she ran only half as far as she rode her bicycle. How far did she ride her bicycle?

CHAPTER REVIEW

Write two equivalent fractions for each.

1. red stars   2. blue stars

Write three equivalent fractions for each fraction.

3. $\dfrac{3}{5}$ 4. $\dfrac{3}{4}$ 5. $\dfrac{1}{3}$ 6. $\dfrac{8}{10}$ 7. $\dfrac{8}{12}$ 8. $\dfrac{6}{8}$

Find the greatest common factor of the two numbers.

9. 12, 8   10. 6, 16   11. 10, 12   12. 15, 21

Change each fraction to simplest form or to a whole number.

13. $\dfrac{4}{6}$ 14. $\dfrac{12}{18}$ 15. $\dfrac{12}{4}$ 16. $\dfrac{18}{6}$ 17. $\dfrac{4}{10}$ 18. $\dfrac{14}{2}$

Change each fraction to a mixed numeral.

19. $\dfrac{8}{3}$ 20. $\dfrac{10}{4}$ 21. $\dfrac{25}{8}$ 22. $\dfrac{24}{5}$

Change each mixed numeral to a fraction.

23. $4\frac{1}{2}$ 24. $6\frac{2}{5}$ 25. $1\frac{7}{9}$ 26. $8\frac{4}{7}$

Find each product in simplest form.

27. $\frac{2}{3} \times \frac{3}{5}$ 28. $6 \times \frac{1}{2}$ 29. $\frac{2}{3} \times \frac{1}{4}$ 30. $\frac{2}{5} \times \frac{5}{11}$

31. $2\frac{1}{3} \times \frac{1}{2}$ 32. $6 \times 2\frac{1}{4}$ 33. $3\frac{1}{3} \times 1\frac{4}{5}$ 34. $3\frac{3}{4} \times 16$

8 Fractions (+, -)

Larry Stepanowicz/Panographics

Adding Fractions

How much juice is in each cup?

How much juice is there?

You can add the fractions in either of these ways.

Add the numerators.

$$\frac{1}{4} + \frac{2}{4} = \frac{1+2}{4} = \frac{3}{4}$$

Use the same denominator.

Add the numerators.
$$\left(\begin{array}{c}\frac{1}{4}\\ +\frac{2}{4}\\ \hline \frac{3}{4}\end{array}\right)$$
Use the same denominator.

There is $\frac{3}{4}$ cup of juice.

This method also works to add three or more fractions.

Add the numerators.
$$\left(\begin{array}{c}\frac{1}{10}\\ \frac{3}{10}\\ +\frac{3}{10}\\ \hline \frac{7}{10}\end{array}\right)$$
Use the same denominator.

$$\begin{array}{r}\frac{6}{8}\\ \frac{1}{8}\\ +\frac{3}{8}\\ \hline \frac{10}{8}\end{array} \quad \text{or} \quad 1\frac{1}{4}$$

How was $\frac{10}{8}$ changed to simplest form?

174

Exercises

Find each sum in simplest form.

1. $\frac{3}{5} + \frac{1}{5}$

2. $\frac{2}{4} + \frac{1}{4}$

3. $\frac{2}{6} + \frac{3}{6}$

4. $\frac{1}{8} + \frac{5}{8}$

5. $\frac{3}{6} + \frac{1}{6}$

6. $\frac{8}{10} + \frac{1}{10}$

7. $\frac{2}{8} + \frac{5}{8}$

8. $\frac{5}{12} + \frac{5}{12}$

9. $\frac{7}{10} + \frac{7}{10}$

10. $\frac{2}{5} + \frac{3}{5}$

11. $\frac{3}{7} + \frac{2}{7}$

12. $\frac{3}{10} + \frac{2}{10}$

13. $\frac{3}{8} + \frac{3}{8}$

14. $\frac{4}{6} + \frac{8}{6}$

15. $\frac{5}{12} + \frac{6}{12}$

16. $\frac{7}{8} + \frac{2}{8}$

17. $\frac{2}{9} + \frac{4}{9} + \frac{1}{9}$

18. $\frac{2}{5} + \frac{3}{5} + \frac{4}{5}$

19. $\frac{3}{10} + \frac{4}{10} + \frac{5}{10}$

20. $\frac{8}{9} + \frac{7}{9} + \frac{5}{9}$

21. $\frac{8}{12} + \frac{5}{12} + \frac{11}{12}$

22. $\frac{3}{8} + \frac{7}{8} + \frac{5}{8}$

23. Rily painted $\frac{1}{4}$ of the house yesterday and $\frac{2}{4}$ of it today. How much of the house did he paint in the two days?

24. Mr. Sellers plowed $\frac{3}{10}$ of his farm one day and $\frac{3}{10}$ of it the next day. How much of his farm did he plow on those two days?

25. Kathy mixed $\frac{3}{4}$ gallon of yellow paint and $\frac{3}{4}$ gallon of blue paint. How much green paint did Kathy make?

26. Mr. and Mrs. Bell ate $\frac{1}{3}$ of a watermelon on Friday, $\frac{1}{3}$ of it on Saturday, and $\frac{1}{3}$ of it the next day. How much of it did they eat?

27. Shirley walked $\frac{3}{8}$ mile to school, $\frac{5}{8}$ mile to the library, and then $\frac{7}{8}$ mile home. How many miles did Shirley walk?

Photri

Least Common Multiple

multiples of 2	multiples of 3	multiples of 4	multiples of 6
$2 \times 0 = 0$	$0 = 3 \times 0$	0	0
$2 \times 1 = 2$	$3 = 3 \times 1$	4	6
$2 \times 2 = 4$	$6 = 3 \times 2$	8	12
$2 \times 3 = 6$	$9 = 3 \times 3$	12	18
$2 \times 4 = 8$	$12 = 3 \times 4$	16	24
$2 \times 5 = 10$	$15 = 3 \times 5$	20	30
$2 \times 6 = 12$	$18 = 3 \times 6$	24	36
and so on	and so on	and so on	and so on

common multiples of 2 and 3

common multiples of 4 and 6

The **least common multiple** of 2 and 3 is 6.

The **least common multiple** of 4 and 6 is 12.

Zero is a multiple of every number. It is never used as the least common multiple.

How do you decide which multiple is the least common multiple?

Here is an easy way to find the least common multiple of 8 and 12. Follow these steps.

Step 1: Start with the larger number. 12

Step 2: Is 12 a multiple of 8? No

Step 3: The next multiple of 12 is 24.
Is 24 a multiple of 8? Yes

The least common multiple of 8 and 12 is 24.

176

Here is how to find the least common multiple of 6 and 10.

Step 1: Start with the larger number.   10

Step 2: Is 10 a multiple of 6?   No

Step 3: The next multiple of 10 is 20.   No
Is 20 a multiple of 6?

Step 4: The next multiple of 10 is 30.   Yes
Is 30 a multiple of 6?

The least common multiple of 6 and 10 is 30.

Exercises

Find the least common multiple of the two numbers.

1. 2 and 4   2. 3 and 4   3. 2 and 8   4. 5 and 10

5. 3 and 9   6. 6 and 8   7. 4 and 7   8. 6 and 10

9. 5 and 6   10. 2 and 5   11. 4 and 8   12. 3 and 5

13. 6 and 9   14. 10 and 15   15. 9 and 12   16. 3 and 11

17. 4 and 10   18. 6 and 14   19. 16 and 3   20. 20 and 30

  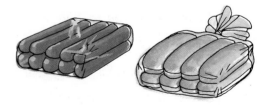

21. You want the same number of bolts and nuts. What is the least number of packages you should buy of each?

22. You want the same number of hot dogs as buns. What is the least number of packages you should buy of each?

Extra Practice—Set B, page 337

Adding Fractions

Here is how to find how much of the bulletin board is covered.

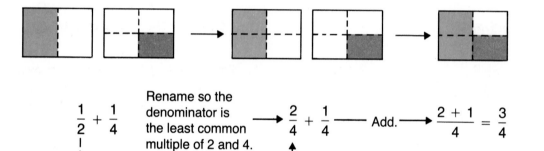

$$\frac{1}{2} + \frac{1}{4}$$

Rename so the denominator is the least common multiple of 2 and 4. $\longrightarrow$ $\frac{2}{4} + \frac{1}{4}$ —— Add. $\longrightarrow$ $\frac{2 + 1}{4} = \frac{3}{4}$

$$\frac{1}{2} = \frac{1 \times 2}{2 \times 2} = \frac{2}{4}$$

Discuss how $\frac{2}{3}$ and $\frac{5}{6}$ are added below.

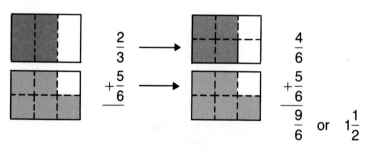

$$\frac{2}{3} \longrightarrow \quad \frac{4}{6}$$

$$+\frac{5}{6} \longrightarrow \quad +\frac{5}{6}$$

$$\frac{9}{6} \quad \text{or} \quad 1\frac{1}{2}$$

How was $\frac{9}{6}$ changed to simplest form?

Exercises

Find each sum in simplest form.

1. $\frac{1}{8} + \frac{1}{4}$

2. $\frac{1}{5} + \frac{3}{10}$

3. $\frac{2}{3} + \frac{1}{9}$

4. $\frac{3}{4} + \frac{1}{8}$

5. $\frac{1}{2} + \frac{3}{8}$

6. $\frac{3}{4} + \frac{3}{8}$

7. $\frac{5}{6} + \frac{7}{12}$

8. $\frac{3}{4} + \frac{5}{8}$

9. $\begin{array}{r} \frac{4}{9} \\ + \frac{1}{3} \\ \hline \end{array}$

10. $\begin{array}{r} \frac{7}{10} \\ + \frac{1}{5} \\ \hline \end{array}$

11. $\begin{array}{r} \frac{1}{12} \\ + \frac{1}{3} \\ \hline \end{array}$

12. $\begin{array}{r} \frac{1}{3} \\ + \frac{1}{6} \\ \hline \end{array}$

13. $\begin{array}{r} \frac{2}{3} \\ + \frac{8}{9} \\ \hline \end{array}$

14. $\begin{array}{r} \frac{1}{4} \\ + \frac{5}{8} \\ \hline \end{array}$

15. $\begin{array}{r} \frac{11}{12} \\ + \frac{1}{4} \\ \hline \end{array}$

16. $\begin{array}{r} \frac{4}{5} \\ + \frac{9}{10} \\ \hline \end{array}$

17. $\begin{array}{r} \frac{5}{6} \\ + \frac{1}{3} \\ \hline \end{array}$

18. $\begin{array}{r} \frac{2}{3} \\ + \frac{5}{12} \\ \hline \end{array}$

19. Randy worked $\frac{3}{4}$ hour one day and $\frac{1}{2}$ hour the next day. How long did he work in all?

20. Beth read $\frac{2}{3}$ of a book one day and $\frac{1}{6}$ of it the next day. How much of it did she read in the two days?

21. Wilma washed $\frac{2}{5}$ of the windows. George washed $\frac{3}{10}$ of the windows. How much of the window-washing job did they do?

22. Geri did $\frac{3}{5}$ of an assignment in school, $\frac{3}{10}$ of it after school, and $\frac{1}{10}$ of it the next morning. How much of the assignment did she get done?

Tennis Anyone?

Jim plays tennis every 3 days, Sue plays every 4 days, and Kim plays every 5 days. They all played tennis today. How long before they all play tennis on the same day again?

Adding Fractions

$$\frac{3}{4} + \frac{5}{6} = \blacksquare$$

To add, rename the fractions so that they have the same denominator.

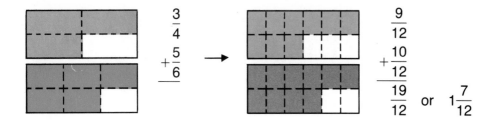

$$\frac{3}{4}$$
$$+\frac{5}{6}$$

$$\frac{9}{12}$$
$$+\frac{10}{12}$$
$$\frac{19}{12} \quad \text{or} \quad 1\frac{7}{12}$$

How was $\frac{19}{12}$ changed to simplest form?

Explain each addition shown below.

$$\frac{1}{2} \quad \overset{\times 5}{\underset{\times 5}{—}} \quad \longrightarrow \quad \frac{5}{10}$$
$$+\frac{1}{5} \quad \overset{\times 2}{\underset{\times 2}{—}} \quad \longrightarrow \quad +\frac{2}{10}$$
$$\frac{7}{10}$$

$$\frac{4}{9} \quad \overset{\times \blacksquare}{\underset{\times \blacksquare}{—}} \quad \longrightarrow \quad \frac{8}{18}$$
$$+\frac{5}{6} \quad \overset{\times \blacksquare}{\underset{\times \blacksquare}{—}} \quad \longrightarrow \quad +\frac{15}{18}$$
$$\frac{23}{18} \quad \text{or} \quad 1\frac{5}{18}$$

What is the least common multiple of 2 and 5?

What is the least common multiple of 6 and 9?

Why are both fractions renamed with denominator 10?

What number should replace each ■?

What number should replace each ■?

The **least common denominator** of two fractions is the least common multiple of their denominators.

180

Exercises

Find each sum in simplest form.

1. $\dfrac{5}{6}$ $+\dfrac{2}{9}$

2. $\dfrac{1}{2}$ $+\dfrac{3}{7}$

3. $\dfrac{7}{8}$ $+\dfrac{1}{3}$

4. $\dfrac{3}{4}$ $+\dfrac{1}{6}$

5. $\dfrac{1}{2}$ $+\dfrac{1}{3}$

6. $\dfrac{2}{3}$ $+\dfrac{1}{5}$

7. $\dfrac{5}{8}$ $+\dfrac{1}{6}$

8. $\dfrac{3}{10}$ $+\dfrac{3}{5}$

9. $\dfrac{3}{5}$ $+\dfrac{2}{5}$

10. $\dfrac{1}{4}$ $+\dfrac{3}{10}$

11. $\dfrac{2}{3}$ $+\dfrac{5}{9}$

12. $\dfrac{7}{9}$ $+\dfrac{3}{5}$

13. $\dfrac{2}{3} + \dfrac{1}{2}$

14. $\dfrac{5}{6} + \dfrac{1}{8}$

15. $\dfrac{4}{5} + \dfrac{3}{10}$

16. $\dfrac{1}{3} + \dfrac{8}{9}$

17. $\dfrac{7}{12} + \dfrac{3}{4}$

18. $\dfrac{1}{5} + \dfrac{5}{6}$

19. $\dfrac{2}{5} + \dfrac{1}{2}$

20. $\dfrac{3}{5} + \dfrac{1}{10}$

21. $\dfrac{2}{3} + \dfrac{1}{4}$

22. $\dfrac{1}{6} + \dfrac{3}{8}$

23. $\dfrac{1}{4} + \dfrac{1}{5}$

24. $\dfrac{1}{2} + \dfrac{5}{6}$

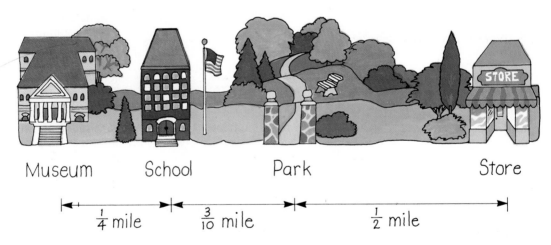

Museum   School   Park   Store

$\dfrac{1}{4}$ mile $\dfrac{3}{10}$ mile $\dfrac{1}{2}$ mile

25. Find the distance from the park to the museum.

26. Find the distance from the store to the school.

27. Mark walked from school to the park and then to the museum. How far did he walk?

28. Rita walked from school to the store and then to the park. How far did she walk?

Mixed Numerals in Addition

Red Clay

$2\frac{1}{4}$ cups flour

$1\frac{1}{8}$ cups salt

$\frac{3}{4}$ cup water

red food coloring

Blue Clay

5 cups flour

$2\frac{1}{2}$ cups salt

$1\frac{2}{3}$ cups water

blue food coloring

To find how much flour and salt are needed to make both recipes, add as shown below.

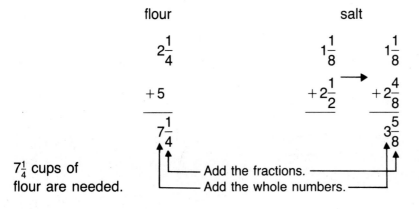

flour

$$2\frac{1}{4}$$
$$\underline{+5}$$
$$7\frac{1}{4}$$

$7\frac{1}{4}$ cups of flour are needed.

salt

$$1\frac{1}{8} \qquad 1\frac{1}{8}$$
$$\underline{+2\frac{1}{2}} \longrightarrow \underline{+2\frac{4}{8}}$$
$$3\frac{5}{8}$$

Rename with the least common denominator.

$3\frac{5}{8}$ cups of salt are needed.

— Add the fractions. —
— Add the whole numbers. —

To find how much water is needed to make both recipes, add as shown below.

$$\frac{3}{4} \qquad\qquad \frac{9}{12}$$
$$\underline{+1\frac{2}{3}} \longrightarrow \underline{+1\frac{8}{12}}$$
$$1\frac{17}{12} \;=\; 1 + \frac{17}{12} \;=\; 1 + 1\frac{5}{12} \;=\; 2\frac{5}{12}$$

$2\frac{5}{12}$ cups of water are needed.

182

Exercises

Find each sum in simplest form.

1. $1\frac{3}{8}$
   $+\ \frac{1}{4}$

2. $2\frac{1}{2}$
   $+2\frac{1}{4}$

3. $1\frac{5}{6}$
   $+4$

4. $1\frac{3}{4}$
   $+4\frac{1}{10}$

5. $2\frac{2}{5}$
   $+1\frac{1}{3}$

6. $1\frac{5}{8}$
   $+3$

7. $4\frac{1}{5}$
   $+\ \frac{3}{4}$

8. $2\frac{1}{2}$
   $+\ \frac{2}{3}$

9. $1\frac{5}{6}$
   $+2\frac{1}{4}$

10. $3\frac{7}{8}$
    $+1\frac{5}{8}$

11. $2\frac{1}{3}$
    $+\ \frac{7}{9}$

12. $1\frac{4}{7}$
    $+1\frac{3}{7}$

13. $7\frac{4}{5}$
    $+\ \frac{1}{2}$

14. $1\frac{3}{4}$
    $+\ \frac{5}{6}$

15. $\frac{8}{9}$
    $+3\frac{1}{6}$

16. $6\frac{1}{3}$
    $+1\frac{1}{2}$

17. $1\frac{5}{9}$
    $+2\frac{5}{6}$

18. $3\frac{7}{10}$
    $+2\frac{1}{2}$

19. $5\frac{3}{4}$
    $+6\frac{3}{5}$

20. $6\frac{4}{9}$
    $+3\frac{3}{4}$

21. $3\frac{5}{8}$
    $+2\frac{1}{4}$

22. $27\frac{1}{2}$
    $+\ 8\frac{3}{4}$

23. $41\frac{7}{10}$
    $+15\frac{2}{5}$

24. $63\frac{2}{3}$
    $+\ 9\frac{3}{6}$

25. $58\frac{3}{8}$
    $+24\frac{5}{8}$

26. Al pitched $4\frac{2}{3}$ innings more than Bo on Sunday. Bo pitched $3\frac{2}{3}$ innings. How many innings did Al pitch?

27. Barney is $12\frac{3}{4}$ inches taller than Paul. Paul is 57 inches tall. How tall is Barney?

28. Vivian is $4\frac{1}{2}$ feet tall. Melissa is $\frac{3}{4}$ foot taller than Vivian. How tall is Melissa?

29. It took Pam $2\frac{1}{3}$ hours to mow the lawn and $1\frac{1}{4}$ hours to trim the hedge. How long did it take her to do both jobs?

Camerique

Practice

1. $\frac{1}{5} + \frac{3}{5}$

2. $\frac{1}{9} + \frac{4}{9}$

3. $\frac{3}{10} + \frac{3}{10}$

4. $\frac{7}{8} + \frac{5}{8}$

5. $\frac{3}{10} + \frac{7}{10} + \frac{9}{10}$

6. $\frac{5}{12} + \frac{5}{12} + \frac{5}{12}$

7. $\frac{7}{8} + \frac{5}{8} + \frac{1}{8}$

8. $\begin{array}{r} \frac{3}{4} \\ +\frac{1}{8} \\ \hline \end{array}$

9. $\begin{array}{r} \frac{1}{3} \\ +\frac{2}{9} \\ \hline \end{array}$

10. $\begin{array}{r} \frac{3}{10} \\ +\frac{1}{5} \\ \hline \end{array}$

11. $\begin{array}{r} \frac{1}{8} \\ +\frac{1}{2} \\ \hline \end{array}$

12. $\frac{1}{12} + \frac{3}{4}$

13. $\frac{5}{6} + \frac{5}{12}$

14. $\frac{2}{3} + \frac{5}{6}$

15. $\frac{1}{2} + \frac{7}{10}$

16. $\begin{array}{r} \frac{2}{5} \\ +\frac{1}{2} \\ \hline \end{array}$

17. $\begin{array}{r} \frac{3}{4} \\ +\frac{1}{9} \\ \hline \end{array}$

18. $\begin{array}{r} \frac{5}{9} \\ +\frac{5}{6} \\ \hline \end{array}$

19. $\begin{array}{r} \frac{3}{4} \\ +\frac{1}{6} \\ \hline \end{array}$

20. $\frac{1}{8} + \frac{5}{12}$

21. $\frac{4}{5} + \frac{3}{4}$

22. $\frac{4}{9} + \frac{1}{6}$

23. $\frac{3}{4} + \frac{2}{3}$

24. $\begin{array}{r} 5\frac{3}{8} \\ +3\frac{2}{5} \\ \hline \end{array}$

25. $\begin{array}{r} 5\frac{3}{8} \\ +1\frac{1}{4} \\ \hline \end{array}$

26. $\begin{array}{r} 7\frac{1}{6} \\ +\ \frac{2}{3} \\ \hline \end{array}$

27. $\begin{array}{r} 9\frac{1}{2} \\ +1\frac{2}{9} \\ \hline \end{array}$

28. $5 + 2\frac{7}{8}$

29. $5\frac{6}{7} + 4\frac{2}{3}$

30. $9\frac{7}{8} + 2\frac{2}{3}$

31. $\frac{5}{6} + 2\frac{1}{2}$

32. $\begin{array}{r} 17\frac{5}{8} \\ 8\frac{1}{8} \\ +21\frac{3}{8} \\ \hline \end{array}$

33. $\begin{array}{r} 7\frac{1}{10} \\ 6\frac{7}{10} \\ +4\frac{9}{10} \\ \hline \end{array}$

34. $\begin{array}{r} 11\frac{1}{3} \\ 4\frac{5}{6} \\ +\ 9\frac{2}{3} \\ \hline \end{array}$

35. $\begin{array}{r} 5\frac{3}{16} \\ 2\frac{5}{8} \\ +7\frac{1}{4} \\ \hline \end{array}$

36. By reading the odometer on his bicycle, Bob found that he rode $8\frac{7}{10}$ miles on Friday, $13\frac{2}{10}$ miles on Saturday, and $11\frac{9}{10}$ miles on Sunday. How far did he ride during the three days?

37. Bob bought some reflector tape. He put $3\frac{1}{4}$ inches of tape on each fender and had $1\frac{1}{2}$ inches left. How much tape did he buy?

184

Fast and Easy Addition

Here is a fast and easy way to add two fractions like $\frac{2}{3}$ and $\frac{4}{5}$.

You can find the numerator like this.

$$10 + 12 = \downarrow$$
$$\frac{2}{3} \times\!\!+\!\!\times \frac{4}{5} = \frac{22}{\blacksquare}$$

You can find the denominator like this.

$$\frac{2}{3} + \frac{4}{5} = \frac{22}{15} = 1\frac{7}{15}$$

Use that method to complete this addition.

$$9 + 8 = \downarrow$$
$$\frac{3}{8} \times\!\!+\!\!\times \frac{1}{3} = \frac{\blacksquare}{\blacksquare} = \blacksquare$$

Exercises

Use that method to find each sum.

1. $\frac{5}{8} + \frac{3}{4}$ 2. $\frac{1}{3} + \frac{1}{4}$ 3. $\frac{2}{3} + \frac{1}{4}$ 4. $\frac{1}{6} + \frac{1}{4}$

5. $\frac{3}{4} + \frac{4}{5}$ 6. $\frac{3}{4} + \frac{5}{6}$ 7. $\frac{2}{9} + \frac{4}{5}$ 8. $\frac{5}{7} + \frac{3}{4}$

9. $\frac{3}{5} + \frac{4}{7}$ 10. $\frac{1}{8} + \frac{1}{9}$ 11. $\frac{3}{8} + \frac{2}{5}$ 12. $\frac{5}{8} + \frac{5}{6}$

Comparing Fractions

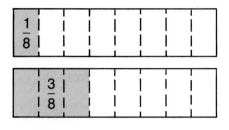

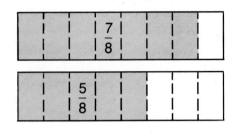

$\frac{1}{8}$ is less than $\frac{3}{8}$.

$\frac{7}{8}$ is greater than $\frac{5}{8}$.

$$\frac{1}{8} < \frac{3}{8}$$

$$\frac{7}{8} > \frac{5}{8}$$

When two fractions have the same denominator, how can you tell which fraction is greater?

Let's compare fractions that have different denominators.

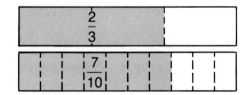

$$\frac{2}{3} < \frac{7}{10}$$

Here is a way to compare fractions without the drawings.

$\frac{2}{3} \bullet \frac{7}{10}$	Rename both fractions with the same denominator.	$\frac{7}{8} \bullet \frac{4}{5}$
$\frac{20}{30} < \frac{21}{30}$	Compare the numerators of the new fractions.	$\frac{35}{40} > \frac{32}{40}$
$\frac{2}{3} < \frac{7}{10}$	How can you decide which fraction is greater?	$\frac{7}{8} > \frac{4}{5}$

Exercises

Write < or > for each ●.

1. $\frac{3}{4}$ ● $\frac{1}{4}$ 2. $\frac{1}{7}$ ● $\frac{2}{7}$ 3. $\frac{7}{10}$ ● $\frac{9}{10}$ 4. $\frac{3}{5}$ ● $\frac{1}{5}$ 5. $\frac{5}{8}$ ● $\frac{3}{4}$

6. $\frac{1}{5}$ ● $\frac{1}{9}$ 7. $\frac{2}{7}$ ● $\frac{2}{3}$ 8. $\frac{3}{5}$ ● $\frac{3}{4}$ 9. $\frac{1}{3}$ ● $\frac{1}{4}$ 10. $\frac{2}{9}$ ● $\frac{3}{10}$

11. $\frac{3}{4}$ ● $\frac{1}{2}$ 12. $\frac{4}{5}$ ● $\frac{9}{10}$ 13. $\frac{2}{3}$ ● $\frac{5}{6}$ 14. $\frac{3}{8}$ ● $\frac{1}{3}$ 15. $\frac{3}{4}$ ● $\frac{2}{3}$

16. Tom ran $\frac{5}{8}$ mile. Rita ran $\frac{3}{4}$ mile. Who ran farther?

17. Jan ran $\frac{4}{5}$ mile and walked $\frac{7}{10}$ mile. Which distance is longer?

18. Juan finished ahead of $\frac{2}{3}$ of the runners. Paul finished ahead of $\frac{3}{5}$ of the runners. Did Paul finish ahead of Juan?

19. $\frac{3}{10}$ of the runners finished ahead of Bob. Dave finished ahead of $\frac{2}{5}$ of the runners. Did Dave finish ahead of Bob?

Quick Trick

$\frac{2}{3} \times \frac{4}{5}$ 2 × 5 ? 3 × 4

10 < 12

So $\frac{2}{3} < \frac{4}{5}$.

$\frac{3}{4} \times \frac{7}{10}$ 3 × 10 ? 4 × 7

30 > 28

So $\frac{3}{4} > \frac{7}{10}$.

Should < or > replace each ●?

1. $\frac{3}{7}$ ● $\frac{5}{8}$ 2. $\frac{2}{9}$ ● $\frac{1}{4}$ 3. $\frac{3}{10}$ ● $\frac{1}{3}$ 4. $\frac{1}{6}$ ● $\frac{2}{11}$ 5. $\frac{3}{5}$ ● $\frac{5}{9}$

6. $\frac{4}{7}$ ● $\frac{5}{9}$ 7. $\frac{5}{12}$ ● $\frac{4}{9}$ 8. $\frac{2}{9}$ ● $\frac{3}{10}$ 9. $\frac{4}{15}$ ● $\frac{2}{9}$ 10. $\frac{7}{16}$ ● $\frac{15}{32}$

Subtracting Fractions

Dan has climbed $\frac{7}{8}$ mile. Fran has climbed $\frac{3}{8}$ mile. How much farther has Dan climbed?

You can subtract fractions in either of these ways.

Subtract the numerators.

$$\frac{7}{8} - \frac{3}{8} = \frac{7 - 3}{8} = \frac{4}{8} = \frac{1}{2}$$

Use the same denominator.

Subtract the numerators.

$$\begin{array}{r} \frac{7}{8} \\ -\frac{3}{8} \\ \hline \frac{4}{8} = \frac{1}{2} \end{array}$$

Use the same denominator.

Dan climbed $\frac{1}{2}$ mile farther.

How was $\frac{4}{8}$ changed to $\frac{1}{2}$?

Explain how to do this subtraction.

$$\frac{7}{9} - \frac{4}{9}$$

188

Exercises

Find each difference in simplest form.

1. $\frac{1}{4} - \frac{1}{4}$

2. $\frac{3}{10} - \frac{1}{10}$

3. $\frac{2}{5} - \frac{1}{5}$

4. $\frac{5}{8} - \frac{3}{8}$

5. $\frac{4}{9} - \frac{2}{9}$

6. $\frac{4}{5} - \frac{2}{5}$

7. $\frac{7}{10} - \frac{3}{10}$

8. $\frac{1}{2} - \frac{1}{2}$

9. $\frac{9}{10} - \frac{3}{10}$

10. $\frac{7}{8} - \frac{5}{8}$

11. $\frac{5}{7} - \frac{3}{7}$

12. $\frac{3}{5} - \frac{2}{5}$

13. $\frac{4}{5} - \frac{4}{5}$

14. $\frac{7}{9} - \frac{1}{9}$

15. $\frac{9}{10} - \frac{1}{10}$

16. $\frac{3}{8} - \frac{1}{8}$

17. $\frac{7}{10} - \frac{1}{10}$

18. $\frac{3}{5} - \frac{1}{5}$

19. $\frac{7}{8} - \frac{1}{8}$

20. $\frac{5}{6} - \frac{1}{6}$

Camerique

21. Toni rode her horse $\frac{3}{10}$ mile. She walked the rest of the way. In all she went $\frac{4}{10}$ mile. How far did she walk?

22. If Louis had walked $\frac{1}{8}$ mile farther, he would have walked $\frac{7}{8}$ mile. How far did Louis walk?

23. Roy hiked $\frac{7}{10}$ mile. Rita hiked $\frac{9}{10}$ mile. Who hiked farther? How much farther?

24. Roberta ran a mile and walked $\frac{3}{10}$ mile. How much farther did she run than walk?

Subtracting Fractions

To find how far Jan still has to go, subtract $\frac{2}{5}$ from $\frac{1}{2}$.

$$\frac{1}{2} \xrightarrow[\times 5]{\times 5} \frac{5}{10}$$

$$-\frac{2}{5} \xrightarrow[\times 2]{\times 2} -\frac{4}{10}$$

$$\frac{1}{10}$$

Why are $\frac{1}{2}$ and $\frac{2}{5}$ renamed?

She has $\frac{1}{10}$ mile to go.

Discuss this subtraction.

How do you decide that the least common denominator should be 6?

How do you change $\frac{2}{3}$ to $\frac{4}{6}$?

How do you get $\frac{3}{6}$?

How is $\frac{3}{6}$ changed to simplest form?

$$\begin{array}{c}\frac{2}{3} \\ -\frac{1}{6}\end{array} \longrightarrow \begin{array}{c}\frac{4}{6} \\ -\frac{1}{6} \\ \hline \frac{3}{6} = \frac{1}{2}\end{array}$$

Exercises

Find each difference in simplest form.

1. $\frac{1}{2}$
    $-\frac{1}{4}$

2. $\frac{5}{6}$
    $-\frac{2}{3}$

3. $\frac{1}{2}$
    $-\frac{1}{6}$

4. $\frac{9}{10}$
    $-\frac{3}{4}$

5. $\frac{2}{5}$
    $-\frac{1}{3}$

6. $\frac{2}{3}$
    $-\frac{4}{9}$

7. $\frac{7}{8}$
    $-\frac{1}{6}$

8. $\frac{3}{4}$
    $-\frac{5}{8}$

9. $\frac{2}{3} - \frac{1}{2}$

10. $\frac{4}{5} - \frac{3}{10}$

11. $\frac{1}{2} - \frac{1}{3}$

12. $\frac{5}{8} - \frac{1}{4}$

13. $\frac{3}{4} - \frac{1}{2}$

14. $\frac{5}{6} - \frac{2}{9}$

15. $\frac{1}{3} - \frac{1}{4}$

16. $\frac{1}{2} - \frac{3}{10}$

17. $\frac{7}{10} - \frac{1}{5}$

18. $\frac{3}{4} - \frac{1}{3}$

19. $\frac{3}{8} - \frac{1}{3}$

20. $\frac{2}{3} - \frac{1}{4}$

21. When Jan crossed the finish line of a $\frac{1}{2}$-mile bike race Paul was $\frac{1}{10}$ mile from the finish line. How far had Paul gone at that time?

22. While Laura was riding $\frac{7}{10}$ mile, Sue rode $\frac{4}{5}$ mile. Who was riding faster? How much farther did she go?

23. Mark rode his bike $\frac{9}{10}$ mile and walked $\frac{3}{4}$ mile. How much farther did he ride than walk?

Extra Practice—Set B, page 339   **191**

Mixed Numerals in Subtraction

Julie lives in Smithton. How much farther is it to Golden City than to Troy?

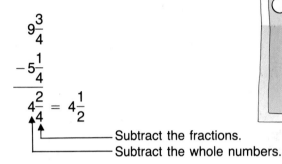

To find the answer, subtract.

$$9\frac{3}{4}$$
$$-5\frac{1}{4}$$
$$4\frac{2}{4} = 4\frac{1}{2}$$

└─── Subtract the fractions.
└──── Subtract the whole numbers.

Golden City is $4\frac{1}{2}$ miles farther.

You can also subtract to find how much farther she lives from Golden City than from Southtown.

$$9\frac{3}{4}$$
$$-8$$
$$1\frac{3}{4}$$

└─── Subtract the fractions.
└──── Subtract the whole numbers.

She lives $1\frac{3}{4}$ miles farther from Golden City than from Southtown.

How can you check to see if the answer is correct?

To find how much farther Julie lives from Golden City than from Lorna, do the subtraction at the right.

$$9\frac{3}{4}$$
$$-\frac{3}{4}$$

Exercises

Find each difference in simplest form.

1. $4\frac{5}{6}$
   $-2\frac{1}{6}$

2. $5\frac{3}{8}$
   $-3\frac{1}{8}$

3. $7\frac{4}{5}$
   $-6\frac{3}{5}$

4. $10\frac{8}{9}$
   $-\;4\frac{5}{9}$

5. $8\frac{7}{8}$
   -2

6. $12\frac{3}{5}$
   -10

7. $25\frac{3}{10}$
   $-\;8$

8. $11\frac{2}{15}$
   $-\;6$

9. $7\frac{2}{3}$
   $-\;\frac{1}{3}$

10. $8\frac{7}{9}$
    $-\;\frac{1}{9}$

11. $16\frac{7}{8}$
    $-\;\frac{5}{8}$

12. $25\frac{7}{10}$
    $-\;\frac{1}{10}$

13. $18\frac{9}{10}$
    $-\;3\frac{3}{10}$

14. $9\frac{4}{5}$
    $-9\frac{1}{5}$

15. $30\frac{8}{9}$
    $-\;\frac{8}{9}$

16. $24\frac{2}{3}$
    $-23\frac{2}{3}$

17. $8\frac{1}{3}$
    $-8\frac{1}{3}$

18. $56\frac{11}{12}$
    $-\;\frac{5}{12}$

19. $22\frac{17}{20}$
    $-\;1\frac{1}{20}$

20. $75\frac{2}{25}$
    -17

21. One route from Middleville to Clayton City is longer than the other. How much longer is it?

22. How much farther is it from Middleville to Sackville than the shorter route from Middleville to Clayton City?

23. How much farther is it from Middleville to Sackville than the longer route from Middleville to Clayton City?

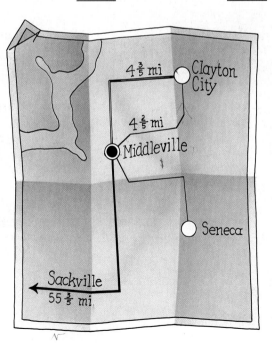

193

Mixed Numerals in Subtraction

Mary has $2\frac{1}{4}$ cups of milk. Her recipe calls for $3\frac{1}{2}$ cups of milk. How much more milk does she need?

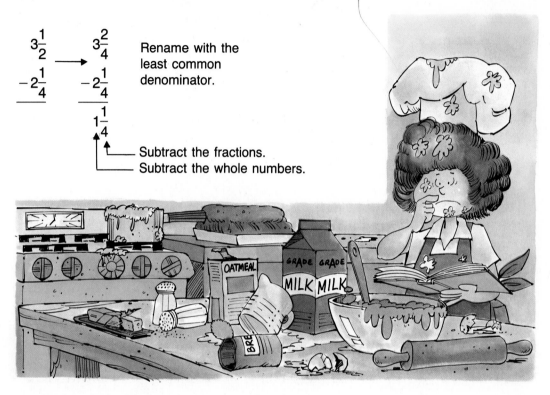

$$3\frac{1}{2} \longrightarrow 3\frac{2}{4}$$
$$-2\frac{1}{4} \qquad -2\frac{1}{4}$$
$$\overline{\qquad\qquad\; 1\frac{1}{4}}$$

Rename with the least common denominator.

└── Subtract the fractions.
└── Subtract the whole numbers.

Mary needs $1\frac{1}{4}$ cups of milk.

Answer these questions about this subtraction.

How do you decide that the least common denominator should be 36?

How do you change $5\frac{7}{12}$ to $5\frac{21}{36}$?

How do you change $\frac{1}{9}$ to $\frac{4}{36}$?

$$5\frac{7}{12} \longrightarrow 5\frac{21}{36}$$
$$-\frac{1}{9} \qquad -\frac{4}{36}$$
$$\overline{\qquad\qquad 5\frac{17}{36}}$$

194

Explain each step in doing this subtraction.

$$4\frac{3}{8} \longrightarrow 4\frac{9}{24}$$
$$-4\frac{1}{6} \qquad -4\frac{4}{24}$$
$$\overline{\qquad\qquad\quad \frac{5}{24}}$$

Exercises

Find each difference in simplest form.

1. $3\frac{2}{3}$
   $-2\frac{1}{6}$

2. $6\frac{1}{4}$
   $-1\frac{1}{5}$

3. $9\frac{3}{4}$
   $-7\frac{1}{6}$

4. $1\frac{7}{8}$
   $-\frac{3}{4}$

5. $4\frac{2}{3}$
   $-2\frac{1}{4}$

6. $5\frac{1}{2}$
   $-4\frac{2}{5}$

7. $2\frac{3}{10}$
   $-\frac{1}{5}$

8. $3\frac{3}{4}$
   $-1\frac{1}{8}$

9. $6\frac{1}{2}$
   $-2\frac{1}{8}$

10. $1\frac{3}{4}$
    $-\frac{2}{3}$

11. $9\frac{7}{8}$
    $-1\frac{2}{3}$

12. $5\frac{2}{3}$
    $-3\frac{3}{5}$

13. $1\frac{5}{6}$
    $-\frac{7}{10}$

14. $6\frac{1}{2}$
    $-6\frac{1}{3}$

15. $3\frac{2}{3}$
    $-\frac{1}{2}$

16. $7\frac{4}{5}$
    $-\frac{2}{3}$

17. $4\frac{1}{9}$
    -2

18. $7\frac{2}{5}$
    $-7\frac{1}{10}$

19. $6\frac{1}{3}$
    $-6\frac{1}{3}$

20. $8\frac{7}{8}$
    $-7\frac{7}{8}$

21. $47\frac{7}{8}$
    $-28\frac{1}{4}$

22. $62\frac{9}{16}$
    $-5\frac{1}{2}$

23. $125\frac{7}{10}$
    $-75\frac{2}{5}$

24. $250\frac{5}{6}$
    $-182\frac{3}{4}$

25. Constance was $64\frac{1}{2}$ inches tall in June. Now she is $65\frac{3}{4}$ inches tall. How much has she grown since June?

26. John grew $2\frac{3}{4}$ inches last year. Horace grew only $2\frac{5}{8}$ inches last year. How much more did John grow than Horace?

Mixed Numerals in Subtraction

Stan filled his new bird feeder with $4\frac{1}{2}$ pounds of feed. The first day the birds ate $1\frac{3}{4}$ pounds of feed. How much feed was left in the feeder?

$$4\frac{1}{2} \quad \rightarrow \quad 4\frac{2}{4}$$
$$-1\frac{3}{4} \qquad\quad -1\frac{3}{4}$$

Rename.

Can you subtract the fractions?

Rename $4\frac{2}{4}$ so that you can subtract the fractions.

$$4\frac{2}{4} \rightarrow = 3 + 1\frac{2}{4} = 3 + \frac{6}{4} = \longrightarrow 3\frac{6}{4}$$
$$-1\frac{3}{4} \qquad\qquad\qquad\qquad\qquad\qquad\quad -1\frac{3}{4}$$
$$\overline{\qquad\qquad\qquad\qquad\qquad\qquad\qquad\qquad 2\frac{3}{4}}$$

There was $2\frac{3}{4}$ pounds of feed left.

Explain how 4 was changed to $3\frac{4}{4}$ below.

$$4 = 3 + 1 = 3 + \frac{4}{4} = 3\frac{4}{4}$$

Exercises

Find the correct number for each ▓.

1. $3\frac{1}{2} = 2\frac{▓}{2}$

2. $6\frac{1}{3} = 5\frac{▓}{3}$

3. $9\frac{2}{5} = 8\frac{▓}{5}$

4. $8 = 7\frac{▓}{2}$

5. $4 = 3\frac{▓}{8}$

6. $12 = 11\frac{▓}{6}$

196

Find each difference in simplest form.

7. $3\frac{1}{6}$
   $-2\frac{5}{6}$

8. $6\frac{2}{5}$
   $-1\frac{3}{5}$

9. $9\frac{1}{4}$
   $-7\frac{3}{4}$

10. $1\frac{3}{8}$
    $-\frac{5}{8}$

11. $4\frac{2}{3}$
    $-2\frac{3}{4}$

12. $5\frac{1}{3}$
    $-4\frac{2}{5}$

13. $2\frac{3}{10}$
    $-1\frac{4}{5}$

14. $3\frac{3}{4}$
    $-1\frac{1}{8}$

15. 4
    $-1\frac{7}{8}$

16. 6
    $-4\frac{3}{5}$

17. 5
    $-2\frac{5}{6}$

18. 1
    $-\frac{3}{10}$

19. $6\frac{1}{2}$
    $-2\frac{5}{8}$

20. $1\frac{3}{4}$
    $-\frac{2}{3}$

21. 9
    $-7\frac{2}{3}$

22. $5\frac{1}{2}$
    $-3\frac{2}{5}$

23. $1\frac{2}{5}$
    $-\frac{7}{10}$

24. $6\frac{3}{10}$
    $-5\frac{5}{6}$

25. 3
    $-2\frac{5}{9}$

26. $17\frac{1}{5}$
    $-6\frac{2}{3}$

27. Jay pitched $5\frac{1}{3}$ innings more than Shawn on Sunday, and $2\frac{2}{3}$ innings less than Shawn on Tuesday. Who pitched more innings? How many more?

28. Jill is $63\frac{1}{2}$ inches tall. Lil is $64\frac{1}{4}$ inches tall. How much taller is Lil?

Three in a Row

$\frac{1}{2}$ $\frac{1}{4}$ $\frac{1}{6}$ $\frac{1}{12}$ $\frac{5}{12}$ $\frac{7}{12}$

Can you place the above fractions in the six circles so that the sum in each line is 1?

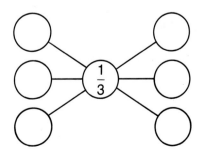

Extra Practice—Set A, page 340

SKILLS REVIEW

Subtract.

1. 316
  −287

2. 888
  −799

3. 604
  −505

4. 200
  −108

5. 370,602
  −361,590

6. 323,232
  −232,323

7. 500,002
  −201,093

8. 365,432
  −265,528

Multiply.

9. 25
  ×8

10. 92
   ×9

11. 73
   ×6

12. 19
   ×5

13. 40
   ×20

14. 28
   ×50

15. 84
   ×10

16. 108
   ×53

17. 142
   ×90

18. 372
   ×127

19. 905
   ×810

20. 397
   ×200

Divide.

21. $6\overline{)54}$

22. $8\overline{)56}$

23. $9\overline{)45}$

24. $5\overline{)30}$

25. $8\overline{)177}$

26. $5\overline{)1237}$

27. $6\overline{)134}$

28. $21\overline{)995}$

29. $53\overline{)960}$

30. $27\overline{)980}$

31. $32\overline{)999}$

32. $80\overline{)1120}$

33. $12\overline{)9660}$

34. $86\overline{)9375}$

35. $24\overline{)9767}$

36. $74\overline{)7890}$

Multiply.

37. $\frac{1}{4} \times \frac{1}{2}$

38. $\frac{2}{5} \times \frac{3}{8}$

39. $\frac{1}{6} \times \frac{3}{4}$

40. $\frac{3}{4} \times \frac{8}{9}$

41. $\frac{7}{10} \times \frac{5}{7}$

42. $\frac{5}{12} \times \frac{2}{3}$

43. $\frac{7}{8} \times \frac{1}{2}$

44. $\frac{3}{10} \times \frac{2}{10}$

45. $2\frac{1}{3} \times 2\frac{1}{4}$

46. $3\frac{1}{3} \times 2\frac{2}{5}$

47. $1\frac{1}{2} \times 3$

48. $\frac{2}{3} \times 4$

Camerique

49. The average weight of a pumpkin from Stan's farm is 22 pounds. If his truck is carrying 5610 pounds of pumpkins, how many pumpkins are on his truck?

50. On Myra's truck are 320 pumpkins. The average weight of each is 19 pounds. Bill's truck is carrying 6023 pounds of pumpkins. Which truck is carrying a heavier load? How much heavier?

51. A marching band has 5 rows of 12 members each. How many members are there?

52. Fran is half as tall as her mother. Her mother is $5\frac{1}{2}$ feet tall. How tall is Fran?

53. 3 more hours of lessons would give Jessica 20 hours of music lessons this month. How many hours of lessons does she have this month?

54. Hillary sold 4 jackets and 2 shirts for $140. He got $100 for the jackets. How much did he get for each jacket?

CHAPTER REVIEW

Find the least common multiple of the two numbers.

1. 3 and 9

2. 5 and 4

3. 6 and 7

4. 8 and 12

Find each sum in simplest form.

5. $\dfrac{3}{5}$
   $+\dfrac{1}{5}$

6. $\dfrac{1}{4}$
   $+\dfrac{1}{4}$

7. $\dfrac{3}{4}$
   $+\dfrac{5}{8}$

8. $\dfrac{5}{6}$
   $+\dfrac{7}{12}$

9. $\dfrac{3}{4}$
   $+\dfrac{4}{5}$

10. $\dfrac{1}{4}$
    $+\dfrac{5}{6}$

11. $1\dfrac{1}{2}$
    $+2\dfrac{1}{3}$

12. $5\dfrac{1}{8}$
    $+3\dfrac{3}{4}$

Write < or > for each ●.

13. $\dfrac{1}{6}$ ● $\dfrac{5}{6}$

14. $\dfrac{3}{5}$ ● $\dfrac{4}{7}$

15. $\dfrac{5}{6}$ ● $\dfrac{2}{3}$

16. $\dfrac{7}{9}$ ● $\dfrac{3}{4}$

Find each difference in simplest form.

17. $\dfrac{7}{9}$
    $-\dfrac{2}{9}$

18. $\dfrac{2}{3}$
    $-\dfrac{1}{3}$

19. $\dfrac{3}{4}$
    $-\dfrac{1}{5}$

20. $\dfrac{3}{5}$
    $-\dfrac{1}{2}$

21. $2\dfrac{1}{2}$
    $-1\dfrac{1}{3}$

22. $3\dfrac{3}{4}$
    $-1\dfrac{2}{5}$

23. $4\dfrac{1}{3}$
    $-2\dfrac{5}{8}$

24. 7
    $-5\dfrac{2}{3}$

25. Phil pitched 8 innings on Saturday and $5\dfrac{2}{3}$ innings on Sunday. How many more innings did he pitch on Saturday than on Sunday?

26. Jill was $51\dfrac{3}{4}$ inches tall in September. Since then she has grown $1\dfrac{1}{2}$ inches. How tall is she now?

9 Decimals

Decimals

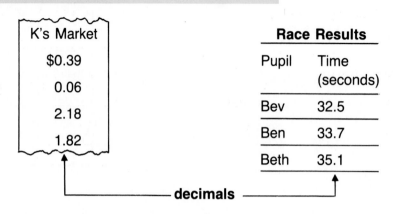

K's Market

$0.39

0.06

2.18

1.82

← decimals →

Race Results	
Pupil	Time (seconds)
Bev	32.5
Ben	33.7
Beth	35.1

The dot in a decimal, like 0.39 or 32.5, is the **decimal point.**

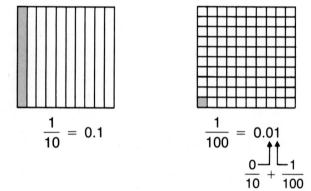

$$\frac{1}{10} = 0.1$$

$$\frac{1}{100} = 0.01$$

$$\frac{0}{10} + \frac{1}{100}$$

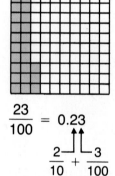

$$\frac{23}{100} = 0.23$$

$$\frac{2}{10} + \frac{3}{100}$$

Here are different ways to name the same number.

Fraction or Mixed Numeral	Decimal	Both are read
$\frac{39}{100}$	0.39	thirty-nine *hundredths*
$22\frac{5}{10}$	22.5	twenty-two **and** five *tenths*
$\frac{6}{100}$	0.06	six *hundredths*
$1\frac{82}{100}$	1.82	one **and** eighty-two *hundredths*

Exercises

Write a decimal for each of these parts of the picture at the right.

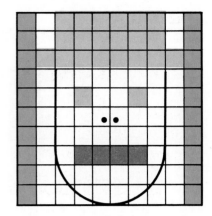

1. green part
2. eyes
3. mouth
4. hat
5. blue part

Write as a decimal.

6. $\dfrac{9}{10}$
7. $\dfrac{9}{100}$
8. $\dfrac{90}{100}$
9. $1\dfrac{2}{10}$
10. $3\dfrac{1}{100}$

11. $\dfrac{7}{10}$
12. $\dfrac{68}{100}$
13. $1\dfrac{4}{10}$
14. $4\dfrac{21}{100}$
15. $5\dfrac{5}{100}$

Write as a fraction or as a mixed numeral.

16. 0.13
17. 0.08
18. 0.5
19. 1.60
20. 1.38

21. 0.3
22. 0.03
23. 0.50
24. 1.9
25. 4.16

Write as a decimal.

26. two and six tenths
27. two and six hundredths

What's Next?

Draw the next two figures in the sequence below.

203

Decimals

Place values	tens	ones	tenths	hundredths	thousandths
	T	O	Ts	Hs	Ths
digits	3	5 .	1	2	8

thirty-five **and** *one hundred twenty-eight thousandths*

You can think of 35.128 as $30 + 5 + \frac{1}{10} + \frac{2}{100} + \frac{8}{1000}$.

You can also write 35.128 as the mixed numeral $35\frac{128}{1000}$.

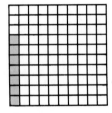  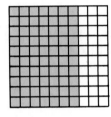

Is 0.07 equal to 0.7?

Is 0.7 equal to 0.70?

  0.07   0.7   0.70

You can find other names for 0.7 like this.

$$\frac{7}{10} = \frac{7 \times 10}{10 \times 10} = \frac{70}{100} = \frac{70 \times 10}{100 \times 10} = \frac{700}{1000}$$

$$0.7 = 0.70 = 0.700$$

You can also name whole numbers as decimals.

$$7.00 = 7 + \frac{0}{100} = 7 + 0 = 7 \qquad\qquad 7.0 = 7 + \frac{0}{10} = 7 + 0 = 7$$

$$7 = 7.0 = 7.00$$

204

Exercises

Write as a decimal.

1. $\dfrac{4}{10}$

2. $\dfrac{4}{100}$

3. $\dfrac{4}{1000}$

4. $\dfrac{444}{1000}$

5. $2\dfrac{5}{10}$

6. $2\dfrac{50}{100}$

7. $2\dfrac{500}{1000}$

8. $2\dfrac{555}{1000}$

9. $6\dfrac{317}{1000}$

10. $1\dfrac{86}{1000}$

11. $5\dfrac{5}{1000}$

12. $10\dfrac{1}{1000}$

Write as a fraction or as a mixed numeral.

13. 0.8

14. 0.08

15. 0.008

16. 0.888

17. 3.2

18. 3.002

19. 3.020

20. 3.200

21. 4.812

22. 6.079

23. 1.004

24. 20.020

Name each whole number or decimal to the tenths place and to the hundredths place.

25. 8

26. 13

27. 4.5

28. 9.0

29. 16.1

30. 240

Write as a decimal.

31. six tenths

32. six hundredths

33. six thousandths

34. sixteen thousandths

35. sixty thousandths

36. six hundred sixty-six thousandths

Write in words.

37. 84.06

38. 200.50

39. 700.090

40. 204.003

Comparing Decimals

Jorge bought the heavier bag of apples. Which bag of apples did he buy?

To tell which is greater, compare the decimals like this.

Write the decimals so the decimal points line up.

Then compare the digits in each place-value position, beginning at the left.

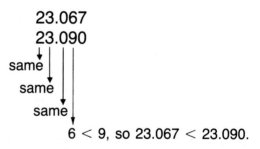

23.067
23.090

same
same
same

6 < 9, so 23.067 < 23.090.

This method works no matter how many digits are to the right of the decimal points.

You can compare 15.125 and 15.1 like this.

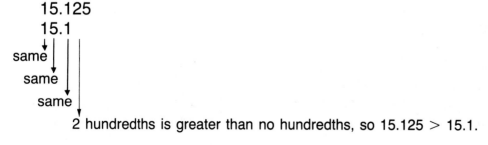

15.125
15.1

same
same
same

2 hundredths is greater than no hundredths, so 15.125 > 15.1.

Exercises

Should <, =, or > replace the ●?

1. 6.210 ● 6.201
2. 19.78 ● 19.87
3. 59 ● 58.9

4. 118.7 ● 181.7
5. 0.609 ● 0.610
6. 54.8 ● 54.80

7. 6 ● 6.0
8. 29.7 ● 2.97
9. 15.34 ● 5.342

10. 0.89 ● 0.09
11. 0.9 ● 0.89
12. 0.090 ● 0.89

13. 61.4 ● 61.400
14. 200 ● 200.0
15. 175 ● 175.001

16. 13.285 ● 13.2
17. 6.315 ● 6.31
18. 4.248 ● 4.25

List the three decimals in order from least to greatest.

19. 2.5, 2.6, 2.7
20. 0.60, 0.70, 0.80
21. 0.3, 0.03, 0.003

22. 1.2, 2.1, 21
23. 0.090, 0.8, 0.007
24. 0.10, 0.08, 0.09

25. 567, 5.67, 56.7
26. 17.0, 1.7, 170
27. 3.8, 3.09, 3.50

28. Which weighs more, the turkey or the pumpkin?

29. Which weighs less, the pumpkin or the apples?

30. List their weights in order from least to greatest.

31. Jessica bought a turkey weighing 18.20 pounds. Is that more, less, or the same weight as the turkey shown at the right?

18.2 pounds

18.235 pounds

18.24 pounds

Adding Decimals

Precipitation Summary

Month	Rain (inches)	Snow (inches)
January	none	10.8
February	0.62	7.2
March	2.16	4

BOLD, Inc.

To find out how much rain fell, add the decimals.

Write the decimals so the decimal points line up.

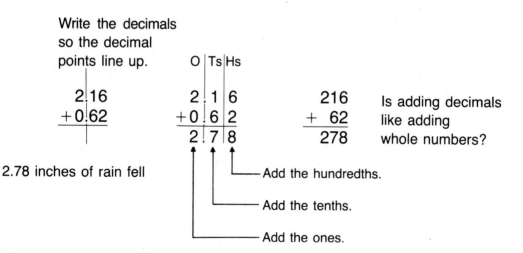

```
   2.16          O  Ts Hs           216      Is adding decimals
 +0.62          2 . 1  6           +  62     like adding
                +0 . 6  2           278      whole numbers?
                2 . 7  8
```

2.78 inches of rain fell

└── Add the hundredths.

└── Add the tenths.

└── Add the ones.

Discuss how the amount of snow that fell was found by adding decimals.

Why was 4 renamed as 4.0?

Why can you say the snowfall was 22.0 inches or 22 inches?

```
   T  O  Ts
   1  1
   1  0 . 8
      7 . 2
 +    4 . 0
   2  2 . 0
```

208

Exercises

1. 0.8
  +0.1

2. 0.8
  +0.6

3. 9.9
  +0.7

4. 2.04
  +5.38

5. 1.1
  +0.9

6. 0.85
  +0.17

7. 2.8
  +0.5

8. 4.67
  +1.92

9. 5.6
  +0.1

10. 0.68
  +0.49

11. 7.8
  +1.5

12. 21.6
  +15.0

13. 8.29
  +1.93

14. 9.85
  +4.79

15. 37.4
  +42.6

16. 0.2
  0.4
  +0.3

17. 0.7
  0.6
  +0.9

18. 0.94
  0.10
  +0.61

19. 5.6
  0.8
  +7.2

20. 1.23
  6.45
  +7.66

21. 16.43
  24.18
  +38.92

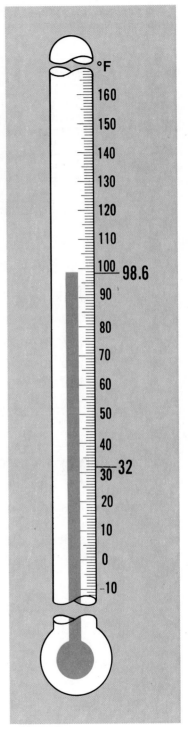

22. The normal body temperature is 98.6 degrees Fahrenheit. When Randy was sick, his temperature was 5.7 degrees above normal. What was his temperature then?

23. On the Fahrenheit scale, the boiling temperature of water is 113.4 degrees higher than normal body temperature. At what temperature does water boil?

24. The coldest temperature ever recorded in Alaska was 79.3 degrees below zero Fahrenheit. The coldest temperature ever recorded on earth was 47.6 degrees lower than that. What was the coldest temperature ever recorded?

Subtracting Decimals

Race Results

Pupil	Time (seconds)
Jill	22.5
Tom	23.7
Sue	25.1

To find how much faster Jill ran the race than the other two, subtract the decimals.

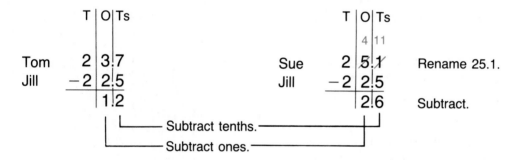

```
        T | O|Ts                          T | O!Ts
                                              4 |11
Tom     2 | 3.7            Sue           2 | 5.1    Rename 25.1.
Jill  − 2 | 2.5            Jill        − 2 | 2.5
        ──────                          ──────
          1.2                             2.6        Subtract.
```

— Subtract tenths. —
— Subtract ones. —

Jill beat Tom by 1.2 seconds.   Jill beat Sue by 2.6 seconds.

Discuss these subtractions.

```
  |Ts|Hs                              O|Ts|Hs
                                        9 |10
   2 |14                             3 |10
  0.3 4 —— Why are these renamed? —— 4.0 0
 −0.2 9                             −1.2 7
 ──────                             ──────
  0.0 5                              2.7 3
   ↑
```
—— Why is 0.0 written here?

Is subtracting decimals like subtracting whole numbers?

Exercises

1. $\begin{array}{r} 0.9 \\ -0.4 \\ \hline \end{array}$	**2.** $\begin{array}{r} 6.5 \\ -4.2 \\ \hline \end{array}$	**3.** $\begin{array}{r} 1.03 \\ -0.01 \\ \hline \end{array}$	**4.** $\begin{array}{r} 2.7 \\ -1.6 \\ \hline \end{array}$	**5.** $\begin{array}{r} 15.67 \\ -\;\;5.34 \\ \hline \end{array}$
6. $\begin{array}{r} 1.1 \\ -0.8 \\ \hline \end{array}$	**7.** $\begin{array}{r} 8.6 \\ -6.7 \\ \hline \end{array}$	**8.** $\begin{array}{r} 5.00 \\ -2.80 \\ \hline \end{array}$	**9.** $\begin{array}{r} 6.1 \\ -5.2 \\ \hline \end{array}$	**10.** $\begin{array}{r} 9.72 \\ -7.62 \\ \hline \end{array}$
11. $\begin{array}{r} 1.6 \\ -0.6 \\ \hline \end{array}$	**12.** $\begin{array}{r} 3.9 \\ -2.8 \\ \hline \end{array}$	**13.** $\begin{array}{r} 13.6 \\ -12.7 \\ \hline \end{array}$	**14.** $\begin{array}{r} 0.81 \\ -0.62 \\ \hline \end{array}$	**15.** $\begin{array}{r} 10.00 \\ -\;\;0.06 \\ \hline \end{array}$
16. $\begin{array}{r} 3.0 \\ -0.5 \\ \hline \end{array}$	**17.** $\begin{array}{r} 0.62 \\ -0.28 \\ \hline \end{array}$	**18.** $\begin{array}{r} 3.00 \\ -1.18 \\ \hline \end{array}$	**19.** $\begin{array}{r} 14.1 \\ -\;\;9.8 \\ \hline \end{array}$	**20.** $\begin{array}{r} 5.00 \\ -0.68 \\ \hline \end{array}$

21. How much more does the largest can hold than the smallest can?

22. How much more does the largest can hold than the next-smaller can?

23. How much less does the smallest can hold than the next-larger can?

24. A 10-liter bucket contains 6.2 liters of water. How much more water is needed to fill the bucket?

25. One bucket contains 6.2 liters. Another bucket contains 7 liters. Find the difference in these amounts.

Liter Quiz

Aaron has an 8-liter pail filled with water. The only other pails he could find are shown. How can he get exactly 6 liters of water in the 8-liter pail? (*Hint:* He can pour water from pail to pail.)

Money

Here is $5.

To find the cost of the paint and the brush, add the decimals.

$$\begin{array}{r} {\scriptstyle 1} \\ \$3.5\,5 \\ +\,1.0\,5 \\ \hline \$4.6\,0 \end{array}$$

When working with money, remember to use the dollar sign.

They cost $4.60.

Subtract to find how much change he should get.

$$\begin{array}{r} {\scriptstyle 4\,|10} \\ \$5.0\,0 \\ -\,4.6\,0 \\ \hline \$0.4\,0 \end{array}$$

His change is $0.40, or 40¢.

Why was $5 written as $5.00 in the subtraction?

Exercises

Add or subtract.

1. $3.20
   +0.35

2. $4.65
   −0.48

3. $8.19
   −1.00

4. $2.46
   +1.24

5. $1.82
  − 0.61

6. $0.21
  + 0.76

7. $1.20
  − 1.08

8. $4.86
  + 1.14

9. $0.53
  + 1.48

10. $0.68
   − 0.62

11. $7.95
   + 2.06

12. $0.90
   + 0.65

13. $5.37
   + 4.58

14. $6.78
   − 5.16

15. $0.49
   + 7.51

16. $0.20
   + 0.30

17. $3.40
   + 2.26

18. $1.00
   − 0.26

19. $5.00
   − 3.49

20. $10.00
   − 8.98

21. Mr. Baxter bought his son a baseball glove and a can of glove oil for his birthday. How much did he spend?

22. Tim charged the Dawsons $7.50 for mowing their lawn and $2.25 for trimming their hedges. How much did he charge for the two jobs?

23. Frank bought the book shown at the right for $1.37 less than shown on the price tag. How much did he pay for the book?

24. Mrs. Johnson had her daughter's picture taken. She could buy 15 small pictures for $8.50 or 15 small pictures and a large picture for $12.95. How much does the large picture cost?

25. Mr. Morris bought a kite for each of his two sons and for his daughter. How much did he spend for the kites?

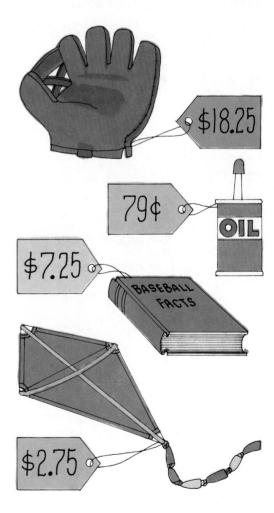

$18.25

79¢

$7.25

$2.75

SKILLS REVIEW

Multiply.

1. 36
   $\times 5$

2. 139
   $\times 3$

3. 300
   $\times 13$

4. 106
   $\times 80$

5. 273
   $\times 18$

6. 596
   $\times 71$

7. 1320
   $\times 7$

8. 562
   $\times 837$

Find each product in simplest form.

9. $\frac{2}{3} \times \frac{1}{5}$

10. $\frac{7}{10} \times \frac{1}{2}$

11. $\frac{6}{7} \times \frac{7}{8}$

12. $1\frac{3}{5} \times \frac{1}{4}$

13. $\frac{3}{10} \times 20$

14. $\frac{7}{10} \times 24$

15. $\frac{9}{10} \times \frac{1}{10}$

16. $2\frac{6}{100} \times 50$

Divide.

17. $7\overline{)921}$

18. $8\overline{)960}$

19. $16\overline{)1117}$

20. $32\overline{)338}$

21. $46\overline{)2175}$

22. $6\overline{)7207}$

23. $98\overline{)9907}$

24. $80\overline{)2450}$

Find each sum or difference in simplest form.

25. $\frac{2}{5}$
    $+\frac{3}{5}$

26. $\frac{2}{3}$
    $+\frac{4}{5}$

27. $1\frac{7}{10}$
    $+ \frac{9}{10}$

28. $4\frac{1}{2}$
    $+1\frac{3}{4}$

29. $\frac{6}{7}$
    $-\frac{3}{7}$

30. $2\frac{57}{100}$
    $-1\frac{42}{100}$

31. $1\frac{1}{10}$
    $- \frac{7}{10}$

32. 5
    $-2\frac{1}{3}$

33. $1\frac{9}{10}$
    $+ \frac{1}{2}$

34. $\frac{78}{100}$
    $-\frac{69}{100}$

35. $7\frac{61}{100}$
    $+1\frac{51}{100}$

36. $5\frac{6}{10}$
    $-4\frac{7}{10}$

214

37. Snow City got $7\frac{3}{4}$ inches of snow on Thursday and $3\frac{1}{2}$ inches on Friday. How much snow fell during the two days?

38. It took Jerry $1\frac{3}{4}$ hours to shovel the driveway and $1\frac{1}{2}$ hours to shovel the walks. How long did it take him to do both jobs?

39. Watertown got 14 inches of snow in January. That was $4\frac{3}{4}$ inches more than in December. How much snow did Watertown get in December?

40. Winterdale got $2\frac{1}{2}$ inches of snow last winter. Five times as much snow fell this winter. How much snow did Winterdale get this winter?

41. Snow fell on Iceton at the rate of $2\frac{1}{2}$ inches per hour for $3\frac{3}{4}$ hours. How much snow did Iceton get?

42. $3\frac{1}{2}$ feet of snow fell on Avalanche City in one week. How many inches of snow was that?

43. It took Sarah 3 hours to shovel the driveway and the walk. If $\frac{1}{6}$ of the time was used to shovel the walk, how long did it take Sarah to shovel the driveway?

44. The ice on Drift Lake was $2\frac{1}{4}$ feet thick last winter. This year the ice is $28\frac{1}{2}$ inches thick. Was the ice thicker this winter or last winter? How much thicker?

Taurus

215

Multiplying Decimals

Animal	Miles per hour
Rabbit	15
Turtle	1.5
Snail	0.15

How far can each animal go in 3 hours?

Rabbit
$$\begin{array}{r} 15 \\ \times 3 \\ \hline 45 \end{array}$$
The rabbit can go 45 miles.

Turtle
$$\begin{array}{r} 1.5 \\ \times 3 \\ \hline \end{array}$$

$$1\frac{5}{10} \times \frac{3}{1} = \frac{15}{10} \times \frac{3}{1}$$

$$= \frac{45}{10} = 4\frac{5}{10}$$

$$\begin{array}{r} 1.5 \\ \times 3 \\ \hline 4.5 \end{array}$$
The turtle can go 4.5 miles.

Snail
$$\begin{array}{r} 0.15 \\ \times 3 \\ \hline \end{array}$$

$$\frac{15}{100} \times \frac{3}{1} = \frac{45}{100}$$

$$\begin{array}{r} 0.15 \\ \times 3 \\ \hline 0.45 \end{array}$$
The snail can go 0.45 mile.

You don't have to use fractions to multiply decimals. Multiply just as you do whole numbers. Then use this pattern to place the decimal point in the answer.

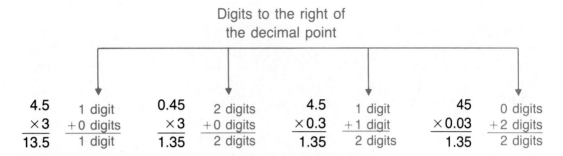

Digits to the right of the decimal point

4.5	1 digit	0.45	2 digits	4.5	1 digit	45	0 digits
×3	+0 digits	×3	+0 digits	×0.3	+1 digit	×0.03	+2 digits
13.5	1 digit	1.35	2 digits	1.35	2 digits	1.35	2 digits

The number of digits to the right of the decimal point in the product is equal to the total number of digits to the right of the decimal points in both factors.

Exercises

Multiply.

1.   2
  ×0.3

2.   20
  ×0.3

3.   3.6
  ×0.4

4. 0.36
  ×4

5.   36
  ×0.4

6.   3
  ×3

7. 0.3
  ×3

8.   3
  ×0.3

9.   30
  ×0.3

10.   30
  ×0.03

11. 49
  ×5

12. 4.9
  ×0.5

13. 0.49
  ×5

14. 0.49
  ×0.5

15. 49
  ×0.05

16. 27
  ×6

17. 2.7
  ×6

18. 0.27
  ×6

19. 2.7
  ×0.6

20. 27
  ×0.06

21. 18
  ×0.3

22. 3.5
  ×0.7

23. 0.81
  ×2

24. 0.58
  ×0.6

25. 94
  ×0.04

Multiplying Decimals

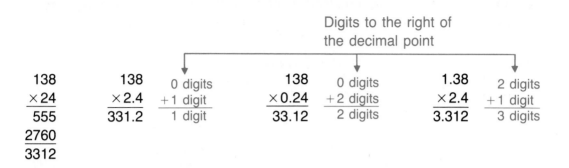

Discuss how the decimal point was placed in each answer above. Study the pattern below.

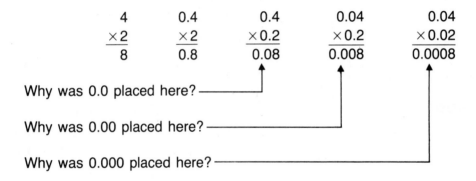

Why was 0.0 placed here?

Why was 0.00 placed here?

Why was 0.000 placed here?

Exercises

Use the examples at the left to write each product.

3
×3
9

1.   3
  ×0.3

2. 0.3
  ×3

3. 0.03
   ×3

4.   30
 ×0.003

687
×14
2748
6870
9618

5. 687
  ×1.4

6. 6.87
  ×14

7. 68.7
  ×14

8.   687
 ×0.014

218

Multiply.

9. 41
 ×2

10. 41
 ×0.2

11. 4.1
 ×0.2

12. 0.41
 ×2

13. 16
 ×0.6

14. 1.6
 ×6

15. 0.16
 ×0.6

16. 0.016
 ×6

17. 2376
 ×3

18. 237.6
 ×0.3

19. 2376
 ×0.30

20. 2376
 ×0.003

21. 816.5
 ×8

22. 91.81
 ×0.7

23. 261
 ×0.15

24. 186.9
 ×0.5

25. 2.675
 ×19

26. 5710
 ×1.6

27. 768
 ×1.01

28. 0.168
 ×321

29. 500
 ×0.68

30. 8.93
 ×6.0

31. 178.5
 ×0.92

32. 176
 ×0.187

33. Standish can drive 35.6 miles on 1 gallon of gasoline. How far can he drive on 5 gallons of gasoline?

34. 1 quart is equal to 0.25 gallon. How many gallons are equal to 26 quarts?

35. Marcy has 37 quarters. How much money is that in dollars and cents?

36. Cindy has 325 nickels. How much money is that in dollars and cents?

37. $\frac{1}{4}$ is equal to 0.25. Express $\frac{3}{4}$ as a decimal.

38. $\frac{1}{8}$ is equal to 0.125. Express $\frac{3}{8}$ as a decimal.

39. 1 kilometer is about 0.62 mile. How many feet is that?

40. A kilogram is about 2.2 pounds. How many ounces is that?

Extra Practice—Set B, page 342

Money Sense

1. Which of these is worth the most?

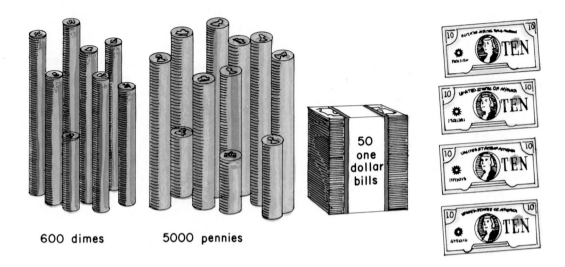

600 dimes   5000 pennies

2. Copy and complete.
   For each amount, you are to have the fewest bills and coins possible.

Amount	$1 bills	Half-dollars (50¢)	Quarters (25¢)	Dimes (10¢)	Nickels (5¢)	Pennies (1¢)
$2.36	2	0	1	1	0	1
$0.85						
$1.35						
$1.91						
$2.74						
$3.47						

Multiplying With a Calculator

Hamburger
$1.95 pound

Edward Hoppe Photography

Paul needs 5.5 pounds of hamburger for a cook-out tomorrow. He used his calculator to find how much it would cost by pressing the keys in this order.

How much will the hamburger cost?

Use a calculator to find each product.

1. 3.002 × 4.5   2. 0.003 × 125   3. 0.05 × 0.36

4. 35.00 × 5.00   5. 75.75 × 36   6. 0.025 × 80

7. 0.001 × 10   8. 0.001 × 100   9. 0.001 × 1000

10. 0.001 × 10,000   11. 365.20 × 1.4   12. 365.2 × 1.4

13. 3652 × 0.14   14. 2 × 2.000   15. 12 × 0.12

221

Ratio

Zoom Airlines has 4 airplanes and 8 pilots. You can compare the number of airplanes to the number of pilots.

We say the **ratio** of airplanes to pilots is

$$4 \text{ to } 8 \quad \text{or} \quad \frac{4}{8}.$$

The **ratio** of two numbers is a comparison by division.

Here is another way to compare the number of airplanes to pilots.

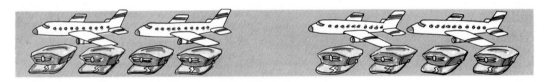

For every 2 airplanes there are 4 pilots. The ratio of airplanes to pilots is

$$2 \text{ to } 4 \quad \text{or} \quad \frac{2}{4}.$$

The ratio of airplanes to pilots is also 1 to 2 or $\frac{1}{2}$.

$\frac{4}{8}$, $\frac{2}{4}$, and $\frac{1}{2}$ all name the same ratio. We call $\frac{1}{2}$ the **simplest ratio** of airplanes to pilots.

The ratio of  's to 's is $\frac{6}{4}$ or $\frac{3}{2}$.
Which of those is in simplest form?

Ratios are not given as mixed numerals like $1\frac{1}{2}$.

Exercises

Write two ratios for each of the following:

1. ⬡'s to ⬤'s   2. ◼'s to ⬤'s   3. ⬤'s to ◼'s   4. ◼'s to ⬡'s

Write each ratio in simplest form.

5. 8 to 12   6. 12 to 8   7. 6 to 10   8. 25 to 15

9. 12 to 20   10. 21 to 14   11. 6 to 9   12. 12 to 15

13. On a test there were 4 A's and 6 B's. What was the ratio of B's to A's?

14. In Fred's class, the ratio of girls to boys is 10 to 7. Does that mean there are only 10 girls and 7 boys?

The ratio of boys to girls in Pam's class is 4 to 5. Could these be the number of boys and girls in her class? Answer *Yes* or *No*.

15. 6 boys
    8 girls

16. 8 boys
    10 girls

17. 30 boys
    24 girls

18. 24 boys
    30 girls

Percent

30% is read "thirty **percent.**"

You can think of % as *hundredths.*

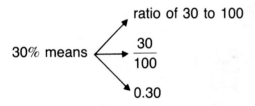

30% means
- ratio of 30 to 100
- $\dfrac{30}{100}$
- 0.30

Give a decimal and a percent to tell how much of the figure is

a. colored red

b. colored blue

c. left white

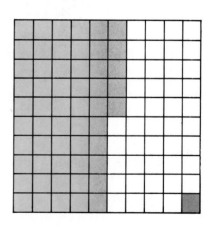

Suppose the entire figure were colored green. What percent of the figure would be green?

Exercises

Write each of these as a percent.

1. $\frac{1}{100}$ 2. $\frac{35}{100}$ 3. 0.68   4. 0.04   5. $\frac{100}{100}$

Write each of these as a decimal.

6. 26%   7. 90%   8. 9%   9. 66%   10. 39%

In the drawing are 100 small squares. What percent of the entire drawing is shown by each of these colors?

11. red   12. white

13. blue   14. purple

15. green

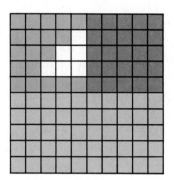

Copy. Express each number in two other ways to complete the table.

	Percent	Fraction	Decimal
16.	17%		
17.		$\frac{31}{100}$	
18.			0.06
19.			0.99

	Percent	Fraction	Decimal
20.	10%		
21.		$\frac{75}{100}$	
22.			0.25
23.	50%		

Estimate what percent of the figure is shown by each of these colors.

24. red   25. blue   26. white

27. Is the sum of your estimates 100?

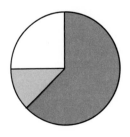

Using Percent

Each child shot 16 free throws. Sally made 50% of her shots. How many free throws did she make?

50% of 16   means   50% × 16.

Here are two ways to find the answer.

$$50\% = \frac{50}{100}$$

$$\frac{50}{100} \times 16 = \frac{50 \times 16}{100}$$

$$= \frac{800}{100}$$

$$= 8$$

50% = 0.50

0.50 × 16

$$\begin{array}{r} 16 \\ \times\,0.50 \\ \hline 8.00 \end{array}$$

Is 8 equal to 8.00?

Sally made 8 free throws.

Dale Moyer/Photo Trends

Discuss this multiplication.

To find 28% of 67, do this. ⟶

$$\begin{array}{r} 67 \\ \times\,0.28 \\ \hline 5\ 36 \\ 13\ 40 \\ \hline 18.76 \end{array}$$

How was the decimal point placed in the product?

Exercises

Find the following:

1. 12% of 32

2. 10% of 80

3. 60% of 200

4. 10% of 50

5. 18% of 200

6. 50% of 48

7. 5% × 100   **8.** 20% × 58   **9.** 15% × 6

10. 38% × 100   **11.** 9% × 15   **12.** 47% × 88

Find the number of shots each pupil made.

	Pupil	Shots attempted	Percent of shots made	Shots made
13.	Angela	30	20%	
14.	Mark	30	50%	
15.	Wilma	30	100%	

16. 50% of the 30 squares are red. Find the number of red squares.

17. 25% of the 30 squares are blue. Find the number of blue squares.

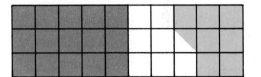

18. A truck is carrying 1620 pounds of apples. If 5% of the apples are rotten, how many pounds of apples are still good?

19. A box of cereal weighs 125 grams. If 32% of the weight is sugar, how many grams of sugar are in 1 box of the cereal?

20. 44% of the pupils in Mary's class are boys. There are 25 pupils in her class. How many are boys?

21. By weight, about 70% of the human body is water. Is more than one half of your body made of water? What percent is not made of water?

Lou Jones

Percent and Money

The regular price of $8 is reduced by 15%.

How much is 15% of $8?

$$0.15 \times 8 = 1.20$$

The price is reduced $1.20.

To find the sale price, subtract $1.20 from $8.

```
      7 10
   $8.00  ←— Regular price
  − 1.20  ←— Reduction
   $6.80  ←— Sale price
```

J.B. Game Store

```
           $ 6.80
             2.92
             3.68
Subtotal   $13.40
     Tax     0.67
   Total   $14.07
```

A sales tax of 5% was added to the cost of the items purchased.

How was the tax computed?

Does your state have a sales tax? If so, what percent is it?

How much sales tax would you pay on an item that costs $8.95 in your state?

What would the item cost, including tax?

228

Exercises

The regular price of an item is $15. That price was reduced by 20%. The sales tax is 5%. Find the following:

1. the amount of the reduction

2. the sale price

3. the sales tax on the sale price

4. the total bill

5. the amount of change you should get from $20

Find the sale price of each item.

6.

7.

Use the sales ticket to do exercises 8-11.

8. Find the subtotal.

9. The sales tax is 5%. Find the amount of sales tax.

10. What is the total?

11. You give the clerk $6. How much change should you get?

12. Link earned $128 mowing lawns. He put 75% of that in the bank and spent the rest. How much did he spend?

13. The price of a yo-yo is $1.36. The sales tax is 5%. How much would you have to pay for the yo-yo?

CHAPTER REVIEW

Write as a fraction or as a mixed numeral and then as a decimal.

1. six and three tenths   **2.** seventy-nine hundredths   **3.** two thousandths

Should <, =, or > replace the ●?

4. 5.301 ● 5.310   **5.** 24.45 ● 24.5   **6.** 0.618 ● 0.608

Find each sum, difference, and product.

7. 0.6
    +0.3

8. 0.78
    +0.63

9. 5.92
    +0.88

10. $17.62
    +18.47

11. 0.8
    −0.6

12. 0.56
    −0.17

13. 1.97
    −0.89

14. $45.63
    −21.71

15. 0.3
    ×6

16. 0.4
    ×0.02

17. 276.5
    ×0.13

18.   916
    ×0.046

19. Write two ratios for △'s to ○'s.

20. Write the ratio of ○'s to △'s in simplest form.

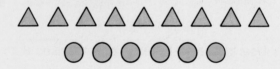

21. Find 25% of 250.   **22.** Find 36% of 86.

Write as a percent.

23. 0.25   **24.** $\frac{3}{100}$ **25.** $\frac{97}{100}$ **26.** 0.01

27. Find the sale price of the tent.

28. The sales tax is 4% of the sale price. Find the amount of sales tax.

29. How much will the tent cost?

SALE
$24
25% off

10 Measurement

Judy Ellefsen

Measurement

On the ruler below, the marks are **1 centimeter** apart. A centimeter is a unit of length.

To find the length of a line segment, lay the ruler along the line segment and read the length *to the nearest centimeter.*

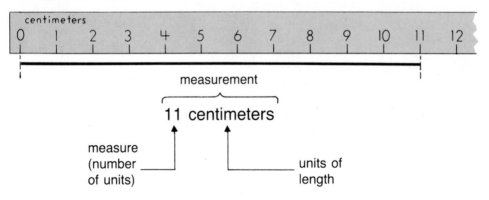

A **measurement** is given by naming the **measure** (number of units) and the **unit** that is used.

Is the length of the line segment at the right closer to 2 or 3 centimeters?

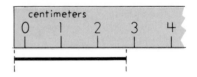

What is the length of that line segment to the nearest centimeter?

Exercises

Find the length of each line segment to the nearest centimeter.

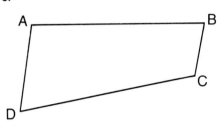

For each figure below, find the length of each side.

3.

4.

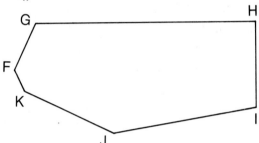

5.

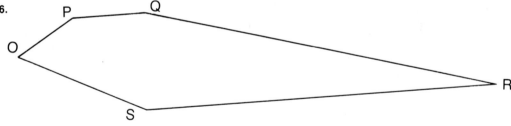

6.

Find the length of each of the following in the figure at the right:

7. side UV

8. side VW

9. diagonal UW

10. side TW

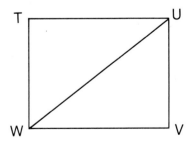

Length

The metric units of length used most often are **meter, centimeter, millimeter,** and **kilometer.**

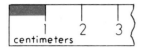

1 centimeter

1 cm

1 millimeter

1 mm

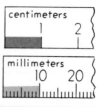

1 cm = 10 mm
1 mm = 0.1 cm

This strip is 10 centimeters long.

If you tape 10 such strips end to end, you will get a strip that is 1 **meter,** or 1 **m,** long.

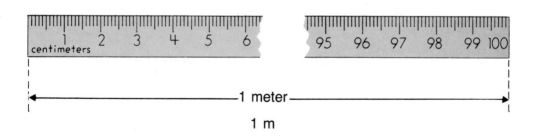

1 meter

1 m

milli means 0.001.   1 millimeter = 0.001 meter

centi means 0.01.   1 centimeter = 0.01 meter

If you lay 1000 meter strips end to end, you will have a strip that is 1 **kilometer,** or 1 **km,** long.

kilo means 1000.   1 kilometer = 1000 meters

Exercises

Use the rulers below to complete the following:

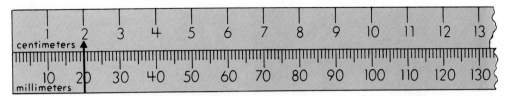

1. 20 mm = ___ cm

2. 10 cm = ___ mm

3. 13 cm = ___ mm

Tell which is longer.

4. 15 mm or 15 cm

5. 23 mm or 2 cm

6. 104 mm or 14 cm

Complete the following:

7. 3 cm = ___ mm

8. 30 cm = ___ mm

9. 50 mm = ___ cm

10. 110 mm = ___ cm

11. 1000 mm = ___ cm

12. 7 cm = ___ mm

13. 80 mm = ___ cm

14. 12 cm = ___ mm

15. 900 mm = ___ cm

16. Ted lives 2 kilometers from school. How many meters is that?

17. Abby lives 3 kilometers from school. How many meters is that?

18. How many more meters must Abby walk than Ted to get to school?

19. Abby is halfway to school. How far is she from school?

Finding Measurements

Mary Elenz Tranter

Each pupil made a list of the objects that were measured. The pupil who made the list below forgot to include the units of length. Tell what unit of length must have been used for each object on the list.

Object	Length
piece of chalk	6
chalkboard	4
height of door	210
width of door	1
book	31

Exercises

Measure each of these to the nearest centimeter.

1. width of a window
2. length of this book
3. thickness of this book
4. your waist
5. length of your desk
6. length of your foot
7. width of this book
8. length of your pencil
9. width of your palm

Measure each of these to the nearest meter.

10. length of the room
11. width of the room
12. height of the door
13. length of the chalkboard
14. your height
15. width of the hallway
16. Which is longer— 3 m or 3 cm?
17. Which is longer— 3 m or 200 cm?
18. Which is shorter— 201 cm or 2 m?

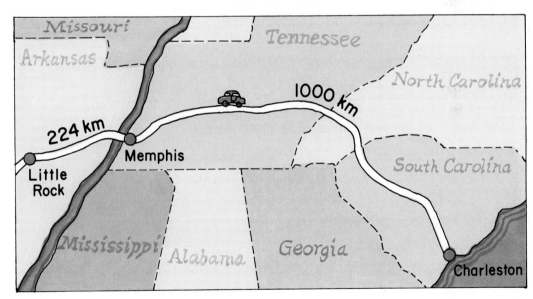

19. On a trip Miss Lewis traveled from Little Rock to Memphis and then on to Charleston. Find how far she traveled.
20. She spent 17 hours driving on the trip. Find her average speed in kilometers per hour.

237

Finding Measurements

The length of the bolt is 84 millimeters.

Since 1 mm = 0.1 cm, it is easy to give the length of the bolt in centimeters.

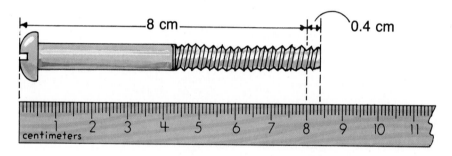

The length of the bolt can also be given as 8.4 centimeters.

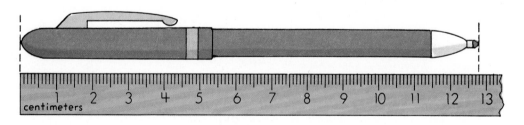

Give the length of the pen in millimeters.

Give the length of the pen in centimeters.

238

Exercises

Give the length of each line segment in millimeters and in centimeters.

1.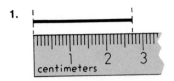

2.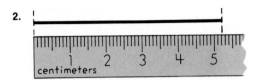

3.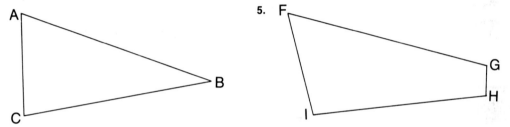

For each figure below, find the length of each side in millimeters and in centimeters.

4.

5.

6.

7.

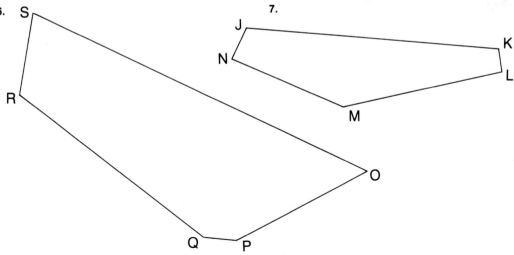

Metric Units

This pencil is 120 millimeters long. How many centimeters is that?

1 m = 1000 mm	1 mm = 0.001 m
1 m = 100 cm	1 cm = 0.01 m
1 cm = 10 mm	1 mm = 0.1 cm
1 km = 1000 m	1 m = 0.001 km

By using the information in the table, you can change from one metric unit to another.

You can change 120 mm to 12 cm like this.

$$120 \text{ mm} = \underline{} \text{ cm}$$

I know $\quad$ 1 mm = 0.1 cm,

so 120 mm = (120 × 0.1) cm.

120 mm = 12 cm

The pencil is 12 cm long.

Study how each of these measurements is changed.

300 m = __ km $\qquad\qquad\qquad$ 1.25 m = __ cm

$\quad$ 1 m = 0.001 km $\qquad\qquad\qquad\quad$ 1 m = 100 cm

300 m = (300 × 0.001) km $\qquad\quad$ 1.25 m = (1.25 × 100) cm

300 m = 0.3 km $\qquad\qquad\qquad\quad$ 1.25 m = 125 cm

240

Exercises

Complete the following:

1. 1.4 m = ___ cm

    1 m = 100 cm

    1.4 m = (1.4 × 100) cm

    1.4 m = ___ cm

2. 13 mm = ___ cm

    1 mm = 0.1 cm

    13 mm = (13 × 0.1) cm

    13 mm = ___ cm

3. 0.08 km = ___ m

4. 27 mm = ___ cm

5. 13 mm = ___ m

6. 300 cm = ___ m

7. 0.6 km = ___ m

8. 7.1 cm = ___ mm

9. 27 cm = ___ mm

10. 68 cm = ___ m

11. 200 mm = ___ m

12. 517 mm = ___ cm

13. 0.4 m = ___ mm

14. 7.3 km = ___ m

15. 1.2 m = ___ cm

16. 12 m = ___ km

17. 1.2 m = ___ mm

Change each measurement below to centimeters.

18. Kevin is 1300 mm tall.
His arm is 492 mm long.
His foot is 195 mm long.
When he grows up, he
hopes to be 2000 mm tall.

19. Martha is 1.3 m tall.
Her arm is 0.5 m long.
Her foot is 0.2 m long.
When she grows up, she
hopes to be 1.6 m tall.

20. Make a list for yourself like those for Kevin and Martha. Use a centimeter as the unit of measure.

21. Which is longer—2 km or 2001 m?

22. Which is shorter—26 mm or 0.3 cm?

23. Which is shorter—5 m or 501 mm?

Capacity

A box this size has a capacity of 1 **liter**.

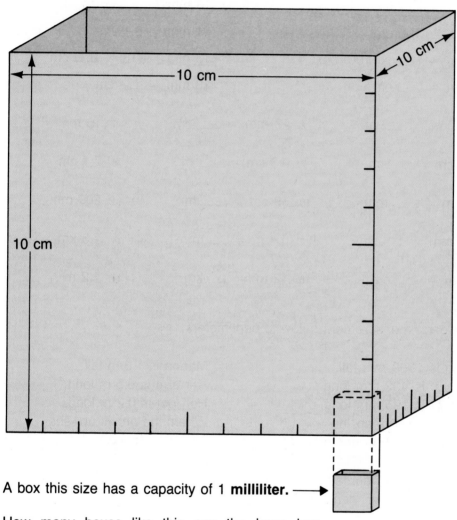

10 cm

10 cm

10 cm

A box this size has a capacity of 1 **milliliter.** ⟶

How many boxes like this can the large box hold?

1 liter = 1000 milliliters

1 L = 1000 mL

0.001 L = 1 mL

Exercises

Would you use liters or milliliters to measure these?

1. amount of ink in a pen

2. amount of oil in a barrel

3. amount of water used for a bath

4. amount of water a parakeet drinks in a day

5. amount of water in an aquarium

6. amount of water used to make one ice cube

7. amount of water used to make a bag of ice cubes

8. amount of perfume in a bottle

Tell which has the larger capacity.

9. a. 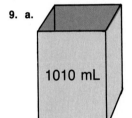 1010 mL   **b.**  1 liter

10. a.  0.75 liter   **b.** 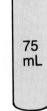 75 mL

11. a. 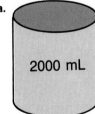 2000 mL   **b.** 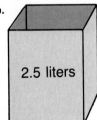 2.5 liters

12. a. 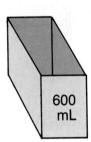 600 mL   **b.** 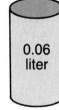 0.06 liter

Choose the best answer: 1 mL, 100 mL, 1 liter, 100 liters.

13. amount of water needed to fill an ice-cube tray

14. amount of gasoline a car's gasoline tank can hold

15. amount of liquid needed to fill an eyedropper

Weight

Some objects are weighed in **grams.**

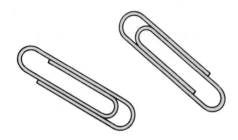

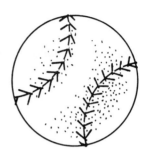

Two paper clips weigh about 1 gram, or 1 **g.**

A baseball weighs about 145 grams, or 145 g.

Heavier objects are weighed in **kilograms.**

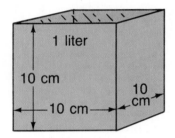

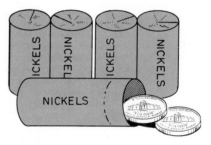

A liter of water weighs about 1 kilogram, or 1 **kg.**

200 nickels weigh about 1 kilogram, or 1 kg.

1 kg = 1000 g	1 g = 0.001 kg

This guinea pig weighs about 500 grams. We also say it weighs about 0.5 kilogram.

500 g = ___ kg

1 g = 0.001 kg

500 g = (500 × 0.001) kg

500 g = 0.5 kg

Exercises

Tell whether you would use grams or kilograms to weigh these.

1. a lawn mower 2. an egg 3. an earthworm 4. yourself

5. a pumpkin 6. a nickel 7. a bale of hay 8. a crayon

9. a letter 10. a dog 11. a box of cereal 12. a magazine

13. an apple 14. a basket of apples 15. a truckload of apples

Choose the correct weight.

16.

   3 grams *or*
   3 kilograms

17.

   225 grams *or*
   225 kilograms

18.

   20 grams *or*
   20 kilograms

19. 2 kilograms are the same as   a. 20 g   b. 2000 g   c. 0.002 g

20. 751 grams are the same as   a. 7.51 kg   b. 0.751 kg   c. 75.1 kg

Complete the following:

21. 2000 g = ___ kg   22. 2 kg = ___ g   23. 1500 g = ___ kg

24. 170 g = ___ kg   25. 0.3 kg = ___ g   26. 0.016 kg = ___ g

27. 200 nickels weigh about 1 kilogram. How much does 1 nickel weigh?

Temperature

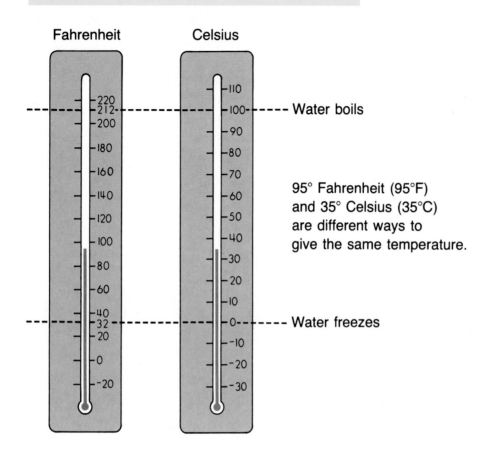

Fahrenheit

Celsius

- - - - 220
      212 - - - - - - - - - - - 100 - - - - Water boils
      200
      180
      160
      140
      120
      100
       80
       60
       40
       32 - - - - - - - - - - - - 0 - - - - Water freezes
       20
        0
      -20

110
100
90
80
70
60
50
40
30
20
10
0
-10
-20
-30

95° Fahrenheit (95°F)
and 35° Celsius (35°C)
are different ways to
give the same temperature.

-10°F means *10° below zero* Fahrenheit.

-10°C means *10° below zero* Celsius.

Someone said the temperature today is 20°. Do you know which scale was used?

You could go swimming outside today. Now do you know which scale was used?

How should you give that temperature?

Exercises

1. What is the Fahrenheit reading when water boils? Freezes?

2. What is the Celsius reading when water boils? Freezes?

3. The temperature is 30°C. Would you build a snowman or go swimming?

4. Find the difference between 87°F and 45°F.

5. What is a shorter way to write 15° below zero Fahrenheit?

6. What is a shorter way to write 15° below zero Celsius?

Lay a straightedge across the temperature scales on page 246 to estimate the following:

7. 68°F = ___°C

8. 45°C = ___°F

9. 10°C = ___°F

10. 180°F = ___°C

11. 0°F = ___°C

12. −25°C = ___°F

13. One day the high temperature was 84° and the low was 61°. Find the difference between the two temperatures. Do you think these are Celsius or Fahrenheit readings?

14. During one week the daily high Celsius readings were 20°, 24°, 22°, 26°, 30°, 29°, and 31°. Find the average high temperature for that week.

15. Your body temperature is about 98.6°F. How would you give your body temperature in degrees Celsius?

16. Bobby's temperature on Monday morning was 40°C. Is that temperature above or below normal?

17. Find the difference between the temperatures at which water boils and freezes on the Fahrenheit scale.

18. Find the difference between the temperatures at which water boils and freezes on the Celsius scale.

Using Customary Units

Length

12 inches = 1 foot

3 feet = 1 yard

5280 feet = 1 mile

Capacity

8 fluid ounces = 1 cup

2 cups = 1 pint

2 pints = 1 quart

4 quarts = 1 gallon

Weight

16 ounces = 1 pound

2000 pounds = 1 ton

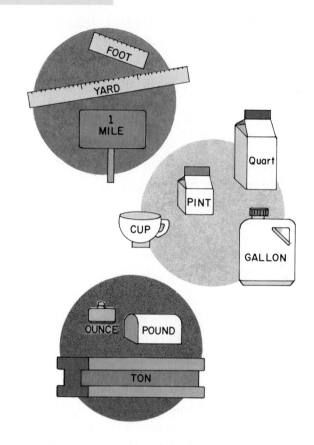

Use the tables above to solve these problems.

1. Tara is 69 inches tall. Gina is 2 inches shorter than Tara. How tall is Gina in feet and inches?

2. Buena had a gallon of milk. She filled 4 cups with milk. How many quarts of milk were left in the gallon container?

3. The paint Amos wants only comes in pint cans. He needs a gallon of the paint. How many pint cans should he get?

4. The paint Carlos wants only comes in quart cans. He needs one-half gallon of the paint. How many quart cans should he get?

5. How many yards in a mile?

6. How many cups in a gallon?

7. Clara poured 2 cups of water into an empty canteen that can hold 2 quarts. How many more cups of water can she pour into the canteen?

8. Karl had a 3-quart jug of water. He drank 4 cups of water from it. How many cups of water were left in the jug?

9. Edna had 2 pounds 4 ounces of wax. She used 12 ounces of the wax to make a candle. How many ounces of wax are left?

10. Vernon measured his height and found it to be $4\frac{1}{2}$ feet. How tall is he in feet and inches? In inches?

11. The Johnsons have a swimming pool that holds 5000 gallons of water. If a gallon of water weighs 8.3 pounds, find the weight of the water in the pool.

12. Stan has 25 ounces of lead. Laurel has 1 pound 8 ounces of lead. Who has the heavier piece of lead? How much heavier?

13. Morgan had a dowel rod 6 feet 4 inches long. He cut a 10-inch piece off one end. How long was the other piece?

14. Lars weighed 9 pounds 3 ounces at birth. On his first birthday he weighed 15 pounds 2 ounces. How much weight did he gain?

15. It takes about 8.5 trees to make 1000 pounds of paper. How many trees are needed to make a ton of paper? Two tons of paper?

16. Polly has 6 yards 6 inches of yarn. Phillip has 20 feet 4 inches of yarn. Who has the longer piece of yarn? How much longer?

Find each answer in simplest form.

1. $\frac{3}{8}$
    $-\frac{2}{8}$

2. $\frac{5}{6}$
    $+\frac{5}{6}$

3. $1\frac{1}{2}$
    $+\ \frac{3}{4}$

4. $2\frac{1}{3}$
    $+1\frac{2}{3}$

5. $\frac{2}{3} \times \frac{1}{3}$

6. $\frac{5}{8} \times \frac{1}{5}$

7. $\frac{7}{10} \times 1\frac{1}{4}$

8. $1\frac{1}{2} \times \frac{2}{3}$

9. $2\frac{1}{4} \times 3\frac{1}{3}$

10. $5 \times \frac{1}{2}$

11. $1\frac{1}{8} \times \frac{2}{3}$

12. $7\frac{1}{2} \times \frac{6}{7}$

13. 0.49
    $+0.61$

14. 16.07
    $+34.93$

15. 0.74
    -0.67

16. 5.281
    -1.136

17. 600
    $\times 0.7$

18. 1.62
    $\times 35$

19. 0.281
    $\times 50$

20. 200
    $\times 0.006$

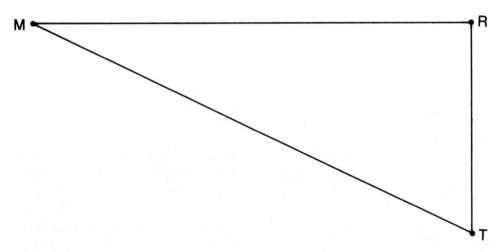

21. Name each angle in the triangle above.

22. Find the measure of each angle. (Use a protractor.)

23. Tell whether each angle is an acute angle, a right angle, or an obtuse angle.

24. Name the sides of the triangle that are perpendicular.

Solving Problems

Horst Schafer/Photo Trends

1. The 1500-meter run is held at the Olympics. Is that distance more than or less than 1 kilometer?

2. Each of the 4 people on a relay team runs 400 meters. How many meters long is the relay race?

3. Another Olympic event is the 50,000-meter walk. Find how many kilometers that is.

4. The 50,000-meter walk was completed in 4 hours. Find the average speed in meters per hour.

5. One woman threw the discus 66.2 meters. Another woman threw it 58.4 meters. Find the difference between these two distances.

6. In the high jump, one man jumped 213.8 centimeters. A second man jumped 9 centimeters higher. How high did the second man jump?

CHAPTER REVIEW

Give the length of each line segment to the nearest unit.

1.
millimeters
10   20   30

2.
centimeters
1   2   3   4   5   6

3.
centimeters
1   2   3   4   5   6   7   8   9   10   11   12

Choose the unit of measure that would be more convenient to find the following:

4. distance from New York to Chicago   a. km   b. cm

5. thickness of a dime   a. m   b. mm

6. your weight   a. g   b. kg

7. amount of water in a swimming pool   a. liters   b. mL

Complete.

8. 100 cm = ___ m   9. 2 liters = ___ mL

10. 0.75 kg = ___ g   11. 600 mL = ___ liters

12. 20 g = ___ kg   13. 130 mm = ___ cm

14. Water freezes at 32°F or ___°C.   15. Water boils at 100°C or ___°F.

16. The weights of three children are 42 kg, 35 kg, and 40 kg. Their average weight is ___ kg.

11 Perimeter, Area, Volume

Joan Kramer and Associates

Perimeter

The distance around a figure is its **perimeter.**

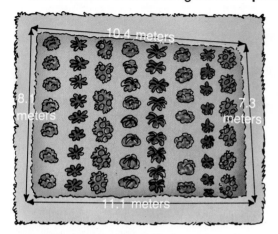

You can find the *perimeter* of the garden by adding the measures of its sides.

$$
\begin{array}{r}
8.1 \\
10.4 \\
7.3 \\
+\,11.1 \\
\hline
36.9
\end{array}
$$

The perimeter is 36.9 meters.

Let p stand for the measure of the perimeter of the rectangle.

$p = 8 + 3 + 8 + 3$

$p = (2 \times 8) + (2 \times 3)$

$p = 2 \times (8 + 3)$

8 units

3 units   3 units

8 units

What is the perimeter of the rectangle?

Which way would you use to find the perimeter?

Exercises

Find the perimeter of each figure.

1.

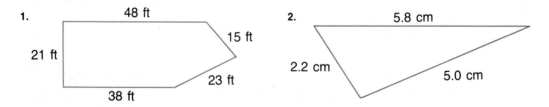

48 ft
15 ft
21 ft
23 ft
38 ft

2.

5.8 cm
2.2 cm
5.0 cm

3.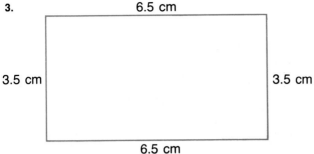

6.5 cm
3.5 cm
3.5 cm
6.5 cm

4.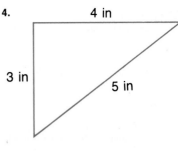

4 in
3 in
5 in

5.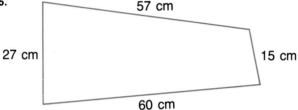

57 cm
27 cm
15 cm
60 cm

6.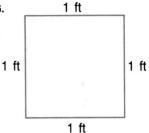

1 ft
1 ft
1 ft
1 ft

7. The perimeter of the triangle at the right is 26 centimeters. Find the length of side AB.

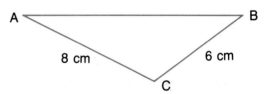

A
B
8 cm
6 cm
C

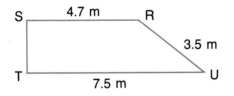

S
4.7 m
R
3.5 m
T
7.5 m
U

8. The perimeter of the figure at the left is 17.8 meters. What is the length of side ST?

9. Mary wants to put a string border around a square picture. Each side is 10 centimeters long. How much string does she need?

10. A rectangular swimming pool is 12 meters long and 8 meters wide. Find the perimeter of the pool.

11. The perimeter of a square lot is 320 meters. How long is each side?

12. The perimeter of a rectangle is 20 centimeters. It is 8 centimeters long. How wide is it?

Area

How many square units like this are needed to cover the inside of the rectangle?

The **area** of the rectangle is *8 square units.*

Units like these shown below are used to find the area of a figure.

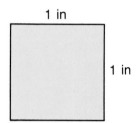

Name:	**square centimeter**	**square millimeter**	**square inch**
Symbol:	**cm²**	**mm²**	**in²**

The following units of area are too large to fit on this page. Tell how you could make a model of each unit.

square meter (m²)   **square foot (ft²)**

square kilometer (km²)   **square mile (mi²)**

Exercises

1 square unit is shown in red for each figure below. Find the area of each figure.

1.
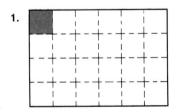

2.
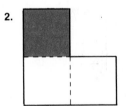

3.
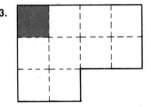

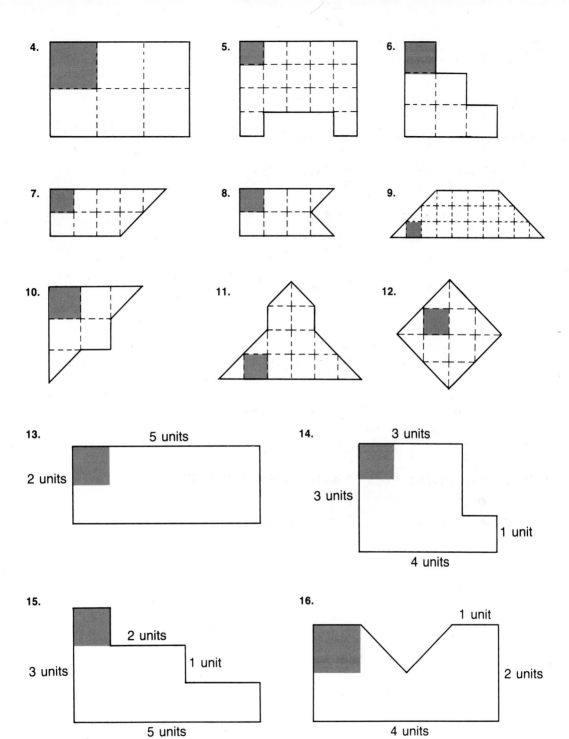

4.

5.

6.

7.

8.

9.

10.

11.

12.

13.
5 units
2 units

14.
3 units
3 units
4 units
1 unit

15.
2 units
3 units
1 unit
5 units

16.
1 unit
2 units
4 units

257

Area of a Rectangle

How many columns of squares are there?

What is the measure of the length?

How many squares are in each column?

What is the measure of the width?

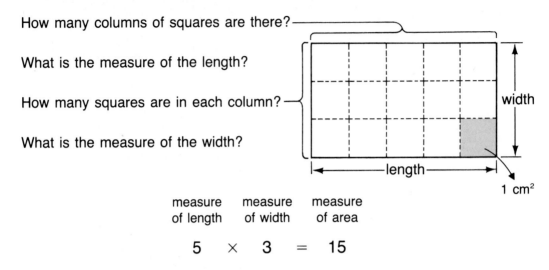

1 cm²

measure of length   measure of width   measure of area

5   ×   3   =   15

The area is *15 square centimeters* or *15 cm².*

By using this idea you can develop a formula for the area of a rectangle.

A **formula** is a math sentence that states a general rule.

A square units w units

l units

measure of area   measure of length   measure of width

$$A = l \times w$$

Exercises

Find the area of each rectangle.

1. $A = l \times w$

$$\begin{array}{r} 15 \\ \times 2.7 \\ \hline \end{array}$$

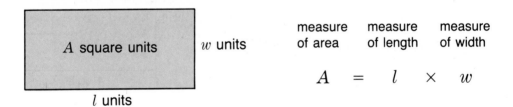

2.7 ft

15 ft

2.

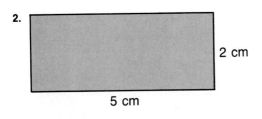

2 cm

5 cm

3.

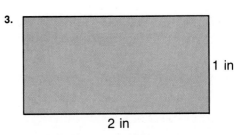

1 in

2 in

4.

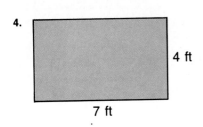

4 ft

7 ft

5.

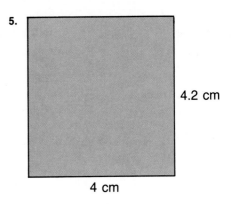

4.2 cm

4 cm

6.

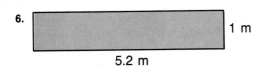

1 m

5.2 m

7. A quart of paint will cover 85 square feet. A wall is 8 feet long and 6 feet tall. Will 1 quart of paint cover 1 wall? 2 walls?

8. A rectangular lawn is 80 feet by 125 feet. One bag of fertilizer will cover 5000 square feet. How many bags of fertilizer are needed?

9. A clubhouse floor is 8 feet long and 11 feet wide. Tile for the floor costs 50¢ per square foot. How much will it cost to tile the floor?

10. A box of tile will cover 45 square feet and sells for $25.50. How much will it cost to tile a floor that is 9 feet wide and 15 feet long?

11. A floor is 12 feet long and 9 feet wide. How many 9-inch–by–9-inch tiles are needed to cover the floor?

12. A rectangular floor is 25 feet long. Its area is 375 square feet. How wide is the floor?

Area of a Right Triangle

What is the area of rectangle ABCD?

Are the two right triangles the same size?

What is the area of each right triangle?

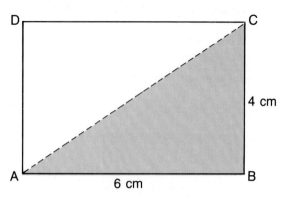

4 cm

6 cm

By using this idea, you can develop a formula for finding the area of any right triangle.

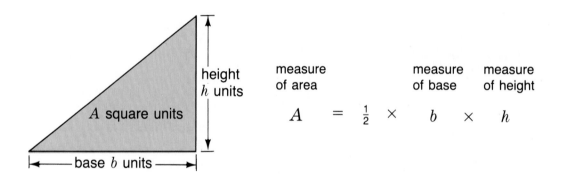

height
h units

A square units

base b units

measure of area		measure of base	measure of height
A	$= \frac{1}{2} \times$	$b \times$	h

You can use the formula to find the area of triangle ABC at the top of the page.

$$A = \frac{1}{2} \times b \times h$$

$$= \frac{1}{2} \times 6 \times 4$$

$$= 12$$

The area is 12 square centimeters.

Exercises

Find the area of each right triangle.

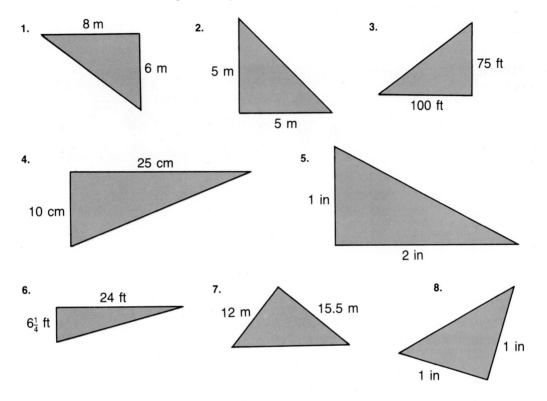

1. 8 m, 6 m

2. 5 m, 5 m

3. 75 ft, 100 ft

4. 25 cm, 10 cm

5. 1 in, 2 in

6. 24 ft, $6\frac{1}{4}$ ft

7. 12 m, 15.5 m

8. 1 in, 1 in

Find the area of the end of each building.

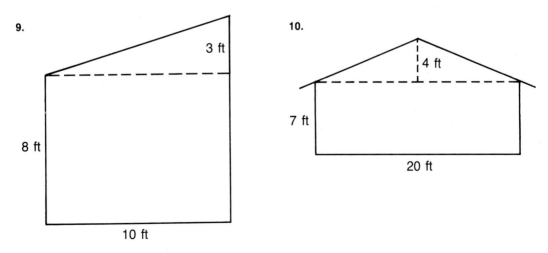

9. 3 ft, 8 ft, 10 ft

10. 4 ft, 7 ft, 20 ft

Solving Problems

1. Sue cut along the diagonal of this rectangular sheet of plastic. Find the area of each piece.

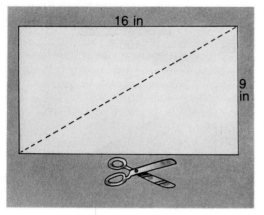

2. A small park has the shape of a right triangle. Find the area of the park.

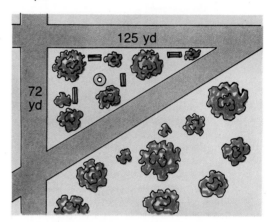

3. Mrs. Avery made a triangular garden in one corner of her yard. Find the area of her garden.

4. If each tomato plant needs 9 square feet, how many tomato plants should she have in her garden?

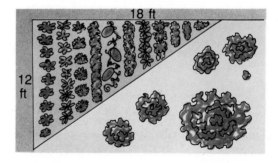

5. Jon is going to put new sails on his sailboat. How many square feet of material does he need for the mainsail?

6. Jon bought 90 square feet of material. Does he have enough for the mainsail and the jib?

7. Jon is spending $2.50 a square foot for the material. How much will the material for the new jib cost?

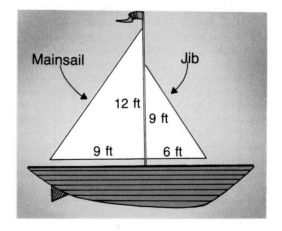

Area and Perimeter

Make and complete a table like this for the perimeter and the area of each rectangle.

Rectangle	l	w	p	A
A				
B				
C				
D				
E				

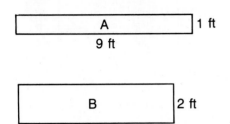

A
9 ft · 1 ft

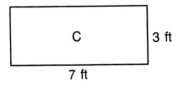

B
8 ft · 2 ft

C
7 ft · 3 ft

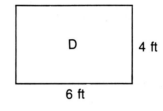

D
6 ft · 4 ft

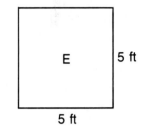

E
5 ft · 5 ft

1. What do you discover about the perimeters?

2. If two rectangles have the same perimeter, do they have the same area?

3. Which rectangle has the greatest area? What is the shape of that rectangle?

4. Peggy has 16 feet of fence. She wants to make a rectangular rabbit pen with the greatest area. How long and how wide should she make the pen?

5. Ronnie has 45 feet of fence for 3 sides of a pen. A barn will form the fourth side. To get the greatest area, how long and how wide should he make the pen?

Volume

Some cubes are already in the box. How many more cubes are needed to fill the box?

How many cubes would be in the box then?

The **volume** of the box is *12 cubic units.*

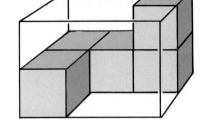

Units like these shown below are used to find the volume.

	cubic centimeter	cubic inch
Name :	**cubic centimeter**	**cubic inch**
Symbol :	**cm³**	**in³**

Tell how you could make a model for each unit.

cubic millimeter (mm³)   **cubic meter (m³)**

cubic foot (ft³)   **cubic yard (yd³)**

Exercises

Find the volume of each figure below in cubic units.

1. 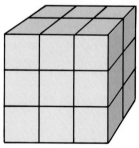   **2.** 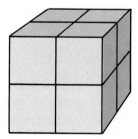   **3.**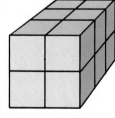

4.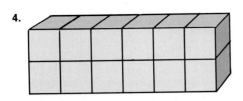

5.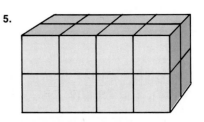

6.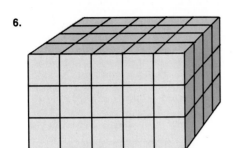

7.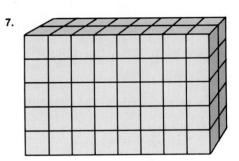

8.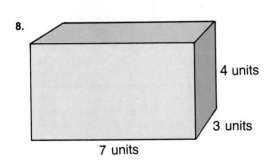

4 units

3 units

7 units

9.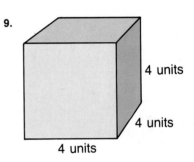

4 units

4 units

4 units

10.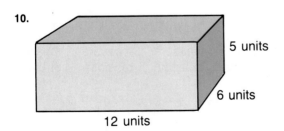

5 units

6 units

12 units

11.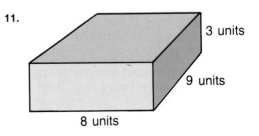

3 units

9 units

8 units

Volume

A rectangular prism has three dimensions, **length, width,** and **height.**

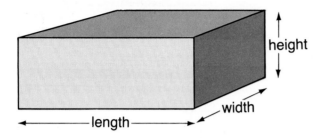

Here is one way to find the volume of a rectangular prism.

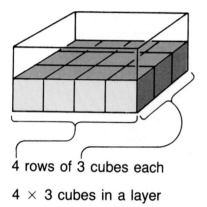

4 rows of 3 cubes each

4 × 3 cubes in a layer

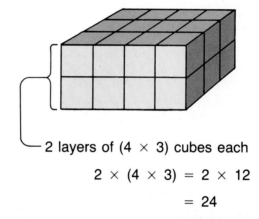

2 layers of (4 × 3) cubes each

$$2 \times (4 \times 3) = 2 \times 12$$
$$= 24$$

The volume is 24 cubic units.

You can also find the volume of the rectangular prism by using this formula.

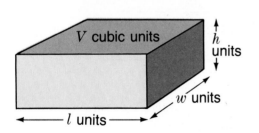

measure of volume	measure of length	measure of width	measure of height
V	=	l	×	w	×	h
	=	4	×	3	×	2
	=	24				

Exercises

Find the volume of each rectangular prism.

1. $V = l \times w \times h$

   $= 6 \times 2 \times 3$

   $= \underline{\hspace{2em}}$

   The volume is ___ cm³.

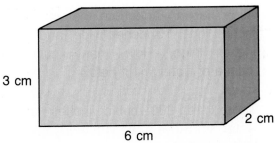

3 cm
6 cm
2 cm

2.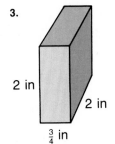

5 ft
4 ft
7 ft

3.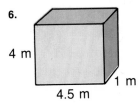

2 in
2 in
$\frac{3}{4}$ in

4.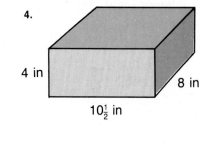

4 in
8 in
$10\frac{1}{2}$ in

5.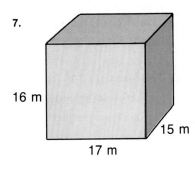

6 cm
2 cm
4 cm

6.

4 m
1 m
4.5 m

7.

16 m
15 m
17 m

8.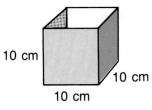

10 cm
10 cm
10 cm

This prism can hold 1 liter of water.

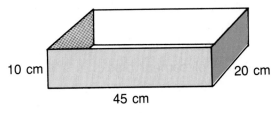

10 cm
20 cm
45 cm

How many liters of water can this prism hold?

Solving Problems

1. Alma has an aquarium that is 24 inches long, 10 inches wide, and 7 inches high. How many cubic inches of water will it hold?

2. There are 800 cubic inches of water in Steve's aquarium. Could he put all that water into a container that is 10 inches by 10 inches by 10 inches?

3. How many cubic inches are there in a cubic foot?

4. How many cubic feet are there in a cubic yard?

5. The Frosts' swimming pool is 6 feet deep. Find the volume of their pool.

6. There are 7.5 gallons per cubic foot of water. How many gallons of water are needed to fill the pool?

7. The Whiz Company packs 25 Whiz Bangs per cubic foot. How many Whiz Bangs can be packed in a crate that is 1 foot by 2 feet by 3 feet?

8. A pile of cement blocks is 20 feet long, 10 feet wide, and 8 feet high. The volume of each block is 1 cubic foot. How many blocks are there?

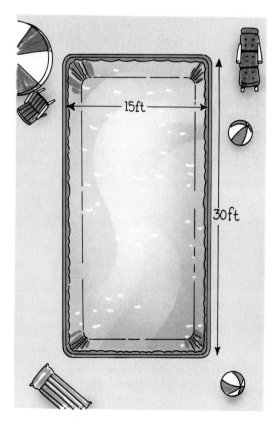

9. Elmer put a small rock in this container and poured in water until the rock was completely under water. Then he measured the depth of the water.

   Then he removed the rock and measured the depth of the water again.

   What is the volume of the rock?

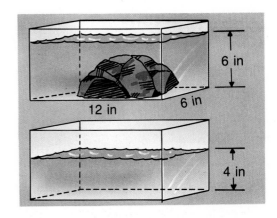

10. A container is 15 inches long, 8 inches wide, and 11 inches high. How many quarts of liquid will it hold? (Hint: 1 quart = 58 cubic inches.)

11. A can is 16 centimeters long, 2.5 centimeters wide, and 10 centimeters high. It is 25% filled with oil. Find the volume of the oil.

Dig This

One man dug a hole 6 feet by 6 feet by 6 feet. Another man dug 2 holes—each hole was 3 feet by 3 feet by 3 feet. Which man dug the most dirt?

Find each answer in simplest form.

1. $\frac{5}{8}$
$+\frac{7}{8}$

2. $1\frac{3}{10}$
$+ \frac{9}{10}$

3. $\frac{2}{3}$
$+\frac{5}{6}$

4. $\frac{3}{4}$
$+\frac{4}{5}$

5. $2\frac{1}{5}$
$+6\frac{7}{10}$

6. $\frac{9}{10}$
$-\frac{3}{10}$

7. $2\frac{4}{5}$
$-\frac{3}{5}$

8. $\frac{1}{2}$
$-\frac{2}{5}$

9. $\frac{7}{8}$
$-\frac{2}{3}$

10. $1\frac{1}{3}$
$-\frac{5}{6}$

11. $\frac{1}{2} \times \frac{1}{5}$

12. $\frac{3}{8} \times \frac{2}{9}$

13. $\frac{1}{3} \times 1\frac{1}{2}$

14. $3 \times 2\frac{1}{3}$

15. $1\frac{1}{4} \times 2\frac{2}{5}$

16. $3\frac{1}{3} \times 4\frac{1}{2}$

Find each sum, difference, or product.

17. 5.92
$+0.88$

18. 1.97
-0.89

19. $45.63
$- 21.71$

20. $17.62
$+ 18.47$

21. 0.3
$\times 6$

22. 4
$\times 0.02$

23. 276.5
$\times 13$

24. 916
$\times 0.046$

At the right is a bill from the hobby shop. The sales tax is 5%. Find the following:

25. the subtotal

26. the tax

27. the amount due

Howe's Hobby House

$1.78
0.56
2.26
6.40

Subtotal

Tax

Amount due

Solve each problem. If the problem cannot be solved, tell what is missing.

28. It took Bonita and Rosa 8 hours to drive home. Rosa drove 25% of the time. How many hours did Bonita drive?

29. Diane's car used 8.6 gallons of gasoline for the trip to see her father. Her car gets 25 miles per gallon. How far did she travel?

30. Homer's car gets 32 miles per gallon. How many gallons of gasoline will his car use to go 128 miles?

31. 63% of the pupils in Donna's class are boys. How many of her classmates are boys?

32. Evan ran the 100-yard dash in 12.30 seconds. Cyril ran it in 12.37 seconds. Who had the better time? How much better was it?

33. A model-plane kit has a regular price of $4.59. It is on sale for $3.89. By how much is the price reduced?

34. The regular price of the baseball bat will be reduced by 10% for a sale. What will be the sale price of the baseball bat?

35. Oran bought a football for $14.95 and a soccer ball for $16.85. How much did he pay for both?

CHAPTER REVIEW

Find the perimeter of each figure.

1.

3 ft   4 ft   1 ft   3 ft   3 ft

2.

4 m   3 m   5 m   2 m   2 m   7 m

Find the area of each rectangle.

3.

6 miles   3 miles

4.

12 m   5 m

Find the area of each right triangle.

5.

7 ft   10 ft

6.

14 m   6 m

Find the volume of each figure.

7.

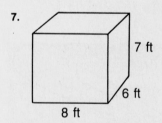
7 ft   6 ft   8 ft

8.

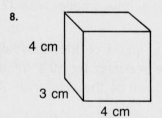
4 cm   3 cm   4 cm

9. A box is 6 feet long, 3 feet wide, and 5 feet high. Find the volume of the box.

10. A tank 5 feet long, 3 feet wide, and 8 feet high is half full of water. Find the volume of the water.

12 Graphs

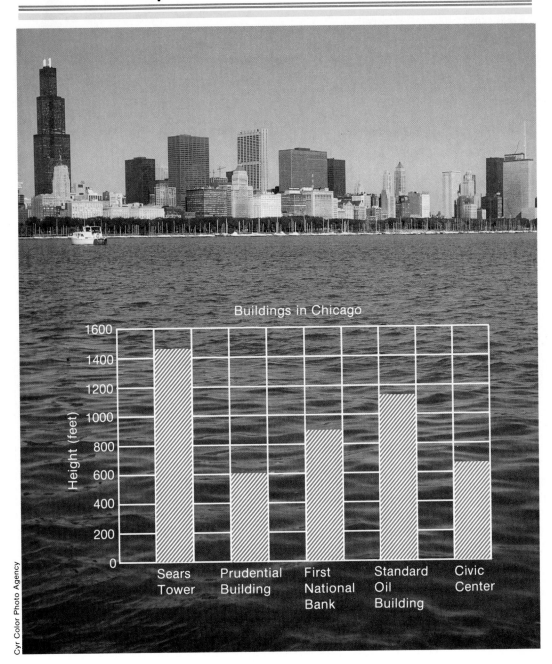

Buildings in Chicago

Grid Game

GRID–DART Rules

Each player has a board with a blue target (4 holes inside it).

Players try to hit each other's target. They take turns calling their shots.

Your opponent tells whether you "Hit" or "Miss" the target.

The first player to hit all four holes in the target wins.

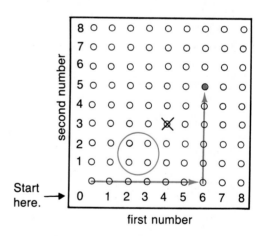

6,5

GRID-DART

When Sue says "Six, five," Alan puts a marker in column 6, hole 5. The marker is not in the target, so Alan says "Miss."

Here is a way to locate the hole for *the pair 6,5,* or (6,5).

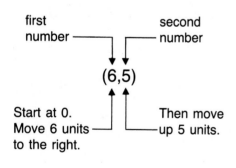

first number ⟶
⟶ second number

(6,5)

Start at 0.
Move 6 units to the right.
Then move up 5 units.

On her next turn, Sue wants to hit the hole marked X. What should she say?

What number pairs does Sue need to win the game?

274

Exercises

The letters on this grid show where Alan placed his darts. Tell the pair of numbers for each letter.

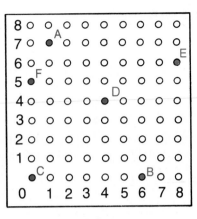

1. A

2. B

3. C

4. D

5. E

6. F

Use grid paper to make these two GRID–DART boards. Mark the hole for each dart.

Your Board

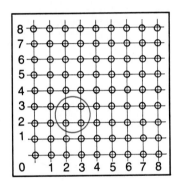

Opponent's darts

7. (6,0)

8. (8,8)

9. (3,4)

10. (7,2)

11. (2,4)

12. (1,1)

13. (1,3)

14. (3,3)

15. (2,3)

16. (3,2)

Opponent's Board

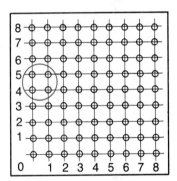

Your darts

17. (7,7)

18. (5,8)

19. (6,4)

20. (8,0)

21. (7,3)

22. (1,6)

23. (0,5)

24. (0,4)

25. (1,4)

26. (1,5)

27. Who won the game?

Ordered Pairs

Here is how to graph (2,7) and (7,2).

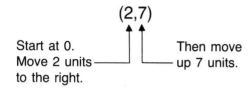

Start at 0.
Move 2 units —
to the right.

Then move
— up 7 units.

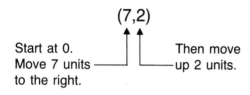

Start at 0.
Move 7 units —
to the right.

Then move
— up 2 units.

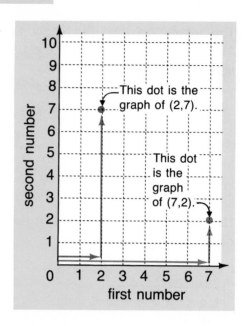

Do (2,7) and (7,2) name the same point?

Since the numbers in each pair are given in a specific order, a pair like (2,7) or (7,2) is an **ordered pair.**

Tell how you would graph each ordered pair below.

(2,6)   (6,2)   (1,1)   (3,0)

Exercises

Write the ordered pair for each of these points.

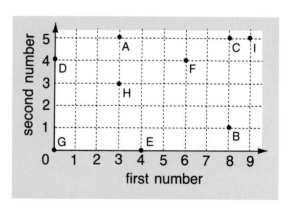

1. A   2. B   3. C

4. D   5. E   6. F

7. G   8. H   9. I

Write the ordered pair for each of
these points.

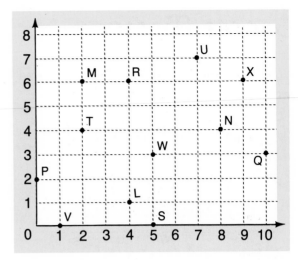

10. L

11. M

12. N

13. P

14. Q

15. R

16. S

17. T

18. U

19. V

20. W

21. X

Draw and label two number lines like those above. Graph each of the following
ordered pairs. Label the graph of each ordered pair with its letter.

22. A(3,5)

23. B(5,3)

24. C(7,0)

25. D(0,7)

26. E(1,2)

27. F(3,0)

28. G(7,6)

29. H(3,3)

30. I(4,2)

31. J(8,2)

32. K(6,7)

33. L(0,1)

34. M(1,1)

35. N(10,0)

36. P(6,5)

37. Q(0,0)

Graph a Picture

Draw two number lines and label each from 0
through 12. Graph each ordered pair. Then use a
straightedge to connect the points *in the order they
were graphed.*

(6,9), (6,12), (7,11), (6,11), (3,3), (6,3), (6,9),

(10,3), (6,3), (6,2), (0,2), (2,0), (11,0), (12,2), (6,2)

Extra Practice—Set A, page 348

Secret Messages

To decode a word, locate each ordered pair and write the letter for that point.

Example: (8,1), (6,6), (0,3)

F   U   N

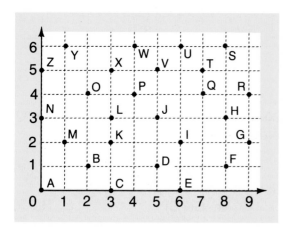

In the following messages, a ▌ is used between words.

1. Decode the message and do what it says.

   (8,6), (6,0), (0,3), (5,1) ▌ (0,0) ▌ (8,6), (6,0), (3,0), (9,4), (6,0), (7,5) ▌ (1,2), (6,0), (8,6), (8,6), (0,0), (9,2), (6,0) ▌ (7,5), (2,4) ▌ (0,0) ▌ (8,1), (9,4), (6,2), (6,0), (0,3), (5,1).

2. Decode this message.

   (1,6), (2,4), (6,6) ▌ (0,0), (9,4), (6,0) ▌ (5,1), (2,4), (6,2), (0,3), (9,2) ▌ (8,1), (6,2), (0,3), (6,0) ▌ (4,6), (6,2), (7,5), (8,3) ▌ (2,4), (9,4), (5,1), (6,0), (9,4), (6,0), (5,1) ▌ (4,4), (0,0), (6,2), (9,4), (8,6).

278

World Grid

Latitude Lines

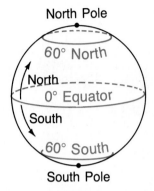

North Pole

60° North

North

0° Equator

South

60° South

South Pole

Longitude Lines

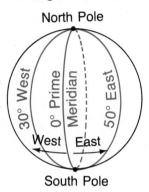

North Pole

30° West

0° Prime Meridian

50° East

West   East

South Pole

Latitude and longitude lines on a globe form a grid. You can use ordered pairs to locate points on the earth. The first number is *latitude.* The second number is *longitude.*

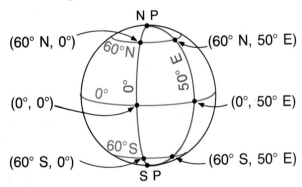

(60° N, 0°)

(60° N, 50° E)

(0°, 0°)

(0°, 50° E)

(60° S, 0°)

(60° S, 50° E)

N P

S P

60°N

0°

0°

50° E

60°S

Use a globe. In what country is each point located?

1. (15° N, 30° E)

2. (45° N, 90° E)

3. (15° S, 45° W)

4. (60° N, 120° W)

5. (60° N, 60° E)

6. (30° S, 120° E)

Name an ordered pair to approximately locate each city.

7. New Orleans, Louisiana

8. Shanghai, China

9. Manila, Philippines

10. Cairo, Egypt

Making Tables

To elect a class president, the pupils voted by ballot. When the ballots were collected, they looked like this.

Can you tell at a glance who won the election? Or, was there a tie vote?

To make it easier to see who won, you could record the votes like this.

Each | stands for one vote.

Eli	⅃⅃⅃⅂	5
Jerry	|||	3
Chan	⅃⅃⅃⅂ ||	7
Cindy	⅃⅃⅃⅂ ⅃⅃⅃⅂	10
Kim	||||	4

Exercises

1. Each child wrote his or her age, in years, on the chalkboard. Using the picture, copy and complete the table below.

Age (years)	9	10	11	12	13
Number of children					

2. Copy the table below. Measure each nail to the nearest centimeter. Complete the table.

Length (cm)	3	4	5	6	7
Number of nails					

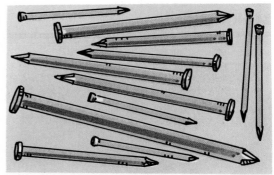

3. Copy and complete the table below.

Name	Number of coins
Pennies	
Nickels	
Dimes	
Quarters	

4. Each child wrote the number of children in his or her family. Copy and complete the table.

Number of children	1	2	3	4	5	6
Number of families						

Raul—4	Paula—4	Janice—2
Phil—2	Jill—3	Kim—3
Gwen—4	Jim—2	Sarah—1
Sue—5	Frank—2	Bill—5
Sam—3	John—1	Bob—4
Jack—6	Joan—6	Dave—2

5. Ask each pupil in class for his or her birthday month. Make a table like the one below to show the results.

Birthday month	Jan.	Feb.	Mar.	Apr.	May	June	July	Aug.	Sept.	Oct.	Nov.	Dec.
Number of pupils												

Making Tables

The satellite makes 1 orbit around the earth in 2 hours.

Number of orbits	1	2	3	4	5
Time (hours)	2	4	6	?	

2 × 2 2 × 3 2 × 4

How many orbits will the satellite make in 4 hours?

Explain how you would complete the table.

Exercises

Copy and complete each table.

1.  12¢

Number of pencils	1	2	3	4
Cost (cents)				

2. A boat travels 15 miles each hour.

Time (hours)	1	2	3	4	5
Distance (miles)					

3. There are 27 feet of tape in 1 roll.

Number of rolls	1	2	3	4	5
Feet of tape					

4. Spritz cologne costs $45 an ounce.

Number of ounces	1	2	3	4
Cost (dollars)				

5. The perimeter of a square is 4 times the length of a side.

Length of a side (cm)	1	2	3	4	5	6
Perimeter (cm)						

6. A car can go 25 miles on each gallon of gasoline.

Number of gallons	1	2	3	4
Distance (miles)				

7.

Number of servings					
Weight (kg)	1	2	3	4	5

1 kilogram will serve 4 people.

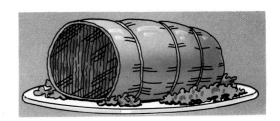

Making Line Graphs

A table, like the one shown below, is actually a list of ordered pairs.

Number of orbits	0	1	2	3	4	5
Time (hours)	0	2	4	6	8	10
Ordered pairs	(0,0)	(1,2)	(2,4)	(3,6)	(4,8)	(5,10)

You already know how to graph such ordered pairs. By doing so, you can show the information by a **line graph.**

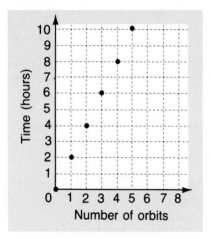

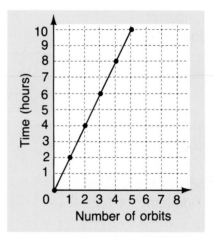

Draw and label two number lines on grid paper. Then graph the ordered pairs.

To make the graph easier to read, draw line segments between the points.

How could you use the line graph to tell how many hours for $2\frac{1}{2}$ orbits?

How could you use the line graph to tell how many orbits in 7 hours?

Exercises

Make a line graph from each table below.

1.

Number of packages	0	1	2	3
Number of pieces	0	4	8	12

2.

Number of tickets	0	1	2	3	4
Cost (dollars)	0	2	4	6	8

3.

Number of sides of a figure	3	4	5	6	7
Number of diagonals	0	2	5	9	14

4.

Number of sides of a figure	0	1	2	3	4
Number of angles	0	1	2	3	4

For each picture below, copy and complete the table. Then make a line graph from each table.

5.

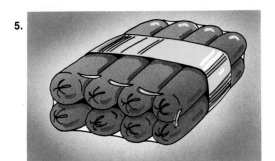

Number of packages	0	1	2	3	4
Number of hot dogs					

6.

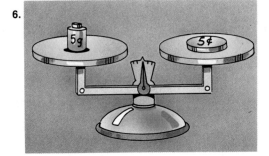

Number of nickels	0	2	4	6
Weight (grams)				

Reading Line Graphs

The table and line graph below show how fast an 8-inch candle melted. The line graph shows more information than the table.

Time (hours)	Height (inches)
0	8
1	7
2	6
3	5
4	4
5	3

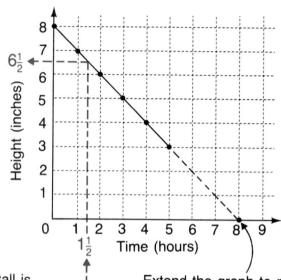

How tall is the candle after $1\frac{1}{2}$ hours? – – – – – ⌐
It is about $6\frac{1}{2}$ inches tall.

Extend the graph to meet the time scale. Then you can predict that in 8 hours the candle would be completely melted.

Exercises

Use the line graph to answer the following:

1. How many miles were traveled in 4 hours?

2. How many hours did it take to go 100 miles?

3. What distance would be traveled in $2\frac{1}{2}$ hours? In 5 hours?

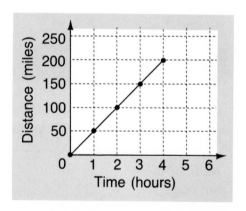

Use the line graph below to answer exercises 4–10.

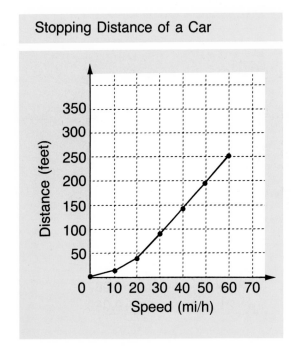

Stopping Distance of a Car

4. How many miles per hour does each segment of the speed scale represent?

5. What distance does each segment of the distance scale represent?

6. How many feet does it take a car traveling 20 miles per hour to stop?

7. Can a car going 60 miles per hour be stopped in less than 200 feet?

8. One car is following another at 40 miles per hour. What is a safe distance between them?

9. It takes 190 feet to stop a car. What is the speed of the car?

10. Predict the stopping distance for 70 miles per hour.

Use the line graph below to answer exercises 11–14.

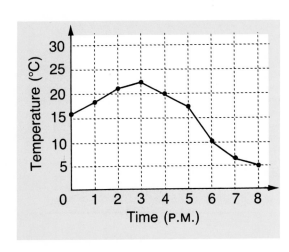

11. At what time was the temperature highest?

12. Between which two hours did the greatest change in temperature occur?

13. At about what time was the temperature 10°C?

14. What was the temperature at about 1:30 P.M.?

287

SKILLS REVIEW

Find each answer in simplest form.

1. $\frac{2}{3} \times \frac{5}{6}$

2. $1\frac{1}{2} \times \frac{2}{3}$

3. $5\frac{1}{2} \times 6$

4. $2\frac{2}{3} \times 1\frac{3}{4}$

5. $\frac{7}{10} + \frac{2}{5}$

6. $\frac{3}{4} + \frac{2}{3}$

7. $2\frac{1}{2} + 1\frac{7}{8}$

8. $1\frac{5}{6} + 2\frac{4}{9}$

9. $\frac{5}{8} - \frac{1}{2}$

10. $1\frac{1}{4} - \frac{1}{8}$

11. $5\frac{1}{2} - 2\frac{3}{10}$

12. $3\frac{1}{3} - 2\frac{3}{4}$

13. $\frac{2}{3} + 2$

14. $10 - \frac{2}{5}$

15. $\frac{5}{8} + \frac{15}{16}$

16. $7\frac{3}{5} - 2\frac{2}{3}$

17. $\begin{array}{r} 0.623 \\ +0.176 \\ \hline \end{array}$

18. $\begin{array}{r} 30.712 \\ +17.297 \\ \hline \end{array}$

19. $\begin{array}{r} 58.62 \\ +\ 1.41 \\ \hline \end{array}$

20. $\begin{array}{r} 60.35 \\ +78.96 \\ \hline \end{array}$

21. $\begin{array}{r} 0.327 \\ -0.113 \\ \hline \end{array}$

22. $\begin{array}{r} 1.62 \\ -0.57 \\ \hline \end{array}$

23. $\begin{array}{r} 57.16 \\ -41.21 \\ \hline \end{array}$

24. $\begin{array}{r} 0.087 \\ -0.069 \\ \hline \end{array}$

25. $\begin{array}{r} 30 \\ \times 0.7 \\ \hline \end{array}$

26. $\begin{array}{r} 156 \\ \times 0.15 \\ \hline \end{array}$

27. $\begin{array}{r} 2.65 \\ \times 25 \\ \hline \end{array}$

28. $\begin{array}{r} 0.087 \\ \times 56 \\ \hline \end{array}$

Use a ruler to find the length of each line segment to the nearest centimeter.

29. _____

30. _____

31. _____

Find the area of each figure below.

32.

2 cm | Rectangle | 5 cm

33.

2 cm | Right Triangle | 6 cm

288

34. Find the cost of three 8-ounce cans of tuna.

35. Find the cost of 8 pounds of bananas.

36. Which costs more—2 small bottles of catsup or 1 large bottle of catsup? How much more?

37. Beryl bought 1 can of tuna, 6 pounds of bananas, and 1 can of soup. How much did she spend?

38. How many 8-ounce cans of tuna are needed to get 72 ounces of tuna?

39. How much can you save by buying 3 cans of soup at the same time rather than one at a time?

40. Kerry bought a 24-ounce can of tuna. The sales tax was 5%. What was his total bill?

41. Mary bought a 16-ounce bottle of catsup and 2 cans of soup. The sales tax was 6%. What was her total bill?

42. Find the cost per ounce of the catsup in the 8-ounce bottle. Find the cost per ounce in the 16-ounce bottle. Which is the better buy?

43. This store also has a 16-ounce can of tuna on sale for $2.72. Which of the three cans of tuna is the best buy?

Bar Graphs

Mrs. Larson made **bar graphs** to show how many books were checked out of the library during one week.

Vertical Bar Graph

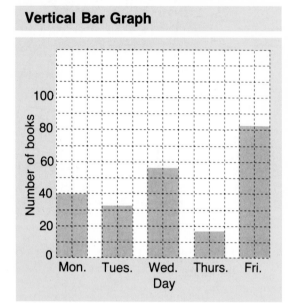

Horizontal Bar Graph

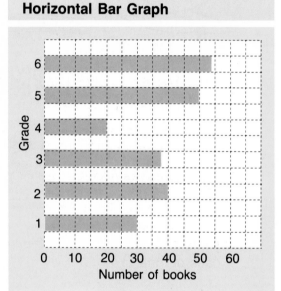

In a bar graph, the width of each bar is the same. So is the amount of space between bars.

Exercises

Use the bar graphs above to answer the following:

1. On which day of the week were the most books checked out?

2. Which grade checked out the fewest books?

3. About how many books did the third grade check out?

4. About how many books were checked out on Thursday?

5. About how many books did the sixth grade check out?

6. Which grade checked out twice as many books as the fourth grade?

Long Jump

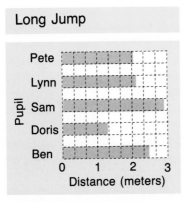

Use the bar graph above to answer the following:

7. Is this a horizontal bar graph or a vertical bar graph?

8. Who made the longest jump?

9. Which two pupils jumped almost the same distance?

10. Who made the shortest jump?

Use the bar graph below. Copy and complete the table.

11. **Pupils Absent**

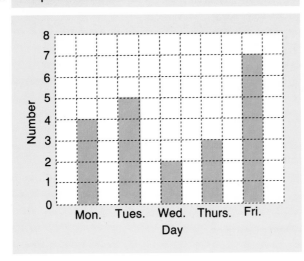

Day	Pupils Absent
Mon.	

291

Making Bar Graphs

The table below shows the results of a class election as given on page 280. Let's make a bar graph from the table.

Pupil	Number of votes		Think of these as ordered pairs.
Eli	5	(Eli,5)	
Jerry	3	(Jerry,3)	
Chan	7	(Chan,7)	
Cindy	10	(Cindy,10)	
Kim	4	(Kim,4)	

Decide whether you will make a vertical or a horizontal graph. Choose the width of each bar and the amount of space between bars. Then make the graph. Here are two possible choices.

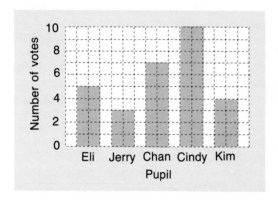 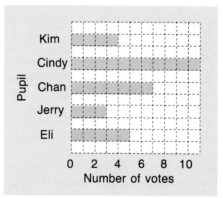

How do you determine the length of each bar?

Do the names have to be in the order shown on these graphs?

Can you suggest an order of the names that would make the graph easier to read?

Exercises

Make a bar graph from each table.

1. Chess-Club Attendance

Month	Number of pupils
Oct.	18
Nov.	20
Dec.	16
Jan.	24
Feb.	22

2. Club Membership

Club	Number of pupils
Chess	26
Checkers	24
Photography	8
Theater	18
Volleyball	20

3. Favorite Subject

Subject	Mathematics	Science	English	Other
Number of votes	12	10	7	3

4. Favorite Color

Color	Red	Blue	Yellow	Green	Orange
Number of votes	9	12	3	8	6

5. Take a vote of a group of pupils on their favorite sport. Make a bar graph to show the results.

6. Make a bar graph to show the birthday months of the pupils in your class.

Circle Graphs

A **circle graph** is used to show how one part of a quantity compares with another part or with the entire quantity.

The inside of the circle represents all of George's allowance. The inside is separated into parts to show how he spends his allowance.

Exercises

Use the circle graph at the right to answer these questions.

1. For what does George spend the most of his allowance?

2. For what does George spend the least of his allowance?

3. The inside of the circle represents what percent of his allowance?

4. What percent of his allowance does George spend on hobbies?

5. What percent of his allowance does George save?

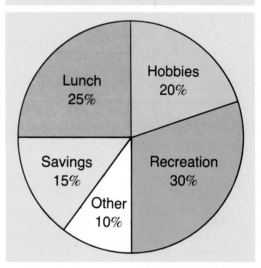

How George Spends His Allowance

6. Does he spend more of his allowance for recreation or for lunches?

7. For what does he spend $\frac{3}{10}$ of his allowance?

8. George's allowance is $10. How much does he spend for recreation?

9. How much of his $10 allowance does he save?

Use the circle graph to answer the following questions:

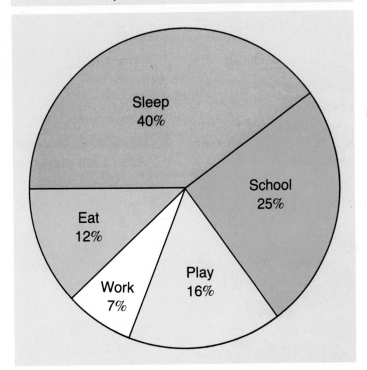

How Laura Spends Her Time Each School Day

Sleep
40%

School
25%

Eat
12%

Work
7%

Play
16%

10. What percent of her time does she spend eating?

11. What percent of her time does she spend sleeping?

12. On what activity does she spend 25% of her time?

13. On what activity does she spend the least time?

14. What percent of her time does she spend working or playing?

15. What percent of the time is Laura awake?

16. What is the sum of the percents in the graph?

17. How many hours a day does she spend in school?

18. How many hours a day does Laura sleep?

19. How many hours a day is Laura awake?

CHAPTER REVIEW

Graph each ordered pair on grid paper. Label the graph of each ordered pair with its letter.

1. A(3,5)
2. B(1,2)
3. C(2,1)
4. D(0,4)

Complete the following:

These are the votes cast in an election for club president.

5. Make a table showing how many votes each pupil received.

6. Make a line graph to show the election results.

7. Make a bar graph to show the election results.

8. Who got the most votes?

9. Who got the fewest votes?

Use the circle graph to answer the following:

10. What did most pupils do during the summer?

11. What percent of the pupils went to camp?

12. How did about $\frac{1}{4}$ of the pupils spend their summer vacation?

How Pupils Spent Summer Vacation

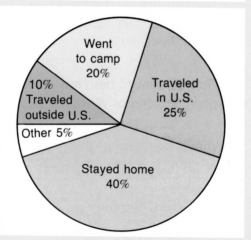

13 Probability

Joan Kramer and Associates

Experimenting

Put these checkers in a box.

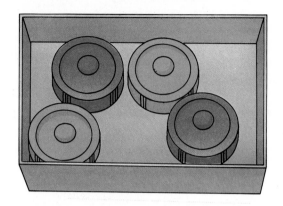

Did you get more red, more black, or the same number of each?

How many checkers are there? How many of them are red?

2 out of 4, or $\frac{2}{4}$, or $\frac{1}{2}$ of the checkers are red.

Jody made 20 draws.
This table shows her results.

Red	⊞⊞ IIII	9 times
Black	⊞⊞ ⊞⊞ I	11 times

Did she get a red checker about $\frac{1}{2}$ of the time?

Exercises

1. Guess how many times you will get a red checker in 30 draws.

2. Try it. Record your results in a table.

3. Did you get a red checker about $\frac{1}{2}$ of the time?

4. Try it again for 40 draws.

5. Did you get a red checker about $\frac{1}{2}$ of the time?

A six-sided pencil has
printing on one side.

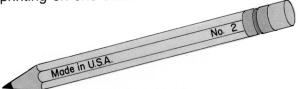

You are to roll the pencil 30 times.

6. 1 out of 6 sides has printing. ▧ of
   the sides have printing.

7. Guess how many times the printed
   side will be on top.

8. Try it. Record your results in a table like this.

Printing		___ times
No printing		___ times

9. Was the printed side at the top about $\frac{1}{6}$ of the
   time?

10. Combine your results with those of a classmate.
    Now you have the results for 60 rolls. Was the
    printed side at the top about $\frac{1}{6}$ of the time?

Print your name on the pencil so 2 sides have printing.

11. Guess how many times a printed side will be
    on top in 30 rolls.

12. Try it. Were the results close to your guess?

13. Guess how many times a printed side will be
    on top in 180 rolls.

Chance

You are to pick one of these hats without looking.

You might pick any one of the hats.

How many hats are there?

How many blue hats are there?

Your chance of picking a blue hat is

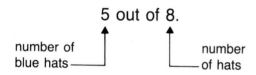

What is your chance of picking a red hat?

What is your chance of picking a yellow hat?

Exercises

To tell which game you will play during recess, draw one of these cards without looking.

What is your chance of playing the following?

1. bombardment

2. volleyball

3. softball

If you spin the pointer, what is the chance of it stopping on

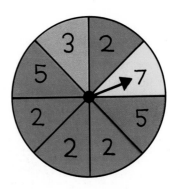

4. 3

5. 2

6. 7

7. 5

8. an odd number

9. an even number

These cards show the prizes in a contest. You are to draw one card without looking.

What is your chance of getting a

10. clock

11. watch

12. baseball

13. radio

You are to draw one of the slips of paper without looking. What is the chance of drawing

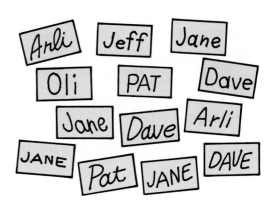

14. Arli

15. Pat

16. Oli

17. Jeff

18. Dave

19. Jane

Probability

You are to draw one of these cards without looking.

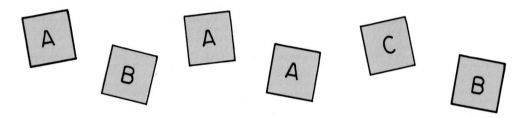

Your chance of drawing an A can be given in these three ways.

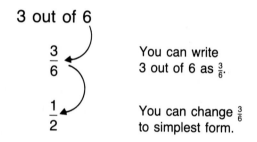

3 out of 6

$\frac{3}{6}$ You can write 3 out of 6 as $\frac{3}{6}$.

$\frac{1}{2}$ You can change $\frac{3}{6}$ to simplest form.

Another word for *chance* is **probability.**

These two sentences have the same meaning.

Your chance of drawing an A is $\frac{1}{2}$.   The probability of drawing an A is $\frac{1}{2}$.

State a probability as a fraction in simplest form.

Exercises

Suppose you draw one of the cards above without looking.

1. What is the probability of getting a B?

2. What is the probability of getting a C?

302

You are to select one pencil without looking. What is the probability of getting a

3. red pencil

4. yellow pencil

5. blue pencil

6. green pencil

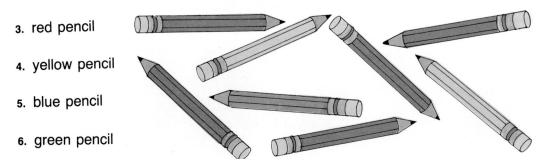

You are to pick one letter from the box without looking. What is the probability of getting

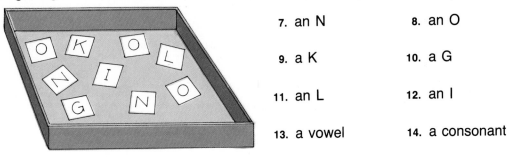

7. an N

8. an O

9. a K

10. a G

11. an L

12. an I

13. a vowel

14. a consonant

A box contains 12 slips of paper numbered 1–12. You draw one slip without looking. What is the probability of getting

15. 10

16. an odd number

17. an even number

18. a number less than 6

19. a number greater than 6

20. a number between 5 and 9

21. a number greater than 11

22. a 2-digit number

23. a 1-digit number

The person before you draws the slip numbered 4 and throws it away. (11 slips are left.) You make the next draw. What is the probability that you will get

24. an even number

25. an odd number

0 and 1 Probabilities

You are to spin the pointer so that it stops on one of the lettered sections.

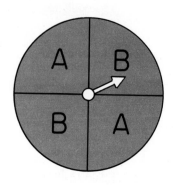

Could the pointer stop on C?

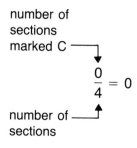

$$\frac{0}{4} = 0$$

number of sections marked C

number of sections

The probability of getting C is 0.

A probability of 0 means the result can never happen.

What is the only color on which the pointer can stop?

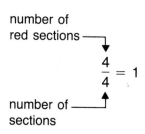

$$\frac{4}{4} = 1$$

number of red sections

number of sections

The probability of getting red is 1.

A probability of 1 means the result will always happen.

Exercises

If you spin the pointer, what is the probability of it stopping on

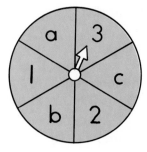

1. a number

2. a letter

3. a green section

4. a blue section

304

If you spin the pointer, what is the probability of it stopping on

5. 15

6. 5

7. an even number

8. 25

9. 10

10. an odd number

The six faces of a die (singular of dice) have 1, 2, 3, 4, 5, and 6 dots. In one roll of a die, what is the probability of the top face showing

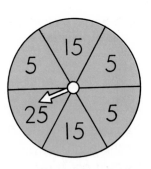

11. 3

12. 6

13. 10

14. an even number

15. 2

16. 1

17. 5

18. an odd number

19. a number less than 7

20. a number less than 6

The keys on a calculator look like this. You are to push one key without looking. What is the probability of pushing

21. 5

22. +

23. B

24. =

25. an odd number

26. a number greater than 7

27. an operation sign

28. a number divisible by 3

29. a number

30. a vowel

31. a number less than 1

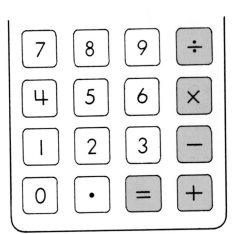

Extra Practice—Set A, page 350

Predicting

In one draw, what is the probability of getting a red marble?

Suppose you make 24 draws, replacing the marble after each draw. Predict the number of times you would get a red marble.

probability of ⎯⎯⎯⎯⎯   ⎯⎯⎯⎯⎯ number
a red marble   of draws

$$\frac{1}{3} \times 24 = 8$$

You could expect to get a red marble 8 times.

Try it. Make 24 draws and keep track of the colors. Did you get a red marble 8 times?

Does probability tell what will *actually* happen or what is *most likely* to happen?

Exercises

Think of drawing one marble from those shown above. Copy and complete this table.

	Color of marble	Probability in 1 draw	Prediction of how many times in 30 draws	Prediction of how many times in 48 draws
1.	red	$\frac{1}{3}$	10	16
2.	blue			
3.	green			
4.	black			

Copy the table. Complete the first two columns. Flip a coin 40 times. Record the results in the last column.

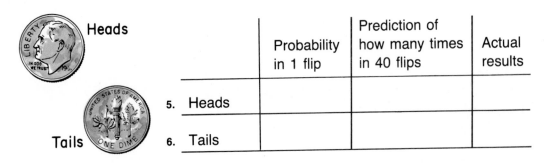

	Probability in 1 flip	Prediction of how many times in 40 flips	Actual results
5. Heads			
6. Tails			

Copy the table. Complete the first two columns. Make slips of paper like those below. Make 56 draws, replacing the slip after each draw. Record the results in the last column.

	Probability in 1 draw	Prediction of how many times in 56 draws	Actual results
7. Art			
8. Su-Lyn			
9. Rosa			

Pierre took a poll of 30 pupils to find their choice for class leader. Use the table he made to predict the results.

10. About how many votes would you expect each pupil to get if 120 pupils voted?

11. About how many votes would you expect each pupil to get if 300 pupils voted?

Pupil	Number of votes
Dave	10
Jane	6
Jon	14

Probability Experiments

In preceding lessons you were able to find a probability without doing an experiment. You could do that because one result was as likely to happen as any other result.

Sometimes the only way you can find a probability is by experimenting to see what happens.

Experiment 1

If you toss a thumbtack, it will land one of these ways.

Point Up   *Point Down*

Make a table like the one below. Toss a thumbtack 50 times and record the results in the table.

	Up	
	Down	
	Total	50

Probability of *Up* $= \dfrac{\text{Number of ups}}{50}$

Probability of *Down* $= \dfrac{\text{Number of downs}}{50}$

Find the probability of *Up*. Find the probability of *Down*.

Make a table like the one below. Combine your results of 50 tosses with those of 5 classmates to complete the table.

Up	
Down	
Total	300

What is the probability of *Up*?

What is the probability of *Down*?

Did you get the same answers as you did for 50 tosses?

To predict future results, would it be better to use the probabilities you got for 50 tosses or for 300 tosses?

Experiment 2

If you toss a spoon, it will land one of these ways.

Up

Down

Make the two tables below.

Toss a spoon 50 times to complete this table.

Up	
Down	
Total	50

Find the probability of *Up*.

Combine your results with those of 5 classmates to complete this table.

Up	
Down	
Total	300

Find the probability of *Down*.

Experiment 3

If you toss a paper cup, it will land one of these ways.

Up

Down

Side

Make a table for 50 tosses. Find the probability for each of the different landing positions.

Combine your results with those of 5 classmates and make a table. Find the probability for each position.

To predict future results, would it be better to use the probabilities you got for 50 tosses or for 300 tosses?

Probability and Percent

A 50% chance of winning is another way to state the probability of winning.

$$50\% \text{ means } \frac{50}{100}. \qquad \frac{50}{100} = \frac{50 \div 50}{100 \div 50} = \frac{1}{2}$$

The probability of winning is 50%, or $\frac{1}{2}$.

Discuss this probability.

The probability of drawing a red marble in one draw is $\frac{3}{4}$.

Explain how $\frac{3}{4}$ is changed to a percent.

$$\frac{3}{4} = \frac{\square}{100}$$

$$4 \times 25 = 100$$

$$\frac{3 \times 25}{4 \times 25} = \frac{75}{100} \quad \text{or} \quad 75\%$$

The probability of drawing a red marble in one draw is $\frac{3}{4}$, or 75%.

Exercises

You pick one of the five cans without looking. Tell a fraction and a percent for the probability of choosing

1. corn

2. beans

3. tomatoes

4. a vegetable

If you spin the pointer, write a fraction and a percent for the probability of the pointer stopping on

5. 2

6. 6

7. 3

8. 4

9. an odd number

10. an even number

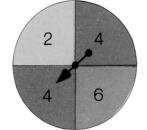

You draw one object below without looking. Write a fraction and a percent for the probability of drawing

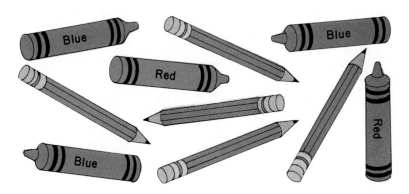

11. a red pencil

12. a red crayon

13. a blue pencil

14. a green crayon

15. a pencil

16. a crayon

17. a pencil or a crayon

18. a magic marker

311

SKILLS REVIEW

Find each answer in simplest form.

1. $\frac{2}{3} + \frac{3}{4}$ 2. $\frac{7}{8} + \frac{1}{2}$ 3. $\frac{9}{10} - \frac{3}{5}$ 4. $\frac{5}{6} - \frac{1}{4}$

5. $1\frac{1}{3} + \frac{2}{5}$ 6. $2\frac{1}{2} + 6\frac{7}{8}$ 7. $5\frac{1}{2} - \frac{3}{4}$ 8. $2\frac{3}{8} - 1\frac{1}{2}$

9. $\frac{7}{8} \times \frac{1}{2}$ 10. $\frac{2}{3} \times \frac{3}{5}$ 11. $\frac{1}{7} \times \frac{7}{10}$ 12. $\frac{9}{10} \times \frac{5}{6}$

13. $1\frac{1}{3} \times \frac{1}{4}$ 14. $6 \times \frac{1}{2}$ 15. $\frac{5}{6} \times 12$ 16. $1\frac{2}{5} \times 1\frac{4}{11}$

Find each sum, difference, or product.

17. $\begin{array}{r} 0.715 \\ +0.193 \\ \hline \end{array}$ 18. $\begin{array}{r} 7.16 \\ -0.76 \\ \hline \end{array}$ 19. $\begin{array}{r} 51.66 \\ + 8.41 \\ \hline \end{array}$ 20. $\begin{array}{r} 52.334 \\ - 2.333 \\ \hline \end{array}$

21. $\begin{array}{r} 68 \\ \times 0.5 \\ \hline \end{array}$ 22. $\begin{array}{r} 3.14 \\ \times 12 \\ \hline \end{array}$ 23. $\begin{array}{r} 5.23 \\ \times 8 \\ \hline \end{array}$ 24. $\begin{array}{r} 6 \\ \times 0.08 \\ \hline \end{array}$

Write each percent as a decimal.

25. 25%   26. 67%   27. 2%   28. 40%

Find the length of a side of each square to the nearest centimeter. Then find the perimeter of each square.

29. A   30. B   31. C   32. D

312

CHAPTER REVIEW

You select one marble without looking.
What is the probability of getting a

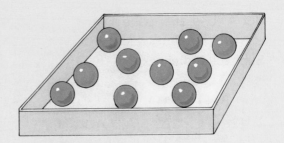

1. red marble

2. blue marble

3. green marble

4. black marble

Copy the table.
Think of spinning the pointer.
Complete the table.

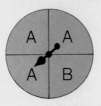

	Pointer lands on	Probability in 1 spin	Prediction of how many times	
			in 24 spins	in 40 spins
5.	A			
6.	B			
7.	C			
8.	red			
9.	blue			

You select one object without looking. Write a fraction and a percent for the probability of drawing a

10. red crayon

11. blue crayon

12. red pencil

13. green crayon

14. crayon

REVIEW AND PRACTICE

Set A (Use after page 11.)

Subtract and check.

$$\begin{array}{r} 81 \\ -37 \\ \hline 44 \end{array} \quad \begin{array}{r} 44 \\ +37 \\ \hline 81 \end{array}$$

1.
$$\begin{array}{r} 76 \\ -61 \\ \hline \end{array}$$

2.
$$\begin{array}{r} 57 \\ -46 \\ \hline \end{array}$$

3.
$$\begin{array}{r} 89 \\ -22 \\ \hline \end{array}$$

4.
$$\begin{array}{r} 95 \\ -55 \\ \hline \end{array}$$

5.
$$\begin{array}{r} 23 \\ -20 \\ \hline \end{array}$$

6.
$$\begin{array}{r} 68 \\ -46 \\ \hline \end{array}$$

7.
$$\begin{array}{r} 40 \\ -15 \\ \hline \end{array}$$

8.
$$\begin{array}{r} 19 \\ -17 \\ \hline \end{array}$$

9.
$$\begin{array}{r} 86 \\ -34 \\ \hline \end{array}$$

10.
$$\begin{array}{r} 33 \\ -16 \\ \hline \end{array}$$

11.
$$\begin{array}{r} 46 \\ -38 \\ \hline \end{array}$$

12.
$$\begin{array}{r} 71 \\ -28 \\ \hline \end{array}$$

13.
$$\begin{array}{r} 62 \\ -49 \\ \hline \end{array}$$

14.
$$\begin{array}{r} 52 \\ -29 \\ \hline \end{array}$$

15.
$$\begin{array}{r} 76 \\ -46 \\ \hline \end{array}$$

16.
$$\begin{array}{r} 83 \\ -67 \\ \hline \end{array}$$

17.
$$\begin{array}{r} 92 \\ -75 \\ \hline \end{array}$$

18.
$$\begin{array}{r} 60 \\ -34 \\ \hline \end{array}$$

Set B (Use after page 13.)

$7 \div 6\overline{)42}$

1. $8\overline{)64}$ 2. $4\overline{)36}$ 3. $5\overline{)30}$

4. $9\overline{)72}$ 5. $3\overline{)24}$ 6. $7\overline{)56}$ 7. $8\overline{)48}$

8. $6\overline{)36}$ 9. $5\overline{)45}$ 10. $7\overline{)63}$ 11. $9\overline{)54}$

12. $4\overline{)48}$ 13. $6\overline{)96}$ 14. $3\overline{)66}$ 15. $5\overline{)75}$

16. $9\overline{)99}$ 17. $7\overline{)84}$ 18. $8\overline{)96}$ 19. $2\overline{)86}$

20. $4\overline{)92}$ 21. $6\overline{)78}$ 22. $5\overline{)60}$ 23. $3\overline{)96}$

Set A (Use after page 17.)

Copy. Put in the commas.

    45,900   **1.** 37518   **2.** 400034   **3.** 10273648

4. 17082   **5.** 214987   **6.** 3120566   **7.** 3728000928

Write the numeral.

8. three thousand six hundred   **9.** five million, forty thousand, two

10. seven hundred twenty-five million, three hundred
two thousand, ninety-seven

11. eighty-eight billion, two hundred sixteen thousand, seventeen

Write in words.

12. 3303   **13.** 20,002   **14.** 2,467,800   **15.** 1,500,000,050

Set B (Use after page 23.)

	1.	2.	3.	4.
261 +715 976	816 + 63	245 +302	721 + 27	520 +428

5.	6.	7.	8.	9.
117 +182	335 + 13	656 +112	402 + 77	760 +124

10.	11.	12.	13.	14.
439 +438	925 + 47	307 +595	598 + 37	184 +232

15.	16.	17.	18.	19.
348 +616	660 + 69	849 +136	217 + 59	391 +459

Set A (Use after page 25.)

22,763
+ 8,129
30,892

1. 42,053
+36,246

2. 625
+9373

3. 8,112
+10,715

4. 7709
+1240

5. 13,792
+32,000

6. 3861
+5004

7. 44,680
+10,106

8. 3192
+4603

9. 54,918
+24,020

10. 358
+2001

11. 1,476
+70,522

12. 2615
+3588

13. 50,635
+13,496

14. 4927
+8494

15. 81,385
+12,755

16. 8147
+3966

17. 81,089
+18,579

18. 6893
+7238

19. 49,607
+27,916

Set B (Use after page 27.)

2,581,768
+7,215,432
9,797,200

1. 612,083
+ 6,113

2. 1,125,714
+ 13,125

3. 321,071
+642,917

4. 1,752,036
+2,146,901

5. 894,658
+ 2,331

6. 2,370,990
+ 103,000

7. 446,703
+123,214

8. 890,634
+2,008,255

9. 342,741
+ 10,243

10. 3,524,710
+ 471,341

11. 600,354
+242,225

12. 1,788,800
+6,545,667

13. 924,707
+ 27,968

14. 2,823,478
+ 65,863

15. 432,543
+441,063

16. 5,995,656
+1,100,665

17. 196,969
+ 67,283

18. 6,702,572
+ 859,278

19. 348,875
+452,125

Set A (Use after page 29.)

Round to the nearest hundred.

1829 ⟶ 1800

1. 622

2. 279

3. 1501

4. 2799

5. 1605

6. 1650

7. 21,549

8. 21,550

9. 21,551

10. 17,979

Round to the nearest thousand.

18,540 ⟶ 19,000

11. 6245

12. 7050

13. 8720

14. 14,562

15. 19,500

16. 26,469

Set B (Use after page 33.)

	1.	**2.**	**3.**	**4.**
6120	217	71,661	729	6718
267	168	269	3	9273
93	319	1,521	76	1468
+1356	+420	+ 4,417	+ 15	+2174
7836				

5.	**6.**	**7.**	**8.**	**9.**
57	726	51,623	400	9871
21	58	27,152	40	652
+67	+272	+ 865	+ 4	+1043

10.	**11.**	**12.**	**13.**	**14.**
17	508	20,127	107	5216
39	817	6,159	29	3072
68	920	760	415	4125
+77	+176	+ 1,124	+ 67	+6157

15.	**16.**	**17.**	**18.**	**19.**
87	601	15,210	28	476
92	58	576	136	25
10	715	2,400	28	913
+44	+216	+ 799	+ 90	+3265

Set A (Use after page 35.)

$$\begin{array}{r} 6253 \\ -4172 \\ \hline 2081 \end{array}$$

1.
$$\begin{array}{r} 7280 \\ -4140 \\ \hline \end{array}$$

2.
$$\begin{array}{r} 491 \\ -73 \\ \hline \end{array}$$

3.
$$\begin{array}{r} 1206 \\ -180 \\ \hline \end{array}$$

4.
$$\begin{array}{r} 3170 \\ -156 \\ \hline \end{array}$$

5.
$$\begin{array}{r} 278 \\ -122 \\ \hline \end{array}$$

6.
$$\begin{array}{r} 9966 \\ -8519 \\ \hline \end{array}$$

7.
$$\begin{array}{r} 905 \\ -64 \\ \hline \end{array}$$

8.
$$\begin{array}{r} 414 \\ -205 \\ \hline \end{array}$$

9.
$$\begin{array}{r} 2800 \\ -387 \\ \hline \end{array}$$

10.
$$\begin{array}{r} 877 \\ -836 \\ \hline \end{array}$$

11.
$$\begin{array}{r} 4000 \\ -308 \\ \hline \end{array}$$

12.
$$\begin{array}{r} 642 \\ -97 \\ \hline \end{array}$$

13.
$$\begin{array}{r} 1513 \\ -276 \\ \hline \end{array}$$

14.
$$\begin{array}{r} 1243 \\ -318 \\ \hline \end{array}$$

15.
$$\begin{array}{r} 571 \\ -443 \\ \hline \end{array}$$

16.
$$\begin{array}{r} 6008 \\ -679 \\ \hline \end{array}$$

17.
$$\begin{array}{r} 503 \\ -94 \\ \hline \end{array}$$

18.
$$\begin{array}{r} 436 \\ -375 \\ \hline \end{array}$$

19.
$$\begin{array}{r} 1002 \\ -793 \\ \hline \end{array}$$

Set B (Use after page 37.)

Estimate.

$$\begin{array}{r} 5972 \\ -4065 \\ \hline \end{array} \longrightarrow \begin{array}{r} 6000 \\ -4000 \\ \hline 2000 \end{array}$$

1.
$$\begin{array}{r} 2075 \\ -987 \\ \hline \end{array}$$

2.
$$\begin{array}{r} 15{,}970 \\ -10{,}959 \\ \hline \end{array}$$

3.
$$\begin{array}{r} 608 \\ -399 \\ \hline \end{array}$$

4.
$$\begin{array}{r} 195{,}861 \\ -90{,}129 \\ \hline \end{array}$$

5.
$$\begin{array}{r} 5998 \\ -4019 \\ \hline \end{array}$$

6.
$$\begin{array}{r} 29{,}076 \\ -10{,}135 \\ \hline \end{array}$$

7.
$$\begin{array}{r} 2799 \\ -1805 \\ \hline \end{array}$$

8. My dictionary has 910 pages. My history book has 392 pages. My dictionary has how many more pages than my history book?

9. 1536 children go to Madison School. If 690 of them are boys, how many girls go to Madison School?

10. A library owns 12,218 books. If 2826 of the books are checked out, how many are in the library?

11. 4107 people entered a 26-mile marathon and 3845 people finished the race. How many did not?

12. A store had 7200 calendars printed. After mailing some to customers, there were 2150 left. How many calendars were mailed?

13. A stadium has 68,750 seats for a football game and 59,500 seats for a baseball game. How many more fans can be seated for a football game?

Set A (Use after page 43.)

1. $\begin{array}{r}2\\ \times 2\\ \hline\end{array}$	2. $\begin{array}{r}2\\ \times 4\\ \hline\end{array}$	3. $\begin{array}{r}4\\ \times 3\\ \hline\end{array}$	4. $\begin{array}{r}3\\ \times 5\\ \hline\end{array}$	5. $\begin{array}{r}6\\ \times 3\\ \hline\end{array}$	6. $\begin{array}{r}4\\ \times 4\\ \hline\end{array}$
7. $\begin{array}{r}3\\ \times 3\\ \hline\end{array}$	8. $\begin{array}{r}5\\ \times 2\\ \hline\end{array}$	9. $\begin{array}{r}7\\ \times 4\\ \hline\end{array}$	10. $\begin{array}{r}6\\ \times 8\\ \hline\end{array}$	11. $\begin{array}{r}5\\ \times 7\\ \hline\end{array}$	12. $\begin{array}{r}8\\ \times 7\\ \hline\end{array}$
13. $\begin{array}{r}7\\ \times 7\\ \hline\end{array}$	14. $\begin{array}{r}7\\ \times 6\\ \hline\end{array}$	15. $\begin{array}{r}6\\ \times 9\\ \hline\end{array}$	16. $\begin{array}{r}9\\ \times 3\\ \hline\end{array}$	17. $\begin{array}{r}8\\ \times 8\\ \hline\end{array}$	18. $\begin{array}{r}4\\ \times 9\\ \hline\end{array}$
19. $\begin{array}{r}4\\ \times 1\\ \hline\end{array}$	20. $\begin{array}{r}3\\ \times 8\\ \hline\end{array}$	21. $\begin{array}{r}5\\ \times 5\\ \hline\end{array}$	22. $\begin{array}{r}9\\ \times 7\\ \hline\end{array}$	23. $\begin{array}{r}2\\ \times 7\\ \hline\end{array}$	24. $\begin{array}{r}0\\ \times 2\\ \hline\end{array}$
25. $\begin{array}{r}4\\ \times 5\\ \hline\end{array}$	26. $\begin{array}{r}1\\ \times 8\\ \hline\end{array}$	27. $\begin{array}{r}6\\ \times 6\\ \hline\end{array}$	28. $\begin{array}{r}8\\ \times 0\\ \hline\end{array}$	29. $\begin{array}{r}9\\ \times 9\\ \hline\end{array}$	30. $\begin{array}{r}1\\ \times 0\\ \hline\end{array}$
31. $\begin{array}{r}7\\ \times 3\\ \hline\end{array}$	32. $\begin{array}{r}8\\ \times 9\\ \hline\end{array}$	33. $\begin{array}{r}1\\ \times 1\\ \hline\end{array}$	34. $\begin{array}{r}6\\ \times 5\\ \hline\end{array}$	35. $\begin{array}{r}2\\ \times 8\\ \hline\end{array}$	36. $\begin{array}{r}5\\ \times 9\\ \hline\end{array}$
37. $\begin{array}{r}4\\ \times 2\\ \hline\end{array}$	38. $\begin{array}{r}9\\ \times 2\\ \hline\end{array}$	39. $\begin{array}{r}7\\ \times 0\\ \hline\end{array}$	40. $\begin{array}{r}8\\ \times 5\\ \hline\end{array}$	41. $\begin{array}{r}8\\ \times 4\\ \hline\end{array}$	42. $\begin{array}{r}9\\ \times 1\\ \hline\end{array}$
43. $\begin{array}{r}0\\ \times 7\\ \hline\end{array}$	44. $\begin{array}{r}0\\ \times 0\\ \hline\end{array}$	45. $\begin{array}{r}7\\ \times 6\\ \hline\end{array}$	46. $\begin{array}{r}2\\ \times 6\\ \hline\end{array}$	47. $\begin{array}{r}7\\ \times 1\\ \hline\end{array}$	48. $\begin{array}{r}1\\ \times 9\\ \hline\end{array}$
49. $\begin{array}{r}7\\ \times 9\\ \hline\end{array}$	50. $\begin{array}{r}9\\ \times 6\\ \hline\end{array}$	51. $\begin{array}{r}5\\ \times 0\\ \hline\end{array}$	52. $\begin{array}{r}3\\ \times 7\\ \hline\end{array}$	53. $\begin{array}{r}0\\ \times 5\\ \hline\end{array}$	54. $\begin{array}{r}2\\ \times 6\\ \hline\end{array}$
55. $\begin{array}{r}1\\ \times 4\\ \hline\end{array}$	56. $\begin{array}{r}3\\ \times 1\\ \hline\end{array}$	57. $\begin{array}{r}1\\ \times 2\\ \hline\end{array}$	58. $\begin{array}{r}9\\ \times 8\\ \hline\end{array}$	59. $\begin{array}{r}6\\ \times 4\\ \hline\end{array}$	60. $\begin{array}{r}7\\ \times 3\\ \hline\end{array}$
61. $\begin{array}{r}0\\ \times 9\\ \hline\end{array}$	62. $\begin{array}{r}8\\ \times 6\\ \hline\end{array}$	63. $\begin{array}{r}5\\ \times 4\\ \hline\end{array}$	64. $\begin{array}{r}8\\ \times 9\\ \hline\end{array}$	65. $\begin{array}{r}2\\ \times 5\\ \hline\end{array}$	66. $\begin{array}{r}9\\ \times 5\\ \hline\end{array}$

	1.	2.	3.	4.	5.
30 ×4 120	70 ×8	60 ×5	80 ×2	70 ×6	90 ×5

6.	7.	8.	9.	10.	11.
20 ×30	60 ×80	10 ×90	40 ×40	80 ×50	90 ×20

12.	13.	14.	15.	16.
500 ×3	200 ×8	700 ×3	600 ×5	300 ×9

17.	18.	19.	20.	21.
700 ×10	500 ×50	900 ×80	400 ×50	100 ×10

22.	23.	24.	25.	26.
300 ×200	700 ×700	100 ×200	500 ×600	800 ×900

Estimate.

275
×86 ⟶ 300
×90
27,000

1.	2.	3.
350 ×4	28 ×34	681 ×29

4.	5.	6.	7.	8.
89 ×15	318 ×9	509 ×51	88 ×22	52 ×84

9.	10.	11.	12.	13.
247 ×12	162 ×222	64 ×45	681 ×53	479 ×558

14.	15.	16.	17.	18.
828 ×702	654 ×395	72 ×28	937 ×450	309 ×34

19. There are 739 boxes. Each box has 24 doo-dads. Estimate the number of doodads in all.

20. You are in school about 188 days each year. Estimate how many days you will have been in school by the time you complete high school.

Set A (Use after page 55.)

48 ×5 240	1. 59 ×2	2. 11 ×7	3. 79 ×0	4. 31 ×8	5. 91 ×1
6. 29 ×9	7. 62 ×6	8. 34 ×4	9. 27 ×8	10. 79 ×3	11. 57 ×7

12. 162 ×6	13. 416 ×2	14. 573 ×9	15. 957 ×6	16. 495 ×5
17. 240 ×4	18. 315 ×9	19. 600 ×5	20. 710 ×6	21. 925 ×8

22. In 1 minute a company can make 528 yo-yos. How many yo-yos can be made in 5 minutes?

23. Drake is driving at a rate of 35 miles per hour. How far can he go in 8 hours?

Set B (Use after page 57.)

63 ×46 2898	1. 16 ×3	2. 16 ×20	3. 16 ×23	4. 51 ×59
5. 91 ×30	6. 37 ×51	7. 12 ×77	8. 60 ×15	9. 24 ×94
10. 73 ×72	11. 76 ×81	12. 57 ×60	13. 50 ×28	14. 42 ×79
15. 80 ×14	16. 19 ×80	17. 83 ×98	18. 62 ×75	19. 93 ×45
20. 99 ×84	21. 54 ×33	22. 82 ×70	23. 67 ×47	24. 92 ×96

	470	1.	170	2.	464	3.	464	4.	464
	×37		×17		×8		×40		×48
	17,390								

5.	174	6.	545	7.	656	8.	300	9.	647
	×52		×81		×73		×70		×38

10.	509	11.	320	12.	462	13.	975	14.	268
	×15		×68		×39		×75		×68

	791	1.	473	2.	528	3.	396	4.	403
	×607		×204		×460		×709		×500
	480,137								

5.	649	6.	167	7.	540	8.	418	9.	427
	×130		×812		×253		×900		×427

10.	159	11.	378	12.	624	13.	880	14.	316
	×774		×683		×916		×382		×879

15.	371	16.	604	17.	591	18.	295	19.	784
	×698		×297		×435		×908		×807

	5269	1.	1427	2.	2805	3.	7069	4.	9124
	×3		×3		×8		×6		×1
	15,807								

5.	8306	6.	4315	7.	6078	8.	5413	9.	7837
	×6		×3		×9		×7		×7

Set A (Use after page 69.)

$$\frac{7}{4)\overline{28}}$$

1. $4)\overline{4}$

2. $2)\overline{14}$

3. $3)\overline{27}$

4. $4)\overline{20}$

5. $3)\overline{0}$

6. $1)\overline{9}$

7. $2)\overline{8}$

8. $8)\overline{48}$

9. $9)\overline{54}$

10. $9)\overline{36}$

11. $3)\overline{9}$

12. $4)\overline{12}$

13. $7)\overline{0}$

14. $8)\overline{8}$

15. $7)\overline{21}$

16. $6)\overline{18}$

17. $9)\overline{72}$

18. $8)\overline{64}$

19. $4)\overline{32}$

20. $5)\overline{15}$

21. $3)\overline{18}$

22. $1)\overline{5}$

23. $5)\overline{40}$

24. $6)\overline{6}$

25. $1)\overline{0}$

26. $7)\overline{49}$

27. $6)\overline{36}$

28. $9)\overline{18}$

29. $3)\overline{6}$

30. $5)\overline{20}$

31. $8)\overline{24}$

32. $7)\overline{63}$

33. $1)\overline{3}$

34. $2)\overline{18}$

35. $5)\overline{25}$

36. $2)\overline{4}$

37. $6)\overline{54}$

38. $7)\overline{7}$

39. $7)\overline{35}$

40. $5)\overline{10}$

41. $3)\overline{21}$

42. $2)\overline{10}$

43. $1)\overline{1}$

44. $8)\overline{16}$

45. $2)\overline{16}$

46. $3)\overline{3}$

47. $7)\overline{14}$

48. $1)\overline{8}$

49. $9)\overline{0}$

50. $4)\overline{16}$

51. $6)\overline{12}$

52. $1)\overline{2}$

53. $1)\overline{6}$

54. $5)\overline{5}$

55. $4)\overline{8}$

56. $5)\overline{0}$

57. $9)\overline{9}$

58. $2)\overline{6}$

59. $1)\overline{4}$

60. $3)\overline{12}$

61. $2)\overline{12}$

62. $1)\overline{7}$

63. $3)\overline{15}$

64. $3)\overline{24}$

65. $4)\overline{36}$

66. $5)\overline{35}$

67. $6)\overline{24}$

68. $8)\overline{32}$

69. $7)\overline{28}$

70. $9)\overline{27}$

71. $4)\overline{24}$

72. $5)\overline{30}$

73. $6)\overline{48}$

74. $4)\overline{28}$

75. $7)\overline{56}$

76. $6)\overline{42}$

77. $9)\overline{81}$

78. $5)\overline{45}$

79. $8)\overline{72}$

80. $6)\overline{30}$

81. $9)\overline{63}$

82. $8)\overline{56}$

83. $8)\overline{40}$

84. $7)\overline{42}$

Set A (Use after page 75.)

$$\begin{array}{r} 14 \\ 4\overline{)56} \\ \underline{4} \\ 16 \\ \underline{16} \\ 0 \end{array}$$

1. $5\overline{)70}$ 2. $7\overline{)91}$ 3. $3\overline{)84}$ 4. $2\overline{)98}$

5. $5\overline{)80}$ 6. $6\overline{)84}$ 7. $7\overline{)875}$ 8. $4\overline{)768}$

9. $8\overline{)184}$ 10. $9\overline{)891}$ 11. $5\overline{)580}$ 12. $2\overline{)996}$

13. $8\overline{)768}$ 14. $3\overline{)828}$ 15. $7\overline{)217}$ 16. $6\overline{)216}$ 17. $5\overline{)220}$

18. $7\overline{)4368}$ 19. $6\overline{)5850}$ 20. $8\overline{)6032}$ 21. $9\overline{)6921}$ 22. $4\overline{)3784}$

Set B (Use after page 76.)

Divide and check.

$$\begin{array}{r} 312 \ \text{R3} \\ 7\overline{)2187} \end{array}$$

$$\begin{array}{r} 312 \\ \times 7 \\ \hline 2184 \\ +\quad 3 \\ \hline 2187 \end{array}$$

1. $3\overline{)650}$ 2. $2\overline{)116}$

3. $4\overline{)729}$ 4. $8\overline{)462}$

5. $9\overline{)595}$ 6. $7\overline{)119}$

7. $3\overline{)725}$ 8. $9\overline{)837}$ 9. $3\overline{)860}$ 10. $8\overline{)683}$

11. $2\overline{)473}$ 12. $5\overline{)3482}$ 13. $7\overline{)7815}$ 14. $6\overline{)5850}$

Set C (Use after page 83.)

$$\begin{array}{r} 27 \ \text{R4} \\ 33\overline{)895} \end{array}$$

1. $25\overline{)573}$ 2. $11\overline{)275}$ 3. $40\overline{)486}$

4. $80\overline{)989}$ 5. $53\overline{)591}$ 6. $75\overline{)975}$ 7. $61\overline{)781}$

8. $31\overline{)350}$ 9. $22\overline{)506}$ 10. $43\overline{)795}$ 11. $88\overline{)968}$

12. $60\overline{)666}$ 13. $82\overline{)902}$ 14. $50\overline{)760}$ 15. $34\overline{)396}$

Set A (Use after page 85.)

$$37\overline{)559}\ \ {}^{15\ R4}$$

1. $18\overline{)632}$
2. $35\overline{)782}$
3. $28\overline{)800}$

4. $46\overline{)599}$
5. $27\overline{)418}$
6. $45\overline{)320}$
7. $77\overline{)385}$

8. $75\overline{)310}$
9. $58\overline{)174}$
10. $86\overline{)260}$
11. $66\overline{)595}$

12. $15\overline{)240}$
13. $39\overline{)313}$
14. $65\overline{)260}$
15. $28\overline{)448}$

16. $47\overline{)752}$
17. $16\overline{)140}$
18. $25\overline{)200}$
19. $75\overline{)975}$

Set B (Use after page 87.)

$$23\overline{)860}\ \ {}^{37\ R9}$$

1. $33\overline{)520}$
2. $62\overline{)368}$
3. $54\overline{)650}$

4. $43\overline{)211}$
5. $24\overline{)832}$
6. $73\overline{)882}$
7. $61\overline{)365}$

8. $84\overline{)410}$
9. $14\overline{)243}$
10. $34\overline{)469}$
11. $94\overline{)470}$

12. $12\overline{)200}$
13. $53\overline{)841}$
14. $44\overline{)202}$
15. $22\overline{)153}$

16. $14\overline{)555}$
17. $83\overline{)569}$
18. $74\overline{)890}$
19. $13\overline{)221}$

Set C (Use after page 88.)

$$6\overline{)7250}\ \ {}^{1208\ R2}$$

1. $7\overline{)72}$
2. $5\overline{)203}$
3. $2\overline{)2140}$

4. $6\overline{)60}$
5. $4\overline{)120}$
6. $8\overline{)1609}$
7. $3\overline{)6121}$

8. $7\overline{)2105}$
9. $8\overline{)8723}$
10. $2\overline{)4017}$
11. $9\overline{)7218}$

12. $23\overline{)460}$
13. $62\overline{)651}$
14. $68\overline{)728}$
15. $47\overline{)470}$

16. $12\overline{)600}$
17. $14\overline{)710}$
18. $89\overline{)900}$
19. $99\overline{)999}$

325

Set A (Use after page 91.)

106 R37
68)7245

1. 16)4864

2. 52)5616

3. 86)8847

4. 20)8198

5. 46)9798

6. 74)5550

7. 93)3372

8. 54)5346

9. 90)9096

10. 30)9210

11. 69)8694

12. 76)6536

13. 57)2108

14. 89)5698

15. 92)9200

16. 97)1939

17. 26)7852

18. 77)8454

19. 56)1512

20. 66)6864

21. 80)7208

22. 72)4032

23. 64)6780

Set B (Use after page 93.)

Find the average for each of the following:

1. 38, 27, 69, 42, 19

2. 58, 76, 60, 33, 72, 91

3. 400, 698, 786, 536

4. 7625, 1237, 9096

5. In 5 hours Arlie drove 240 miles. Find his average speed in miles per hour.

6. A plane flew 1812 miles in 3 hours. Find the average speed in miles per hour.

Pupil	Scores			
Beth	88	74	92	82
Rob	100	80	90	90
Otto	77	95	88	92
Kim	87	87	87	91

7. Find Beth's average score.

8. Find Rob's average score.

9. Find Otto's average score.

10. Find Kim's average score.

Set A (Use after page 99.)

For each problem, write what you know and what you are to find.

1. 87 people saw the afternoon show, and 153 people saw the evening show. How many people saw the show?

2. One part of the show is 18 minutes long. The other part is 34 minutes long. How long is the entire show?

3. Tickets cost $2 each. How much do 16 tickets cost?

4. There are 12 shows each week. How many shows are there in 8 weeks?

5. 84 seats are arranged in rows of 6 seats each. How many rows are there?

6. At one show there were 52 adults and 35 children. How many more adults were there?

7. 48 small lemonades and 35 large lemonades were sold. How many more small lemonades were sold?

8. The longest show was 197 minutes long. How long was that show in hours and minutes?

Set B (Use after page 101.)

Tell how you would solve each problem.

1. Jack is 12 years old. Janet is 3 years older than Jack. How old is Janet?

2. Clare is 132 centimeters tall. Ira is 141 centimeters tall. How much taller is Ira?

3. Jake read 132 pages one day and 214 pages the next day. How many pages did he read?

4. The bus took 3 hours to go 126 miles. Find the average speed in miles per hour.

5. A bike costs $125. It is on sale for $89. How much was the price reduced?

6. Rich has 18 rare coins. Each coin is worth $5. How much are the 18 coins worth?

7. 575 milliliters of water was boiled until only 428 milliliters were left. How much water was turned to steam?

8. The 25 pupils in art class used 500 sheets of construction paper. Find the average number of sheets used by each pupil.

Solve each problem. Watch for extra or missing information. If the problem cannot be solved, tell what is missing.

Attendance	
Day	Number of people
Friday	14,384
Saturday	26,028
Sunday	9,016

1. Find the total attendance for the 3 days.

2. How many more people were there on Saturday than on Friday?

3. How many more people were there this weekend than last weekend?

4. 416 people came on 8 buses. Find the average number of people per bus.

5. 6202 adults were there on Friday. How many children were there on Friday?

6. 10,000 adults were there on Saturday. How many more adults were there on Saturday than on Sunday?

7. The average daily attendance is 17,000 people. Is that more or less than the average attendance for these 3 days?

Jim, Tom, Bill, Paul, and Ken own bikes of colors red, brown, silver, black, and blue. Use the clues below to find the color of each boy's bike.

While on their way to see Tom, the owners of the brown and black bikes met Paul and Bill. The owners of the brown and red bikes then left Jim and Paul and continued on to see Tom. The number of letters in the color of Paul's bike is the same as the number of letters in his name.

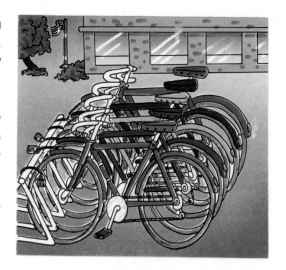

Solve each problem.

1. There are 6 rows of cars with 15 cars in each row. Only 7 of the cars are taxicabs. How many are not taxicabs?

2. Each rack holds 16 bikes. There are 2 racks. All but 5 of the spaces are full. How many bikes are there?

3. 1 ton is 2000 pounds. A newborn blue whale weighs 3 tons. When full-grown, it will weigh 40 times that much. How many pounds will it weigh when it is full-grown?

4. A camel weighs 1300 pounds. A bear weighs 750 pounds. An elephant weighs 4 times as much as the bear and the camel together. How much does the elephant weigh?

5. 13,492 people came to the circus on Friday, 23,423 on Saturday, and 18,432 on Sunday. Find the average daily attendance.

Set B (Use after page 119.)

Name the shape of each object.

1.
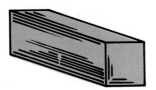

2.

3.
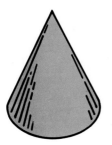

4.
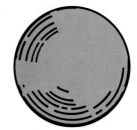

Name each figure.

1. 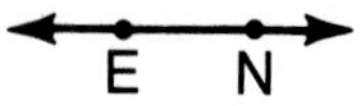 E   N

2. 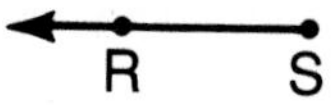 R   S

3. 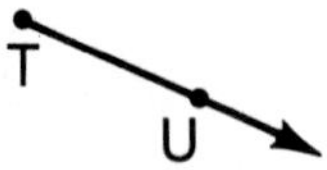 T
U

4. 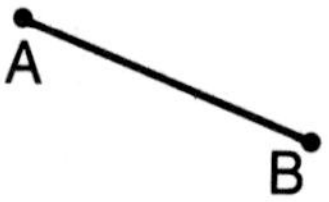 A
B

Tell whether each pair of line segments is congruent.

5.

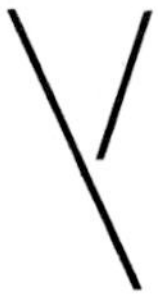

6. ─────
    ───

7.

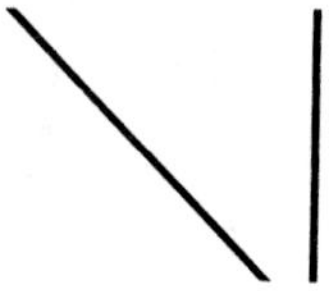

8.

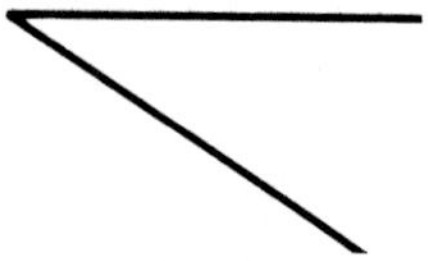

Copy the table. Measure each angle and complete the table.

Name of angle	Measure of angle	Kind of angle
1.		
2.		
3.		

1. 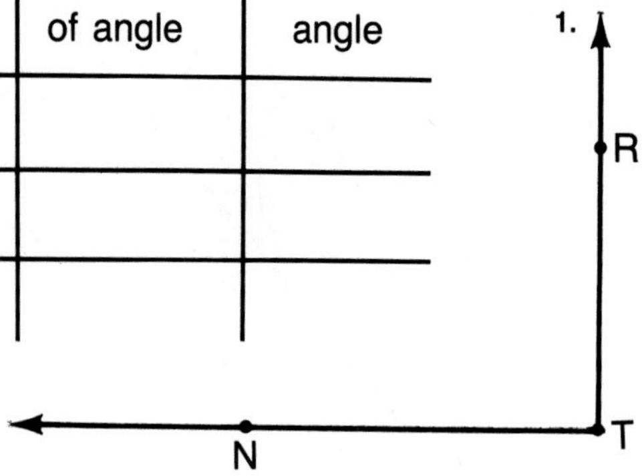 R
N   T

2. 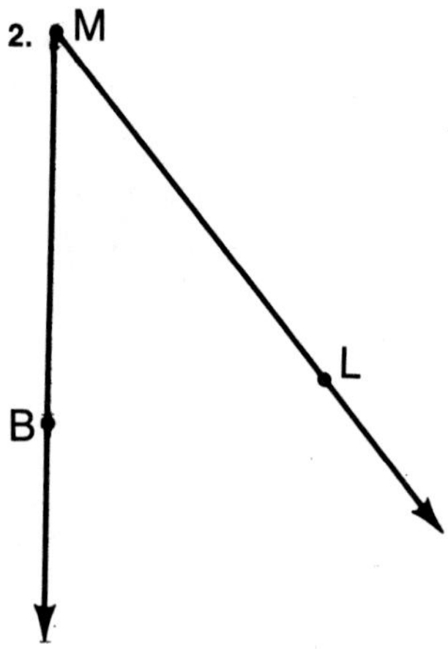 M
B   L

3. 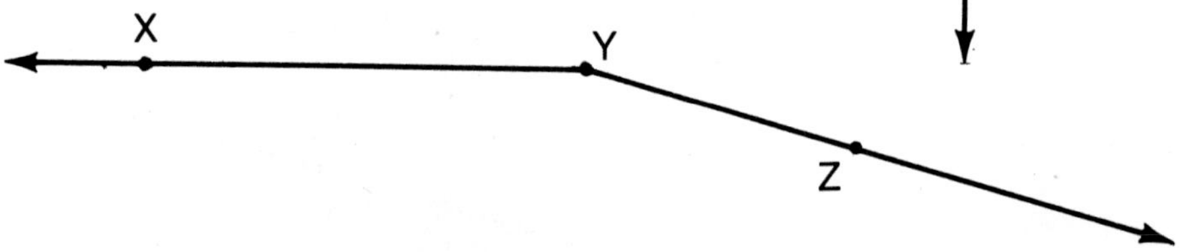 X   Y
Z

4. Draw an angle having a measurement of 150°.

330

Measure each of the angles on this page and tell which angles are congruent.

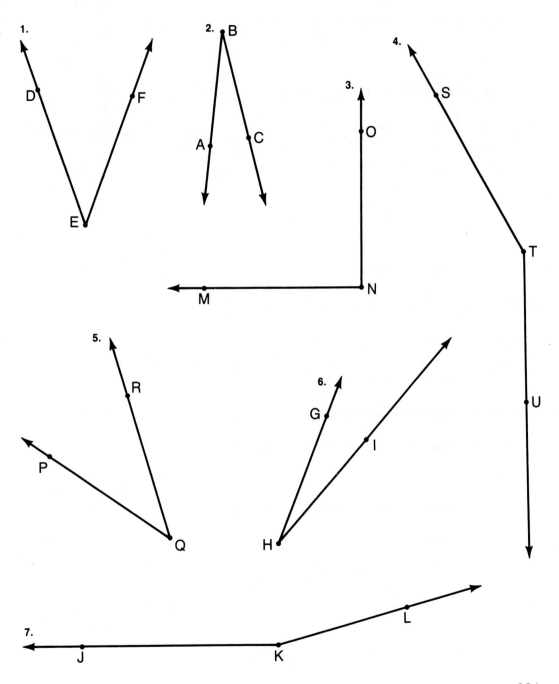

Name the following:

1. a radius   2. a diameter

3. a point inside the circle

4. a point outside the circle

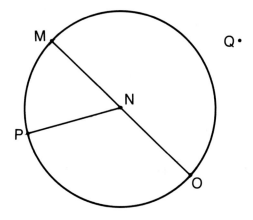

5. If line segment PN is 6 units long, then line segment MO is ___ units long.

6. If line segment MN is 8 units long, then line segment NO is ___ units long.

7. Is line segment MN a diameter?   8. Is line segment NO a radius?

Set B (Use after page 137.)

Give the name for each figure.

1.

2.
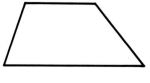

3.
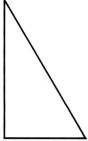

4.
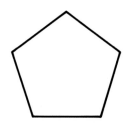

5.
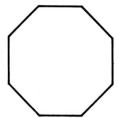

Tell whether the line segments are parallel.

1.

2.

3.

Measure the angles in each figure. Tell whether the lines are perpendicular.

4.

5.

6. Use a protractor to draw two perpendicular lines.

333

Set A (Use after page 149.)

$\overset{\times 4}{\underset{\times 4}{\frac{3}{5}}} = \frac{\square}{20}$ $\frac{3}{5} = \frac{12}{20}$

1. $\frac{1}{4} = \frac{\square}{8}$ 2. $\frac{1}{9} = \frac{\square}{90}$

3. $\frac{5}{6} = \frac{\square}{42}$ 4. $\frac{3}{8} = \frac{\square}{56}$ 5. $\frac{1}{10} = \frac{\square}{100}$ 6. $\frac{1}{5} = \frac{\square}{25}$

7. $\frac{3}{4} = \frac{\square}{20}$ 8. $\frac{2}{9} = \frac{\square}{27}$ 9. $\frac{1}{12} = \frac{\square}{60}$ 10. $\frac{6}{1} = \frac{\square}{4}$

11. $\frac{3}{10} = \frac{\square}{30}$ 12. $\frac{4}{5} = \frac{\square}{50}$ 13. $\frac{5}{4} = \frac{\square}{100}$ 14. $\frac{9}{10} = \frac{\square}{100}$

Set B (Use after page 151.)

$\overset{\div 3}{\underset{\div 3}{\frac{9}{24}}} = \frac{\square}{8}$ $\frac{9}{24} = \frac{3}{8}$

1. $\frac{2}{10} = \frac{\square}{5}$ 2. $\frac{6}{9} = \frac{\square}{3}$

3. $\frac{27}{36} = \frac{\square}{4}$ 4. $\frac{60}{72} = \frac{\square}{6}$ 5. $\frac{9}{15} = \frac{\square}{5}$ 6. $\frac{8}{12} = \frac{\square}{3}$

7. $\frac{10}{20} = \frac{\square}{2}$ 8. $\frac{6}{21} = \frac{\square}{7}$ 9. $\frac{10}{16} = \frac{\square}{8}$ 10. $\frac{12}{18} = \frac{\square}{3}$

11. $\frac{8}{10} = \frac{\square}{5}$ 12. $\frac{18}{36} = \frac{\square}{2}$ 13. $\frac{10}{45} = \frac{\square}{9}$ 14. $\frac{12}{30} = \frac{\square}{5}$

Set C (Use after page 153.)

Give the greatest common factor for the following:

$\overset{2}{\text{2 and 6}}$

1. 6 and 8   2. 2 and 4

3. 3 and 9   4. 8 and 2   5. 4 and 5   6. 6 and 5

7. 12 and 4   8. 6 and 3   9. 7 and 8   10. 9 and 12

11. 12 and 8   12. 9 and 6   13. 2 and 7   14. 10 and 5

15. 4 and 6   16. 12 and 16   17. 8 and 10   18. 7 and 9

19. 10 and 12   20. 14 and 16   21. 8 and 11   22. 10 and 15

Find each product in simplest form.

$$\overset{1}{\underset{3}{\cancel{6}}} \times \overset{2}{\underset{1}{\cancel{4}}} = \frac{2}{3}$$

1. $\frac{2}{5} \times \frac{1}{4}$ 2. $\frac{1}{2} \times \frac{6}{7}$ 3. $\frac{3}{4} \times \frac{5}{6}$

4. $\frac{5}{8} \times \frac{4}{5}$ 5. $\frac{1}{3} \times \frac{9}{10}$ 6. $\frac{4}{5} \times \frac{1}{8}$ 7. $\frac{1}{4} \times \frac{6}{11}$

8. $\frac{1}{5} \times \frac{5}{6}$ 9. $\frac{7}{9} \times \frac{3}{4}$ 10. $\frac{3}{5} \times \frac{1}{6}$ 11. $\frac{5}{6} \times \frac{1}{3}$

12. $\frac{2}{3} \times \frac{3}{10}$ 13. $\frac{5}{16} \times \frac{8}{10}$ 14. $\frac{7}{8} \times \frac{1}{7}$ 15. $\frac{5}{7} \times \frac{3}{10}$

16. $\frac{10}{11} \times \frac{1}{12}$ 17. $\frac{3}{7} \times \frac{2}{9}$ 18. $\frac{5}{6} \times \frac{9}{10}$ 19. $\frac{3}{10} \times \frac{8}{9}$

20. Vera has $\frac{2}{3}$ gallon of paint. She poured $\frac{3}{8}$ of it into a smaller can. How much paint is in the smaller can?

21. Gerald has $\frac{1}{2}$ gallon of paint. Pat has $\frac{1}{3}$ as much paint as Gerald. How much paint does Pat have?

22. Bart has $\frac{3}{4}$ gallon of paint. He poured $\frac{1}{3}$ of it into a smaller can. How much paint was left in the larger can?

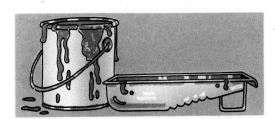

Change each fraction to a whole number or a mixed numeral.

$$\frac{8}{3} = 2\frac{2}{3}$$

1. $\frac{6}{5}$ 2. $\frac{5}{3}$ 3. $\frac{8}{2}$ 4. $\frac{15}{3}$

5. $\frac{12}{5}$ 6. $\frac{16}{3}$ 7. $\frac{24}{6}$ 8. $\frac{19}{4}$ 9. $\frac{23}{6}$ 10. $\frac{13}{2}$

11. $\frac{42}{7}$ 12. $\frac{34}{7}$ 13. $\frac{30}{10}$ 14. $\frac{45}{8}$ 15. $\frac{64}{9}$ 16. $\frac{45}{15}$

Set A (Use after page 164.)

Change each mixed numeral to a fraction.

$4\frac{1}{4} = \frac{17}{4}$

1. $1\frac{1}{5}$　　2. $3\frac{2}{3}$　　3. $1\frac{1}{10}$　　4. $4\frac{1}{2}$

5. $2\frac{3}{5}$　　6. $1\frac{1}{6}$　　7. $2\frac{5}{7}$　　8. $1\frac{1}{4}$　　9. $2\frac{2}{9}$　　10. $1\frac{7}{8}$

11. $3\frac{3}{8}$　　12. $4\frac{1}{3}$　　13. $2\frac{1}{12}$　　14. $3\frac{4}{5}$　　15. $5\frac{1}{2}$　　16. $3\frac{3}{10}$

Set B (Use after page 167.)

Find each product in simplest form.

$1\frac{3}{5} \times 1\frac{3}{4} = \frac{14}{5}$　or　$2\frac{4}{5}$

1. $\frac{1}{2} \times 3\frac{1}{3}$　　2. $\frac{4}{5} \times 10$

3. $\frac{3}{4} \times 1\frac{7}{9}$　　4. $\frac{3}{8} \times 6$　　5. $1\frac{1}{2} \times 1\frac{5}{9}$　　6. $\frac{1}{4} \times 4$

7. $3\frac{1}{3} \times 1\frac{1}{5}$　　8. $\frac{1}{3} \times 1\frac{4}{5}$　　9. $\frac{5}{12} \times 3$　　10. $\frac{5}{8} \times 1\frac{1}{15}$

11. $\frac{3}{5} \times 1\frac{2}{3}$　　12. $1\frac{1}{4} \times 2\frac{2}{5}$　　13. $\frac{3}{10} \times 5$　　14. $3\frac{1}{2} \times 1\frac{4}{7}$

15. $\frac{9}{10} \times 4\frac{1}{6}$　　16. $2\frac{2}{3} \times 3\frac{3}{4}$　　17. $\frac{8}{15} \times 1\frac{1}{4}$　　18. $1\frac{4}{5} \times 4\frac{1}{6}$

19. Jim set a new school high-jump record of $5\frac{1}{2}$ feet. How many inches is that?

20. Allen weighs 78 pounds. Joy weighs $\frac{2}{3}$ as much as Allen. How much does Joy weigh?

21. Harry drove his car 50 miles per hour for $6\frac{1}{2}$ hours. How far did he drive?

22. How far would you go if you went $\frac{1}{3}$ of the way around a $4\frac{1}{2}$-mile track?

23. A recipe calls for $2\frac{2}{3}$ cups of water. If Ada wants to make $\frac{1}{2}$ of a recipe, how much water does she need?

24. Each pizza was cut into 8 pieces. The girls ate $3\frac{1}{4}$ pizzas. How many pieces of pizza did they eat?

Set A (Use after page 175.)

Find each sum in simplest form.

$\frac{2}{9} + \frac{7}{9} = \frac{9}{9}$ or 1

1. $\frac{4}{8} + \frac{3}{8}$

2. $\frac{1}{2} + \frac{1}{2}$

3. $\frac{1}{5} + \frac{3}{5}$

4. $\frac{2}{6} + \frac{5}{6} + \frac{5}{6}$

5. $\frac{3}{7} + \frac{1}{7}$

6. $\frac{3}{8} + \frac{2}{8}$

7. $\frac{1}{6} + \frac{4}{6}$

8. $\frac{5}{6} + \frac{1}{6} + \frac{5}{6}$

9. $\frac{7}{10} + \frac{6}{10}$

10. $\frac{2}{3} + \frac{2}{3}$

11. $\frac{5}{8} + \frac{6}{8}$

12. $\frac{7}{10} + \frac{9}{10} + \frac{4}{10}$

13. $\frac{2}{3} + \frac{1}{3}$

14. $\frac{1}{10} + \frac{6}{10}$

15. $\frac{6}{8} + \frac{1}{8}$

16. $\frac{3}{4} + \frac{2}{4} + \frac{3}{4}$

17. $\frac{4}{9} + \frac{3}{9}$

18. $\frac{1}{7} + \frac{5}{7}$

19. $\frac{2}{4} + \frac{2}{4}$

20. $\frac{3}{4} + \frac{3}{4} + \frac{3}{4}$

21. $\frac{4}{7} + \frac{4}{7}$

22. $\frac{3}{6} + \frac{4}{6}$

23. $\frac{4}{5} + \frac{4}{5}$

24. $\frac{7}{8} + \frac{7}{8} + \frac{5}{8}$

25. $\frac{8}{9} + \frac{4}{9}$

26. $\frac{5}{10} + \frac{6}{10}$

27. $\frac{11}{12} + \frac{8}{12}$

28. $\frac{5}{12} + \frac{4}{12} + \frac{3}{12}$

29. $\frac{2}{9} + \frac{5}{9}$

30. $\frac{3}{6} + \frac{2}{6}$

31. $\frac{3}{10} + \frac{6}{10}$

Set B (Use after page 177.)

Find the least common multiple of the two numbers.

2 and 9 ⟶ 18

1. 3 and 6

2. 4 and 12

3. 8 and 5

4. 9 and 15

5. 8 and 3

6. 10 and 2

7. 14 and 8

8. 6 and 9

9. 10 and 4

10. 3 and 5

11. 6 and 8

12. 10 and 20

13. 20 and 5

14. 15 and 10

15. 9 and 12

16. 8 and 16

17. 4 and 5

18. 6 and 7

19. 12 and 16

20. You want the same number of bolts and nuts. What is the least number of packages of each you should buy?

Bolts
8 for $1.50

Nuts
12 for $1.75

Set A (Use after page 181.)

Find each sum in simplest form.

$\frac{3}{5} + \frac{9}{10} = 1\frac{1}{2}$

1. $\frac{1}{2} + \frac{1}{6}$

2. $\frac{3}{8} + \frac{1}{4}$

3. $\frac{2}{3} + \frac{5}{12}$

4. $\frac{1}{8} + \frac{1}{2}$

5. $\frac{1}{5} + \frac{9}{10}$

6. $\frac{1}{3} + \frac{11}{12}$

7. $\frac{3}{8} + \frac{1}{3}$

8. $\frac{2}{3} + \frac{4}{9}$

9. $\frac{5}{6} + \frac{7}{12}$

10. $\frac{7}{8} + \frac{1}{2}$

11. $\begin{array}{r} \frac{3}{10} \\ + \frac{1}{2} \\ \hline \end{array}$

12. $\begin{array}{r} \frac{1}{5} \\ + \frac{1}{6} \\ \hline \end{array}$

13. $\begin{array}{r} \frac{3}{4} \\ + \frac{7}{10} \\ \hline \end{array}$

14. $\begin{array}{r} \frac{1}{5} \\ + \frac{3}{8} \\ \hline \end{array}$

15. $\begin{array}{r} \frac{3}{4} \\ + \frac{3}{7} \\ \hline \end{array}$

16. $\begin{array}{r} \frac{5}{8} \\ + \frac{5}{12} \\ \hline \end{array}$

17. $\begin{array}{r} \frac{4}{9} \\ + \frac{1}{6} \\ \hline \end{array}$

18. $\begin{array}{r} \frac{2}{5} \\ + \frac{3}{4} \\ \hline \end{array}$

Set B (Use after page 183.)

Find each sum in simplest form.

$\begin{array}{r} 1\frac{5}{9} \\ + 3\frac{5}{6} \\ \hline 4\frac{25}{18} \quad \text{or} \quad 5\frac{7}{18} \end{array}$

1. $\begin{array}{r} 1\frac{1}{5} \\ + 1\frac{3}{10} \\ \hline \end{array}$

2. $\begin{array}{r} \frac{1}{2} \\ + 5\frac{3}{8} \\ \hline \end{array}$

3. $\begin{array}{r} 1\frac{9}{10} \\ + 6 \\ \hline \end{array}$

4. $\begin{array}{r} 3\frac{1}{2} \\ + 4\frac{1}{4} \\ \hline \end{array}$

5. $\begin{array}{r} 3\frac{1}{6} \\ + \frac{11}{12} \\ \hline \end{array}$

6. $\begin{array}{r} 3\frac{3}{4} \\ + 6\frac{3}{4} \\ \hline \end{array}$

7. $\begin{array}{r} 4\frac{1}{6} \\ + 3\frac{1}{8} \\ \hline \end{array}$

8. $\begin{array}{r} 1\frac{2}{3} \\ + 1\frac{1}{12} \\ \hline \end{array}$

9. $\begin{array}{r} 8 \\ + 8\frac{7}{8} \\ \hline \end{array}$

10. $\begin{array}{r} 3\frac{1}{4} \\ + \frac{7}{10} \\ \hline \end{array}$

11. $\begin{array}{r} 7\frac{1}{3} \\ + 2\frac{5}{9} \\ \hline \end{array}$

12. $\begin{array}{r} 1\frac{3}{5} \\ + 1\frac{9}{10} \\ \hline \end{array}$

13. $\begin{array}{r} 1\frac{8}{9} \\ + 2\frac{2}{3} \\ \hline \end{array}$

14. $\begin{array}{r} 9\frac{2}{3} \\ + 10\frac{1}{6} \\ \hline \end{array}$

15. $\begin{array}{r} 9\frac{7}{8} \\ + \frac{1}{4} \\ \hline \end{array}$

16. $\begin{array}{r} 5\frac{5}{8} \\ + 7\frac{8}{12} \\ \hline \end{array}$

17. $\begin{array}{r} 4\frac{3}{4} \\ + 5\frac{5}{8} \\ \hline \end{array}$

18. $\begin{array}{r} 6\frac{5}{6} \\ + 2\frac{2}{9} \\ \hline \end{array}$

19. On a fishing trip, Wanda caught a $3\frac{1}{2}$-pound fish and a $4\frac{3}{4}$-pound fish. How much did the two fish weigh?

20. Wanda fished $2\frac{1}{2}$ hours in the morning and $1\frac{1}{4}$ hours in the afternoon. How long did she fish?

Set A (Use after page 189.)

Write $>$ or $<$ for each ●.

1. $\frac{3}{5}$ ● $\frac{1}{5}$
2. $\frac{1}{6}$ ● $\frac{3}{6}$
3. $\frac{2}{9}$ ● $\frac{4}{9}$
4. $\frac{3}{8}$ ● $\frac{5}{8}$

5. $\frac{3}{5}$ ● $\frac{2}{3}$
6. $\frac{3}{8}$ ● $\frac{2}{6}$
7. $\frac{1}{4}$ ● $\frac{1}{5}$
8. $\frac{3}{4}$ ● $\frac{5}{8}$

9. $\frac{3}{10}$ ● $\frac{2}{9}$
10. $\frac{3}{4}$ ● $\frac{3}{5}$
11. $\frac{1}{6}$ ● $\frac{2}{9}$
12. $\frac{1}{5}$ ● $\frac{3}{10}$

Find each difference in simplest form.

$\frac{3}{4} - \frac{1}{4} = \frac{2}{4}$ or $\frac{1}{2}$

13. $\frac{5}{6} - \frac{1}{6}$
14. $\frac{5}{8} - \frac{3}{8}$

15. $\frac{8}{10} - \frac{5}{10}$
16. $\frac{5}{9} - \frac{2}{9}$
17. $\frac{5}{12} - \frac{1}{12}$
18. $\frac{4}{5} - \frac{3}{5}$

19. $\frac{8}{9} - \frac{2}{9}$
20. $\frac{5}{16} - \frac{1}{16}$
21. $\frac{9}{14} - \frac{5}{14}$
22. $\frac{7}{20} - \frac{2}{20}$

Set B (Use after page 191.)

Find each difference in simplest form.

$\frac{2}{3} - \frac{3}{5} = \frac{1}{15}$

1. $\frac{1}{2} - \frac{1}{5}$
2. $\frac{11}{12} - \frac{5}{6}$

3. $\frac{3}{4} - \frac{1}{12}$
4. $\frac{1}{3} - \frac{1}{6}$
5. $\frac{7}{10} - \frac{3}{5}$
6. $\frac{3}{4} - \frac{3}{8}$

7. $\frac{3}{8} - \frac{1}{4}$
8. $\frac{3}{5} - \frac{3}{10}$
9. $\frac{5}{6} - \frac{1}{2}$
10. $\frac{7}{8} - \frac{3}{4}$

11. $\begin{array}{r} \frac{1}{4} \\ -\frac{1}{8} \\ \hline \end{array}$
12. $\begin{array}{r} \frac{4}{5} \\ -\frac{3}{4} \\ \hline \end{array}$
13. $\begin{array}{r} \frac{1}{8} \\ -\frac{1}{10} \\ \hline \end{array}$
14. $\begin{array}{r} \frac{1}{5} \\ -\frac{1}{6} \\ \hline \end{array}$

15. $\begin{array}{r} \frac{3}{5} \\ -\frac{1}{2} \\ \hline \end{array}$
16. $\begin{array}{r} \frac{5}{6} \\ -\frac{5}{8} \\ \hline \end{array}$
17. $\begin{array}{r} \frac{2}{3} \\ -\frac{3}{8} \\ \hline \end{array}$
18. $\begin{array}{r} \frac{3}{10} \\ -\frac{1}{4} \\ \hline \end{array}$

19. $\begin{array}{r} \frac{5}{6} \\ -\frac{5}{9} \\ \hline \end{array}$
20. $\begin{array}{r} \frac{3}{8} \\ -\frac{1}{5} \\ \hline \end{array}$
21. $\begin{array}{r} \frac{9}{16} \\ -\frac{1}{4} \\ \hline \end{array}$
22. $\begin{array}{r} \frac{8}{9} \\ -\frac{5}{12} \\ \hline \end{array}$

Find each difference in simplest form.

$$3\tfrac{1}{3}$$
$$-1\tfrac{1}{2}$$
$$\overline{1\tfrac{5}{6}}$$

1. $5\tfrac{2}{5}$ $-2\tfrac{1}{2}$

2. $2\tfrac{1}{3}$ $-1\tfrac{2}{9}$

3. 5 $-3\tfrac{1}{2}$

4. $2\tfrac{2}{3}$ $-1\tfrac{2}{5}$

5. $2\tfrac{1}{2}$ $-\tfrac{3}{4}$

6. 7 $-1\tfrac{4}{5}$

7. $1\tfrac{1}{4}$ $-\tfrac{1}{2}$

8. $6\tfrac{1}{5}$ $-4\tfrac{1}{3}$

9. 8 $-6\tfrac{7}{8}$

10. $4\tfrac{3}{4}$ $-1\tfrac{7}{8}$

11. $8\tfrac{2}{3}$ $-6\tfrac{7}{9}$

12. 2 $-\tfrac{3}{4}$

13. $3\tfrac{1}{2}$ $-1\tfrac{4}{5}$

14. $6\tfrac{1}{4}$ $-5\tfrac{1}{4}$

15. $4\tfrac{7}{8}$ $-1\tfrac{1}{4}$

16. $1\tfrac{1}{3}$ $-\tfrac{3}{4}$

17. $12\tfrac{1}{4}$ $-9\tfrac{3}{10}$

18. $2\tfrac{3}{10}$ $-\tfrac{4}{5}$

19. 5 $-4\tfrac{1}{6}$

20. $1\tfrac{2}{5}$ $-\tfrac{3}{10}$

21. $7\tfrac{1}{6}$ $-2\tfrac{2}{3}$

22. $10\tfrac{1}{8}$ $-9\tfrac{3}{4}$

23. 10 $-6\tfrac{7}{8}$

24. $6\tfrac{3}{5}$ $-\tfrac{9}{10}$

Write as a decimal.

$\tfrac{4}{10} = 0.4$

1. $\tfrac{3}{10}$

2. $\tfrac{5}{10}$

3. $\tfrac{45}{100}$

4. $\tfrac{7}{100}$

5. $\tfrac{57}{1000}$

6. $\tfrac{20}{100}$

7. $\tfrac{200}{1000}$

8. $1\tfrac{3}{100}$

9. $6\tfrac{273}{1000}$

10. $23\tfrac{6}{10}$

11. $8\tfrac{2}{1000}$

Write <, >, or = for each ●.

12. 3.23 ● 3.32

13. 0.02 ● 0.002

14. 63 ● 63.00

15. 128.25 ● 128.249

16. 32.8 ● 32.800

17. 9.6 ● 9.601

18. 45.233 ● 40.233

19. 0.010 ● 0.01

20. 3.001 ● 3.09

	1.	2.	3.	4.
3.73 +9.68 13.41	2.15 +3.72	0.1 +0.5	1.24 +0.70	36.3 +41.6

5.	6.	7.	8.	9.
76.7 +23.7	5.17 +0.09	0.93 +0.91	31.8 + 1.5	5.4 +6.9

10.	11.	12.	13.	14.
6.21 +0.57	7.6 +0.1	1.8 +2.2	5.0 +6.6	2.41 +0.57

15.	16.	17.	18.	19.
0.62 0.43 +0.86	13.3 27.7 + 6.9	6.1 7.8 +2.1	9.37 12.36 + 0.07	25.2 67.6 + 7.2

20. Alfredo rode his bike 3.6 kilometers on Friday, 12.12 kilometers on Saturday, and 16.5 kilometers on Sunday. How far did he ride his bike those 3 days?

	1.	2.	3.	4.
3.21 −1.65 1.56	0.7 −0.5	6.27 −1.12	3.89 −0.75	5.6 −1.0

5.	6.	7.	8.	9.
8.0 −4.9	1.2 −0.5	29.6 − 9.8	7.81 −1.94	0.39 −0.33

10.	11.	12.	13.	14.
3.05 −0.73	0.79 −0.30	18.3 − 9.6	4.05 −0.26	0.80 −0.08

15.	16.	17.	18.	19.
5.00 −0.60	8.8 −5.1	9.54 −8.78	16.00 − 9.49	1.07 −0.37

20. Jordan rode his bike 4.34 kilometers. Andrea rode her bike 5.03 kilometers. How much farther did Andrea ride?

Set A (Use after page 213.)

	$7.05 − 4.30 $2.75	1.	$5.12 − 1.02	2.	$0.89 − 0.62	3.	$6.50 − 3.25	4.	$3.00 − 0.76
5.	$0.31 + 0.86	6.	$7.15 + 2.68	7.	$0.97 + 0.05	8.	$2.08 + 1.47	9.	$6.88 + 0.34
10.	$1.00 − 0.60	11.	$3.27 − 1.19	12.	$0.07 − 0.05	13.	$9.99 − 7.26	14.	$10.00 − 7.26
15.	$0.76 + 0.97	16.	$5.93 + 9.78	17.	$0.03 + 0.67	18.	$7.68 + 6.35	19.	$56.52 + 4.89
20.	$0.98 − 0.95	21.	$6.71 + 4.29	22.	$0.83 − 0.75	23.	$7.15 + 1.95	24.	$18.00 − 7.62

Set B (Use after page 219.)

	0.395 ×37 14.615	1.	3.95 ×37	2.	39.5 ×37	3.	395 ×3.7	4.	395 ×0.37
5.	34 ×1.9	6.	18 ×0.6	7.	0.06 ×4	8.	0.92 ×28	9.	0.005 ×4
10.	6.8 ×6	11.	7.2 ×5	12.	0.53 ×85	13.	0.014 ×37	14.	0.716 ×80
15.	3.42 ×0.6	16.	2.3 ×0.04	17.	562 ×0.24	18.	2.81 ×1.6	19.	73.2 ×4.06
20.	0.6 ×0.7	21.	0.30 ×5.5	22.	9.1 ×0.7	23.	22.2 ×2.22	24.	1.01 ×0.1

342

Write each ratio in simplest form.

$\bigstar$'s to $\bullet$'s $\frac{2}{4} = \frac{1}{2}$ **1.** $\bullet$'s to $\blacksquare$'s **2.** $\blacktriangle$'s to $\bigstar$'s

3. $\blacksquare$'s to $\bullet$'s **4.** $\bigstar$'s to $\blacktriangle$'s **5.** $\bullet$'s to $\blacktriangle$'s

6. $\bigstar$'s to $\blacksquare$'s **7.** $\blacksquare$'s to $\bigstar$'s **8.** $\blacktriangle$'s to $\bullet$'s

Write each as a decimal and as a percent.

$\frac{3}{100} = 0.03 = 3\%$ **1.** $\frac{29}{100}$ **2.** $\frac{50}{100}$ **3.** $\frac{70}{100}$ **4.** $\frac{7}{100}$

5. $\frac{33}{100}$ **6.** $\frac{11}{100}$ **7.** $\frac{37}{100}$ **8.** $\frac{8}{100}$ **9.** $\frac{100}{100}$

10. $\frac{84}{100}$ **11.** $\frac{56}{100}$ **12.** $\frac{95}{100}$ **13.** $\frac{60}{100}$ **14.** $\frac{75}{100}$

Copy. Express each number in two other ways to complete the table.

	Percent	Fraction	Decimal		Percent	Fraction	Decimal
15.	20%			**19.**			0.15
16.			0.28	**20.**		$\frac{95}{100}$	
17.		$\frac{5}{100}$		**21.**			0.10
18.	9%			**22.**	100%		

Set A (Use after page 227.)

Find the following:

22% of 200 = 44

1. 25% of 60

2. 13% of 72

3. 75% of 100

4. 100% of 75

5. 10% of 750

6. 2% × 7

7. 68% × 29

8. 31% × 100

9. 83% × 78

10. 62% × 500

11. 8% × 268

12. Last year, Bob attempted 55 free throws. If he made 60% of the free throws, how many did he make?

13. 45% of the pupils in Paul's class are girls. Are there more girls or boys in the class?

14. If 70% of your body is water, how many pounds of water make up your body?

Set B (Use after page 229.)

1. A coat that sells for $24 is reduced 30%. Find the reduced price.

2. A hat that sells for $4 is reduced 20%. Find the reduced price.

3. An item costs $32. The sales tax is 5%. Find the cost of the item plus sales tax.

The regular price of an item is $25. That price was reduced by 40%. The sales tax is 6%. Find the following:

4. the amount of the reduction

5. the sale price

6. the sales tax on the sale price

7. the total bill

8. the amount of change you should get from $20

344

Find the length of each line segment to the nearest centimeter.

1. ━━━━━━━   2. ━━━━━━━━━━━━━━━━

3. ━━━━━━━   4. ━━━━━━━━━━━━━━━━━

5. ━━━━━━━━━━━━━━━━━━━━

Complete the following.

0.8 m = __80__ cm   6. 3 mm = ___ cm   7. 46 m = ___ km

8. 600 cm = ___ m   9. 0.5 km = ___ m   10. 1 m = ___ mm

11. 20 cm = ___ mm   12. 30 cm = ___ m   13. 3000 mm = ___ m

14. 0.06 km = ___ m   15. 2 m = ___ cm   16. 500 mm = ___ cm

Set B (Use after page 243.)

Would you use liters or milliliters to measure these?

1. amount of liquid in an aquarium   2. amount of medicine in a shot

3. amount of water an elephant drinks in a day   4. amount of water a gerbil drinks in a day

5. Arrange these measurements from least to most.

1.9 liters

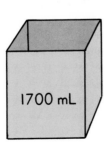
1700 mL

1.3 liters

1901 mL

Set A (Use after page 245.)

Tell whether you would use grams or kilograms to weigh these.

1. a pen

2. an orange

3. a watermelon

4. a book of matches

5. a box of matches

6. a person

7. a car

8. a potato

9. a sack of potatoes

10. a truckload of potatoes

Complete the following:

11. 1000 g = ___ kg

12. 5 kg = ___ g

13. 1500 g = ___ kg

14. 500 g = ___ kg

15. 0.6 kg = ___ g

16. 0.03 kg = ___ g

Set B (Use after page 255.)

Find the perimeter of each figure.

1.
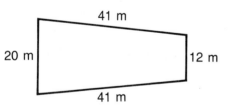

2.
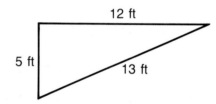

3.
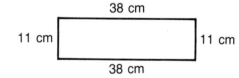

4.
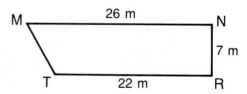

5. The perimeter of the figure at the right is 64 meters. Find the length of side MT.

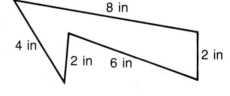

Find the area of each rectangle and right triangle.

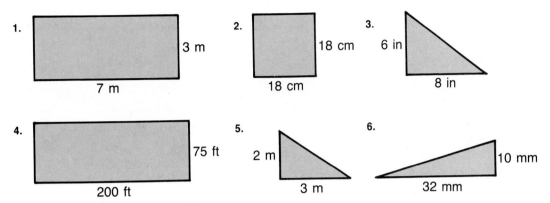

1. 3 m, 7 m

2. 18 cm, 18 cm

3. 6 in, 8 in

4. 75 ft, 200 ft

5. 2 m, 3 m

6. 10 mm, 32 mm

7. A rectangular garden is 24 feet long and 32 feet wide. Find the area of the garden.

8. A square has sides that are each 25 cm long. Find the area of the square.

Find the volume of each rectangular prism.

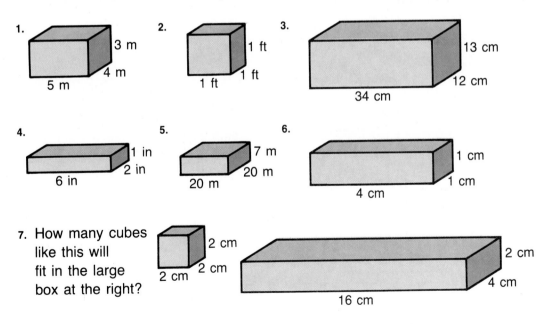

1. 3 m, 4 m, 5 m

2. 1 ft, 1 ft, 1 ft

3. 13 cm, 12 cm, 34 cm

4. 1 in, 2 in, 6 in

5. 7 m, 20 m, 20 m

6. 1 cm, 1 cm, 4 cm

7. How many cubes like this will fit in the large box at the right?

2 cm, 2 cm, 2 cm

2 cm, 4 cm, 16 cm

Write the ordered pair for each of these points.

1. A

2. B

3. C

4. D

5. E

6. F

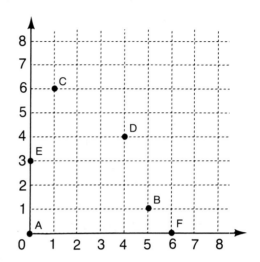

Draw and label two number lines like those at the right. Graph each of these ordered pairs.

7. (6,5)

8. (0,7)

9. (1,2)

10. (3,1)

11. (2,0)

12. (3,4)

Copy and complete each table. Then make a line graph.

1. For $1 you can buy 3 cans of soup.

Cost (dollars)	1	2	3	4	5
Number of cans	3				

2. A golden eagle can fly 2 miles in 1 minute.

Time (minutes)	1	2	3	4	5
Distance (miles)	2				

3. Each car has 5 tires.

Number of cars	1	2	3	4
Number of tires	5			

4. Two buttons weigh three ounces.

Buttons	2	4	6	8	10
Weight	3	6			

Use the graph below to answer the following:

1. Who earned the most points?

2. Who earned the fewest points?

3. Which two pupils earned the same number of points?

4. Who earned twice as many points as Ida?

5. Estimate the number of points earned by all the pupils.

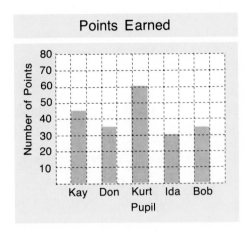

6. Make a bar graph from this table.

Test Grades	A	B	C	D	F
Number of Pupils	6	8	10	3	1

Use the circle graph to answer the following:

1. What percent of the money is spent on refreshments?

2. On what is 25% of the money spent?

3. What fractional part of the money is for entertainment?

4. How is $\frac{1}{4}$ of the money spent?

5. What fractional part of the money is for "other" items?

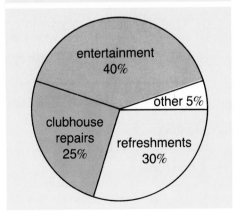

If you spin the pointer once, what is the chance it will stop on

1. 1   2. 2   3. 3

4. red   5. blue

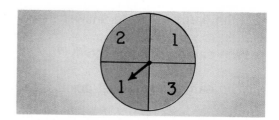

You are to pick one of the marbles without looking. What is the probability that you pick a

6. red marble   7. blue marble

8. green marble   9. marble

You push one button without looking. What is the probability that you push

10. A   11. B   12. C

13. a letter   14. an even number

15. a number

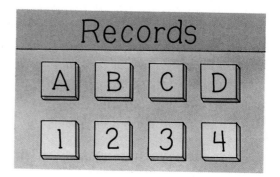

Copy. Use the buttons above to complete the table.

	Probability in 1 try	Prediction of how many times in 32 tries	Prediction of how many times in 80 tries
16. a vowel			
17. a consonant			
18. a number			

Glossary

addend Any of the numbers to be added.

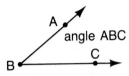

$8 + 5 = 13$

addends

$$\begin{array}{r} 8 \\ +5 \\ \hline 13 \end{array}$$

angle A figure formed by two rays having the same endpoint.

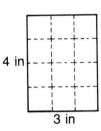

angle ABC

area The number of square units that fit inside a figure. The area of this figure is 12 square inches.

4 in

3 in

average The quotient obtained when the sum of a set of numbers is divided by the number of addends.

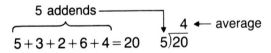

5 addends

$5+3+2+6+4=20$

$$5\overline{)20}$$ → 4 ← average

centimeter A unit of length in the metric system (one hundredth of a meter).

1 centimeter or 1 cm

circle A curved figure (in a plane) with all points the same distance from a point called the center.

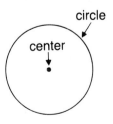

circle

center

circumference The distance around a circle.

composite number A whole number greater than 1 that has more than two factors.

cone A figure that is shaped like this.

congruent figures Figures having the same size and shape.

cube A figure that is shaped like this. Each of its six faces is a square.

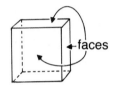

faces

cylinder A figure shaped like this.

decimal A numeral with place values based on 10. The following are decimals:

342   5.6   12.48

denominator The bottom number in a fraction. The denominator in the fraction $\frac{3}{4}$ is 4.

diagonal A line segment—other than a side or an edge—that joins two corners of a figure.

351

diameter A line segment that joins two points on a circle and passes through the center.

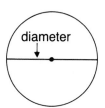

difference The number you get by subtracting one number from another.

$$48 - 29 = 19$$

$$\begin{array}{r} 48 \\ -29 \\ \hline 19 \end{array}$$

difference → 19

digit Any of the symbols 0, 1, 2, 3, 4, 5, 6, 7, 8, and 9 when used in a decimal.

dividend The number to be divided.

$$32 \div 4 = 8 \qquad 4\overline{)32}$$

dividend

divisor The number by which the dividend is divided.

$$32 \div 4 = 8 \qquad 4\overline{)32}$$

divisor

equation A number sentence containing an equal sign.

equivalent fractions Two or more fractions that name the same number or amount.

$\frac{1}{3}, \frac{2}{6},$ and $\frac{3}{9}$ are equivalent fractions.

estimate To guess the result before doing the computation.

352

even number Any whole number whose numeral has 0, 2, 4, 6, or 8 in the ones place.

factor Any of the numbers to be multiplied.

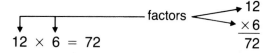

$$12 \times 6 = 72$$

$$\begin{array}{r} 12 \\ \times 6 \\ \hline 72 \end{array}$$

formula A math sentence that states a general rule.

fraction A name for numbers like $\frac{1}{2}$, $\frac{5}{6}, \frac{8}{3},$ and $\frac{4}{4}$.

gram A unit of mass (weight) in the metric system (one thousandth of a kilogram).

graph A diagram that shows how two sets of information are related (bar graph, line graph, circle graph).

greater than A comparison of two numbers that are not the same—one number is more than the other.

$8 > 5$ is read "8 is greater than 5."

greatest common factor The greatest common factor of two or more numbers.

Factors of 6: 1, 2, 3, 6
Factors of 15: 1, 3, 5, 15

3 is the greatest common factor of 6 and 15.

kilogram A unit of mass (weight) in the metric system (1000 grams).

kiloliter A unit of capacity in the metric system (1000 liters).

kilometer A unit of length in the metric system (1000 meters).

least common denominator The least common multiple of the denominators of two or more fractions.

$$\begin{array}{r} \frac{1}{4} \\ +\frac{1}{6} \\ \hline \end{array}$$ The least common multiple of 4 and 6 is 12, so 12 is the least common denominator of $\frac{1}{4}$ and $\frac{1}{6}$.

least common multiple The least common multiple (other than zero) of two or more numbers.

Multiples of 4: 4, 8, 12, 16, ⋯
Multiples of 6: 6, 12, 18, 24, ⋯

12 is the least common multiple of 4 and 6.

less than A comparison of two numbers that are not the same—one number is less than the other.

$7 < 9$ is read "7 is less than 9."

line segment Any part of a line that joins two points.

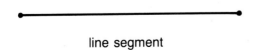

line segment

liter A unit of capacity in the metric system (one thousandth of a kiloliter).

meter A unit of length in the metric system (one thousandth of a kilometer).

milligram A unit of mass in the metric system (one thousandth of a gram).

milliliter A unit of capacity in the metric system (one thousandth of a liter).

A container this size holds a milliliter of liquid.
1 cm
1 cm
1 cm

millimeter A unit of length in the metric system (one thousandth of a meter).

1 millimeter or 1 mm

mixed numeral A numeral formed by naming a whole number and a fraction. Numerals like $1\frac{1}{2}$ and $54\frac{5}{8}$ are mixed numerals.

multiple A product of two whole numbers is a multiple of both whole numbers.

numeral A name for a number.

numerator The top number in a fraction. The numerator of the fraction $\frac{5}{8}$ is 5.

odd number Any whole number whose numeral has 1, 3, 5, 7, or 9 in the ones place.

ordinal *First, second, third, fourth, fifth,* and so on, are ordinals. They are used to order members of a group.

parallel lines Two or more lines (in the same plane) that never meet or cross.

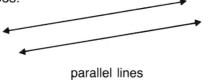

parallel lines

parallelogram A quadrilateral whose opposite sides are parallel.

percent (%) The ratio of some number to 100.

13% can be written $\frac{13}{100}$ or 0.13.

perimeter The distance around a figure. The perimeter of this figure is $3+5+3+5$ or 16 inches.

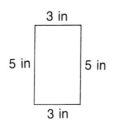

3 in
5 in   5 in
3 in

perpendicular lines Two lines that form right angles.

pi The ratio of the circumference of a circle to the length of a diameter. Pi is approximately equal to 3.14.

place value The value of the place or position of a digit in a numeral.

place values   5 0 3 7

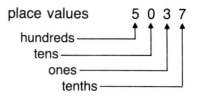

hundreds
tens
ones
tenths

prime number A whole number that is greater than 1 and has only itself and 1 as factors.

probability The chance that a given outcome or event will occur.

product The number you get when one number is multiplied by another.

$3 \times 15 = 45$

     15
    $\times 3$
     45

product

proportion An equation stating that two ratios are equal.

$\frac{2}{3} = \frac{4}{6}$ is called a proportion.

quadrilateral A figure that has four sides.

quadrilaterals

quotient The number you get when one number is divided by another.

quotient

$42 \div 6 = 7$ $6\overline{)42}$ → 7

354

radius A line segment that joins the center of a circle with any point on the circle.

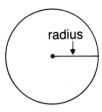
radius

ratio A comparison of the number of members of two sets. This can be given in several ways.

3 to 2   3:2 $\frac{3}{2}$

reciprocals Two numbers whose product is 1. Since $\frac{3}{4} \times \frac{4}{3} = 1$, $\frac{3}{4}$ and $\frac{4}{3}$ are reciprocals.

rectangle A figure with four sides and four right angles.

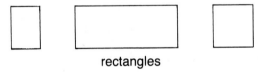
rectangles

remainder The number that is left over, or remains, after a division is completed.

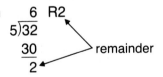

$$\begin{array}{r} 6 \;\; R2 \\ 5\overline{)32} \\ 30 \\ \hline 2 \end{array}$$
remainder

right angle An angle that has a measurement of 90°.

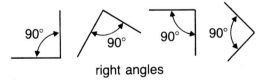
right angles

simplest form (1) A fraction is in simplest form if 1 is the only whole number factor of both the numerator and the denominator. (2) A mixed numeral is in simplest form if the fraction is in simplest form and names a number less than 1.

sphere A figure shaped like this.

square A rectangle with all four sides the same length.

sum The number you get when you add two numbers.

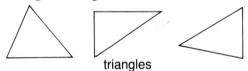

$$33 + 28 = 61$$

$$\begin{array}{r} 33 \\ +28 \\ \hline 61 \end{array}$$
sum

triangle A figure with three sides.

triangles

volume The number of cubic units that fit inside a figure. The volume of this figure is 12 cubic centimeters.

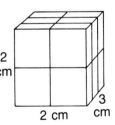
2 cm

2 cm   3 cm

whole number Any of the numbers 0, 1, 2, 3, 4, 5, and so on.

Table of Measures

Length

1 centimeter = 10 millimeters

1 decimeter = 10 centimeters

1 meter = 10 decimeters

1 meter = 100 centimeters

1 meter = 1000 millimeters

1 dekameter = 10 meters

1 hectometer = 10 dekameters

1 kilometer = 10 hectometers

1 kilometer = 1000 meters

1 foot = 12 inches

1 yard = 3 feet

1 yard = 36 inches

1 mile = 5280 feet

1 mile = 1760 yards

Area

1 square centimeter = 100 square millimeters

1 square meter = 10,000 square centimeters

1 are = 100 square meters

1 hectare = 100 ares

1 square foot = 144 square inches

1 square yard = 9 square feet

1 acre = 43,560 square feet

1 square mile = 640 acres

Volume

1 cubic centimeter = 1000 cubic millimeters

1 cubic decimeter = 1000 cubic centimeters

1 cubic meter = 1000 cubic decimeters

1 cubic foot = 1728 cubic inches

1 cubic yard = 27 cubic feet

Capacity

1 liter = 1000 milliliters

1 kiloliter = 1000 liters

1 cup = 8 fluid ounces

1 pint = 2 cups

1 quart = 2 pints

1 gallon = 4 quarts

Weight

1 gram = 1000 milligrams

1 kilogram = 1000 grams

1 metric ton = 1000 kilograms

1 pound = 16 ounces

1 ton = 2000 pounds

Index

A

Acute angle, 128–129

Addition
of decimals, 208–209
estimating sums in, 30–31
of fractions, 174–175, 178–181,
184, 185
mixed numerals in, 182–184
of several addends, 32–33
solving problems with, 33
of whole numbers, 8–9, 22–27,
32–33, 49

Angles, 124–125
acute, 128–129
congruent, 132–133
drawing, 130
measures of, 126–130
naming, 124–125
obtuse, 128–129
right, 128–129, 140
sides of, 124–125
vertices of, 124–125

Area, 256
estimating, 256–257
and perimeter, 263
of a rectangle, 258–259, 263
of a right triangle, 260–261
solving problems with, 262
units of, 256

Average, 92–93

B

Bar graphs, 290–293

C

Calculators
addition with, 39
and decimals, 221

finding averages with, 94
subtraction with, 39

Capacity, 242–243

Celsius scale, 246–247

Centimeter, 232–241

Chance, 300–302

Checking
division, 12–13, 76
subtraction, 10–11

Circle, 134–135
diameter of, 134–135
graph, 294–295
radius of, 134–135

Circle graphs, 294–295

Comparing
decimals, 206–207
fractions, 186–187
whole numbers, 18–19

Congruent figures
angles, 132–133
line segments, 122–123

Cubic units, 256

Customary units
of capacity, 248
of length, 248
solving problems with, 248–249
of weight, 248

D

Decimal point, 202

Decimals
addition of, 208–209
and calculators, 221
comparing, 206–207

equivalent, 206–207
and fractions, 204–205
and mixed numerals, 204–205
and money, 212–213
multiplication of, 216–219
and percent, 224–225
place values in, 202–203
solving problems with, 209, 213, 219
subtraction of, 210–211

Degrees, 126, 246

Denominator, 144

Diagonal, 123

Diameter, 134–135

Dividend, 13, 68

Divisibility, 78–79

Division
checking, 12–13, 76
remainders in, 74–76
of whole numbers, 68–88, 90–91
zero in, 88

Divisor, 13, 68

E

Endpoints, 120

Equivalent fractions, 146–149

Estimating
area, 256–257
differences, 36
products, 50–51
sums, 30–31

F

Factor, 42
greatest common, 152–153

Fahrenheit scale, 246–247

Formula, 258
for area of a rectangle, 258
for area of a right triangle, 260
for volume of a rectangular prism, 266

Fractions, 144–145
addition of, 174–175, 178–181, 184, 185
comparing, 186–187
and decimals, 204–205
equivalent, 146–149
and mixed numerals, 162–167
multiplication of, 156–159, 165
and percent, 224–225
and probability, 302
and ratios, 222–223
renaming, 148–149
in simplest form, 154–155, 158
subtraction of, 188–191
for whole numbers, 161

G

Gram, 244–245

Graphs
bar, 290–293
circle, 294–295
line, 284–287
of an ordered pair, 276–277

Greatest common factor, 152–153

H

Hexagon, 136–137

I

Inequalities, 18–19, 186–187, 206–207

K

Kilogram, 244–245

Kilometer, 234–241

L

Least common denominator, 180

Least common multiple, 176–177

Length, 232–235

Line graphs, 284–287

Line segments, 120–123
    congruent, 122–123
    parallel, 138–139
    perpendicular, 140–141

Lines, 120–121
    intersecting, 138
    parallel, 138–139
    perpendicular, 140–141
    skew, 139

Liter, 242–243

M

Measurement, 232
    of angles, 256–263
    of capacity, 242–243, 248–249
    of length, 232–235, 248–249
    solving problems with, 248–249, 251,
       262, 268–269
    of temperature, 246–247
    of volume, 264–267
    of weight, 244–245, 248–249

Meter, 234–241

Metric units
    centimeter, 232–241
    gram, 244–245
    kilogram, 244–245
    kilometer, 234–241
    liter, 242–243
    meter, 234–241
    milliliter, 242–243
    millimeter, 234–241

Milliliter, 242–243

Millimeter, 234–241

Mixed numerals
    in addition, 182–184
    and fractions, 162–167
    in multiplication, 166–167
    renaming, 162–165
    simplest form, 166–167
    in subtraction, 192–195

Multiplication
    of decimals, 216–219
    estimating products in, 50–51
    factors, 42
    of fractions, 156–159, 165
    mixed numerals in, 166–167
    of more than two factors, 42–43
    of whole numbers, 8–9, 42–47, 52–63
    zero in, 44–47

N

Numerator, 144

O

Obtuse angle, 128–129

Octagon, 136–137

Ordered pairs, 274–279

P

Parallel lines, 138–139

Parentheses, 42

Pentagon, 136–137

Percent, 224
    and decimals, 224–225
    and fractions, 224–225
    and money, 228–229
    of a number, 226–227
    and probability, 310–311
    and ratio, 224–225
    solving problems with, 227, 229

Perimeter, 254–255, 263

Perpendicular lines, 140–141

Place value, 14–17, 48

Polygons, 136–137

Probability, 302–303
    and chance, 300–301
    experiments, 298–299, 308–309
    as percent, 310–311
    predicting with, 306–307
    of 0 and 1, 304–305

Problem solving, 98–115
  with addition and subtraction, 33
  with averages, 93
  with decimals, 209, 213, 219
  with different operations, 33, 65, 89,
    168–169, 199
  with extra information, 108–109
  with measurement, 248–249, 251, 262,
    268–269
  and missing information, 110–111
  with percent, 227, 229
  with two operations, 114–115

Product, 42

Protractor, 126

Pyramid, 118

Q

Quadrilateral, 136–137

Quotient, 13, 68

R

Radius, 134–135

Ratio, 222–223
  and percent, 224–225
  simplest form of, 222

Ray, 120–121

Rectangle, 123, 258–259, 263

Rectangular prism, 118, 266–267

Remainders, 74–76

Right angle, 128–129, 140

Right triangle, 260

Rounding numbers, 28–29

S

Sales price, 228–229

Sales tax, 228–229

Simplest form
  of fractions, 154–155, 158
  of mixed numerals, 166–167
  of ratios, 222

Skew lines, 139

Space figures, 118

Square units, 256

Subtraction
  checking, 10–11
  of decimals, 210–211
  estimating differences in, 36
  of fractions, 188–191
  mixed numerals in, 192–195
  solving problems with, 33
  of whole numbers, 8–9, 34–35, 49

T

Tables
  for graphs, 280–283
  of measures, 356

Temperature, 246–247

Triangle
  angles of, 125
  area of a right, 260–261
  right, 260
  sides of, 136–137

U

Unit of measure, 232

V

Vertex of an angle, 124

Volume, 264–265
  of a rectangular prism, 266–267
  solving problems with, 268–269
  units of, 264

W

Weight, 244–245

Z

Zero
  in division, 88
  in multiplication, 44–47
  probability, 304–305